Praise for *The Mighty Hughes*

"Craig McInnes has written a richly textured, must-read book on the tour de force who is Ted Hughes. This is the story of a man who has led an extraordinary life at the centre of some of the most remarkable events in BC and Canadian political history. This is an inspirational account of a true Canadian hero—a giant in legal, public and political circles."

MAUREEN MALONEY QC, Professor of Public Policy, Simon Fraser University, and former BC Deputy Attorney General and Dean of Law

"We used to say that if Ted Hughes did not exist, we would have to invent him. But as Craig McInnes makes clear in this remarkable biography, Ted was his own invention—a public servant who established his credibility and integrity case by case, year by year, making some of the toughest judgement calls ever faced in this country."

VAUGHN PALMER *Vancouver Sun*

"Craig McInnes has wonderfully captured the forces that shaped the life and career of Ted Hughes, whose remarkable contributions to the legal and social fabric of Canada will continue to inspire for generations to come those who would give a powerful voice to the most vulnerable in our communities."

DANIEL SHAPIRO QC, Chief Adjudicator, Indian Residential Schools Adjudication Secretariat

"Craig McInnes' biography of Ted Hughes provides engaging insight into Ted's life, career and unshakeable reputation for integrity, wisdom, sound advice, the ability to untangle other people's messes, and his belief in the value of politicians, good government and the dignity of all individuals. The Mighty (and Fearless) Hughes is the model and high benchmark for all independent adjudicators in the country."

DAVID PHILLIP JONES QC, Administrative lawyer in private practice, Conflict of Interest Commissioner for Yukon and for NWT

"*The Mighty Hughes* effectively captures the many roles of Ted Hughes in public service, as a thoughtful and indefatigable listener of marginalized groups and issues of social injustice, along with his stature as a fearless and forceful speaker of truth to those in power."

MICHAEL J. PRINCE Lansdowne Professor of Social Policy, University of Victoria

"Craig McInnes' brilliant book, *The Mighty Hughes*, captures the road Ted travelled, proving that truth, principle and a strong moral compass can protect public interest and enhance the body politic. To understand BC politics, buy this book."

BOB PLECAS former deputy minister, author of *Bill Bennett: A Mandarin's View*

CRAIG MCINNES

The Mighty Hughes

FROM PRAIRIE LAWYER TO WESTERN CANADA'S MORAL COMPASS

A BIOGRAPHY OF E.N. "TED" HUGHES

Victoria | Vancouver | Calgary

Heritage House Publishing Company Ltd.
heritagehouse.ca

CATALOGUING INFORMATION AVAILABLE
FROM LIBRARY AND ARCHIVES CANADA

978-1-77203-205-5 (hardcover)
978-1-77203-206-2 (epub)
978-1-77203-207-9 (epdf)

Edited by Audrey McClellan
Proofread by Lenore Hietkamp
Cover design by Jacqui Thomas
Interior design by Setareh Ashrafologhalai
Cover photograph by Debra Brash, *Times Colonist*
Interior photos used with permission from the Hughes family collection, unless otherwise noted.

The interior of this book was produced on 100% post-consumer recycled paper, processed chlorine free, and printed with vegetable-based inks.

Generous financial support of this project by the Law Foundation of Saskatchewan and the Law Foundation of British Columbia is gratefully acknowledged.

We acknowledge the financial support of the Government of Canada through the Canada Book Fund (CBF) and the Canada Council for the Arts, and the Province of British Columbia through the British Columbia Arts Council and the Book Publishing Tax Credit.

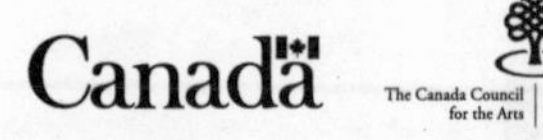

21 20 19 18 17 1 2 3 4 5
Printed in Canada

Contents

Preface 1

Introduction 4

Part I Saskatchewan

Origins 12

University and a Growing Interest in Politics 21

Helen 26

Country Lawyer and Budding Politician 34

A Powerful Patron 45

Family 52

Judge Hughes 67

Life Means Life 78

Marriage 84

Hospitals 86

Thatcher v. Thatcher 90

A New Opportunity and a Bitter Crash 98

Part II British Columbia

A New Beginning: From Master of the Court to Civil Servant 108

Breaking Down Barriers 118

Rising from Conflict 125

Calling in the Cops: Peter Toigo and the Expo Lands 134

Making Room at the Top for BC 139

Blue Boxes, Secret Tapes and the Wild West 143

Fantasy Gardens 162

Vander Zalm: Round Two 175

Conflict Commissioner: Some Honourable Members 182

Smackdown 192

Part III Canada and First Nations

Payback: Harvey Pollock and Indigenous Justice 204

Hate and Death 214

Riot 219

APEC and Chretien: The National Arena 225

Residential Schools 238

Stan Hagen and the Moral Fixer 248

Loss 254

Lighting a Candle 257

Positive Press: The Benefits of a Lifelong Affair with Newspapers 267

Never Shy or Retiring 272

Appendix 1: List of Reports by E.N. "Ted" Hughes 276

Appendix 2: Awards Presented to E.N. "Ted" Hughes 280

Selected Bibliography and Sources 282

Index 286

Preface

EARLY ON, I told a friend of Ted Hughes that I was working on his biography.

"Oh," she replied. "You must be writing a hagiography."

Hughes evokes that reaction. He may not merit the life story of a saint, but he swims in a sea of superlatives, all earned. With his enormous capacity, and appetite, for work, his unshakable and unfashionable belief that politics should be an honourable profession, his addiction to public service and his insistence that equality means little if it doesn't include women and Indigenous Canadians, he has fairly been called Canada's moral authority and the most credible man in British Columbia.

I first encountered Ted in the mid-'90s when I was a reporter for the *Globe and Mail* covering the legislature in Victoria. He was already a legend in the press gallery. He was past the normal retirement age of 65 and just getting started on his third career as Canada's go-to guy for restoring faith in institutions at all levels by offering his rare combination of honesty, integrity, wisdom, administrative competence and a no-nonsense approach to getting the job done.

More than two decades later, Paul Fraser, who followed Ted's pioneering footsteps as the conflict-of-interest commissioner for the BC legislature, approached me about writing this biography. Ted had just finished the largest public inquiry ever held in Manitoba, and Fraser thought that at the age of 87 he might finally be getting ready to retire, and that his work was too important to be forgotten.

I was honoured to be asked and excited at the opportunity, but I still had to make a living, and Ted had to be persuaded that it was a good idea. Paul set out to raise some money and get Hughes on board. While reluctant at first, in the end Ted was persuaded that the story of his life could and should be an extension of his life's work.

Paul started a campaign, enlisting the support initially of Kathleen Keating, Dan Shapiro and John Waddell, who as Friends of Ted Hughes arranged for the backing of the law school of the University of Saskatchewan and significant financial support from the law foundations of British Columbia and Saskatchewan. Many of Ted's friends and former colleagues also made generous donations, in addition to contributing their recollections and stories.

I got help early on from Vaughn Palmer, my former colleague at the *Vancouver Sun*, who accessed his encyclopedic memory and extensive files from decades of insightful coverage of the BC political scene to point me in the right direction and pull me back on track when I went astray.

My friend Verna Laliberte gave me the technical support to set up a database to organize the hundreds of newspaper clippings and other publications Ted's work has inspired over six decades and several provinces. As a former journalist, I was interested to discover that, more often than not, the written record of his work compiled by reporters at the time of distant events was more reliable than even the most acute memories.

Other journalists helped me along the way, including my friends at the press gallery who had for decades feasted on Ted's ability to make news. Tom Hawthorn and Paul Willcocks gave me early encouragement and insight into what it takes to write a book.

I am indebted as well to Ted's cousin Catherine Crawford, who in the 1990s compiled an extensive history of the Hughes family on which I drew heavily for my description of his early years.

I also need to thank the dozens of friends and colleagues who agreed to be interviewed, with a special thanks to Bob Plecas, who was extremely helpful early on, and Kathleen Keating, who among others reviewed portions of the manuscript. Audrey McClellan, the editor for Heritage House, patiently showed me how much there was left to do to turn a manuscript into a book after I thought I was done.

And none of this would have been possible without love and support from my wife, Vivian Smith, my inspiration for all things and my toughest editor.

The result is this book, in which any errors or omissions are mine. It is not exactly an authorized biography in that, from the beginning, Ted said he wanted it to be my narrative and he wasn't going to dictate the contents. But it couldn't have been written without the access to his personal papers he provided, his help in many hours of interviews, and the cooperation and financial support of his friends, family and former colleagues, who gave generously of their time and money. And I am biased. I wouldn't have taken it on if I wasn't already persuaded that Ted was a more than worthy subject for a biography, not a saint but a truly good man, who through his work and the way he treats everyone with genuine respect made Canada a better place to live.

The narrative is written from a particular time and place. Unless otherwise noted, the quotes are from interviews conducted between 2014 and 2016. Throughout the narrative I switch between "Ted" and "Hughes" when referring to my subject. I think of him both ways—formally with the respect he deserves, and affectionately as Ted. As I write this, Ted and his wife, Helen, are alive and well. My hope is that the story of his extraordinary life will be around to entertain and inspire long after we are all gone.

Introduction

THE UNION CLUB of British Columbia was founded in 1879 on the model of a classic London club for gentlemen, complete with a library and billiards room. For more than a century it has been a private refuge for the well-heeled and well-connected in Victoria. While no longer literally an old boys' club, the dark mahogany and leather-panelled rooms still ooze class and privilege, with the subtext that important people come here to discuss important things, issues that will affect not just their personal fortunes but the future and well-being of the city and the province.

On this occasion, lunch is in the McKenzie Private Dining Room and Lounge, reached by descending a wide stairway past a large sombre portrait of Sir Winston Churchill, who club historians note once dined in the larger formal dining room upstairs.

Seating is limited to 38 by the size of the room, described in club literature as "classically Edwardian in its relaxed formality, complete with chandeliers and period furniture." The setting is formal but the invitation specifies casual dress. "Our honoured guest wants us all to be informally comfortable."

The honoured guest is Ted Hughes. The occasion is a celebration to mark his retirement, although few among the guests are entirely persuaded that even at 87 he is really through. For a decade Ted has been telling reporters that every new assignment, while significant, is probably his last. Although he is more than two decades beyond what used to be considered normal retirement age, no one would be shocked if he used the tribute lunch to announce he had accepted another assignment.

Badly stooped but otherwise apparently undimmed by age, Ted and Helen, his wife of 60 years, warmly greet the guests as they arrive, checking with each other to make sure no one goes unnoticed. They behave as though they are the hosts, responsible for everyone's comfort and enjoyment, rather than the honoured guests.

The gathering is small relative to the vast cast of former colleagues and admirers who would have been delighted to honour a unique and distinguished career in public service, and a body of work that has played such a key role in the history of the province and the country. As political scientist Norman Ruff put it for a televised retrospective on Hughes' career two years earlier, "If Ted Hughes hadn't come to BC in 1980, we would have had to invent him to ever hope to protect the values that we've wanted to see maintained in the government of the province."

The gathering may not be large, but it is all he wanted. "It's just not me," Hughes says of the more grandiose plans that had been proposed earlier to mark his retirement. For a man with such a large presence on the public stage, he has maintained a remarkably small personal profile. The organizers, who had previously booked the ballroom at Government House for a formal dinner with more than 160 guests, knew that when, as a judge, administrator or commissioner, Hughes made a decision, it usually stuck. And what the Hon. Edward Norman Hughes, OC, QC, LLD (Hon.), wanted was to be surrounded by the people who were most important in his and Helen's lives: family and the people who were both colleagues and friends, people who knew him well enough to affectionately call him Ted.

No one sent their regrets. It is, a former Victoria city councillor gushes to her neighbour as the tributes start to flow from the podium and waiters quietly distribute elegantly plated crème caramel and coriander shortbread, "an incredible privilege to be in this room."

The assembly makes up in lustre what it lacks in size, bringing together judges, lawyers, former federal and provincial cabinet ministers, senior civil servants, mayors, veteran journalists and successful entrepreneurs.

And the location is more in tune with Hughes' role in the history of the province. The first president of the Union Club was Sir Matthew Baillie Begbie. The first judge in the colony of British Columbia, he was an imposing, wilful man who followed a legal code and acted with the courage of his convictions at a time when the rule of law was an insecure notion in the mining camps and boom towns of the BC Interior. Later dubbed "the hanging judge" for his strict adherence to the law, Begbie appeared in the province as the proverbial right man in the right place at the right time.[1]

Hughes also has a knack for stumbling into pivotal events that often turn on his judgment and his unshakable conviction that the only option is to interpret the law as he sees it and to stand up for the institutions he represents. He is the Boy Scout who will never grow up. That often put him offside with politicians, some of whom were his bosses. More often than not it was politicians who had to back down in the encounters that built the legend of "the Mighty Hughes" among reporters in British Columbia over the three decades since he arrived

1 Begbie's role, like many of the effects of colonization, has come under new scrutiny recently as Canada's First Nations call for a retelling of the history of Canada from their point of view. In April 2017, the Law Society of BC announced it was taking down a statue of Begbie that was in the lobby of its office building in Vancouver. The statue was offensive to Indigenous people because of Begbie's role in the hanging of six Tsilhqot'in chiefs in 1864.

in the province. He once told journalists that independent officers of the legislature could play a crucial role as long as they "have the jelly to say what needs to be said."

Jelly never seemed to be in short supply when Hughes was on any stage.

As *Vancouver Sun* columnist Vaughn Palmer quips during the lunch, "Had I been asked 'what would Ted like as a going-away present,' I would have said a premier's head on a platter, but he's already had one of those, maybe more than one."

The extraordinary role Hughes had in bringing some order to the political Wild West he found when he arrived in British Columbia was just one chapter in a career that spanned more than six decades. By the time he arrived in Victoria at the age of 53, he had already been a lawyer and a judge for almost 30 years. When he and Helen, a force in her own right, left Saskatoon, the city held a farewell at the civic auditorium for them both and named a street in honour of Helen's service on city council.

Ted's law office in Saskatoon was on the same floor of the Royal Bank building as the local Progressive Conservative Party headquarters, which were frequented by John Diefenbaker when he was in town. That coincidence led to a lifelong friendship that first propelled and then sidetracked Hughes' legal career and later found him traipsing around Ottawa searching for a rumoured trust fund as one of the executors of the former prime minister's estate.

And while most young lawyers and judges found enough to do in their day jobs, Hughes served on hospital boards, first as a member and then as chair, both provincially and nationally. That was no mere honorary role during the bitter Saskatchewan doctors' strike after Premier Tommy Douglas introduced provincial medicare.

So if the assembled guests at the Union Club are skeptical that Hughes is really retiring, they have cause.

They have been involved in one or more of the other chapters in his life, assignments that for many people would have constituted a career in themselves, but that for Ted have never been enough.

Eight and a half years earlier, when Hughes completed his damning review of BC's Ministry of Children and Family Development and showed again his talent for cutting through bafflegab, he told reporters, "The sand has gone pretty much through the egg timer."

He said that in 2006, before serving for another two years as the first chief adjudicator of the national program providing compensation for Indigenous children abused in residential schools, a job that he had assured a *Regina Leader-Post* reporter in May 2004 would be his last. "I've done a lot of interesting things in my life, and I really believe if this is successful, I'll be closing out my career with the most meaningful thing that I've ever participated in."

But five years later, in 2009, he was investigating a Northwest Territories premier for potential conflicts of interest stemming from his affair with a clerk. In 2011, at the age of 83, he took on the inquiry into the death of five-year-old Phoenix Sinclair after successive failures of the child protection system in Manitoba.

"A lot of interesting things" hardly begins to cover the ground Hughes has travelled since his first job in 1951 as a country lawyer in North Battleford, where he was sent out to community chicken dinners to troll for clients. On one level, his career has followed a path he imagined, at least in part, when he was in high school in Saskatoon. He took Latin so he would qualify for law school, and skipped sports to become a debater. On another level, growing up during the Depression and the Second World War, he was always aware that outside forces can trump career planning. Although he prepared himself for law school, he fully expected to follow his older brother into the military when he graduated from high school. Instead, his final year coincided with the end of the fighting, and he was able to cross the river and go to the University of Saskatchewan.

The political career he envisioned while president of the Saskatchewan Young Conservatives never panned out, even though politics came to play a large role in his career, and the work he took on would, in turn, have a significant impact on how the game of politics is played in Canada.

Hughes became a public figure in British Columbia through his entanglement with politicians, first when he was forced to render opinions as the deputy attorney general and then as the province's first conflict-of-interest commissioner. As he took on MLAs and several premiers, it soon became clear who was more credible. When Ted Hughes spoke, people in power were well advised to listen.

In the late 1990s he found himself on a national stage, seeking (unsuccessfully) to have the prime minister, Jean Chretien, come and explain his role in the security planning for the 1997 Asia Pacific Economic Cooperation (APEC) summit, which was characterized by civil rights violations and immortalized by film of an RCMP officer pepper-spraying a CBC camera operator.

Through it all, Hughes stood up for the notion that public servants and politicians must first and foremost serve the public and not their own personal interests. The challenges he faced and overcame, in British Columbia and across Canada, with his unique combination of political savvy, grounding in the law, warmth and respect for others, intellect and force of will, forged the reputation for unquestionable integrity, sound judgment, administrative efficiency and courage to speak truth to power that he carried through another two decades of public service across the country.

Part I

Saskatchewan

Origins

AS IT DID for millions of men and women of his generation, the First World War changed the direction of Private William "Bill" James Hughes' life and changed the world into which his son Edward Norman "Ted" Hughes would be born in 1927, on a scale that was global and personal. The piece of metal that smashed into Bill's shoulder blade on September 16, 1916, in the midst of the fight for Courcelette during the Battle of the Somme, also shattered his plan to return to the physically demanding work on the homestead southwest of Saskatoon that he had staked with his brother John Edward Percy eight years earlier.

Bill Hughes was one of 10 children born to John and Mary Hughes in Worthen, England. Bill was the oldest, born in 1884. His brother John, who was always known by his middle name, Percy, came along 21 months later. Their father John was a tailor and draper in the small town in Shropshire near the Welsh border.

The economy in England in the first part of the 20th century was flat, with few jobs for young men. In 1906, Percy joined the thousands leaving for Australia and Canada in search of a better life after reading an ad in a London paper that said "Men wanted in the harvest fields of Western Canada; passage six pounds with the privilege of returning in six months for the same amount."

Percy found work as promised, thrashing wheat near Virden, Manitoba, for two dollars a day with no lunch or coffee break. A succession of jobs followed, and by the spring of 1908 he decided to become a homesteader in recently opened territory in the new province of Saskatchewan. He filed a claim for a quarter section of unbroken prairie 80 kilometres past the end of the Goose Lake rail line that ended in Zealandia, 100 kilometres southwest of Saskatoon.

Percy's first survey of his new home was by bicycle, which he rented in Saskatoon and rode over the rough tracks that passed for roads. It took five days to get to the homestead and back, with winds so strong that at times he had to get off and walk. It was a hard introduction to a hard life.

Bill followed his brother to Canada in 1908 and staked a quarter section of his own adjacent to Percy's. He filed his papers in January 1909.

For the Hughes brothers, the first task was to build a shelter. Like other settlers, they used the material at hand. On a treeless landscape, home was a hut made with pieces of sod cut from the virgin prairie with a team of oxen. With no suitable timber nearby to support the roof, the brothers set off with a neighbour, two teams of oxen and a team of horses to the South Saskatchewan River, a trip they expected to take a week. When they reached the river there were no trees big enough for the job, and the men had to travel another two days before finding anything useful. They ran out of food on the way back but managed to bag three partridges. Later, when they stumbled on a homesteader's shack, the settler gave them some bread and jam but wouldn't part with any of his grain for their horses and oxen. As they left, they "purloined" six sheaves of oats to keep their teams going.

Winter arrived before the roof was finished. They also had to gather fuel to get through the bitterly cold months, mostly sagebrush and dried cattle manure along with a few green pole ends.

"Under these circumstances and on a poor diet, we got through somehow," Ted's father wrote 50 years later in his contribution for a local history, *Memoirs of Hillsburgh*.

The first crop—23 acres of flax—failed in summer when no rain fell. To earn some income, the brothers hauled water from their well to a restaurant in the village six kilometres away. Two-thirds of the water would slop out of the barrels on the rough wagon road, but if they timed it right, they got a free meal in addition to 75 cents for the one barrel they were able to fill. Such were the details that made a difference between surviving or being defeated by the harsh demands of homesteading in rural Saskatchewan in the early 20th century.

Crops improved over the next couple of years, but Bill and Percy still took other jobs. Percy followed his father's trade as a tailor. Bill worked on a dam. At the same time they had to ensure they met the requirements for securing title to their homesteads by increasing the value of their land through cultivation and building.

In 1912, Bill acquired the patent for his land. The improvements he listed on the application were a 14-by-16-foot sod house valued at $150, a well and 20 rods (about 100 metres) of fencing valued at $20.

After their father died in Worthen in 1910, the brothers were able to save enough to help their mother and seven younger siblings—six sisters and a brother—come to Saskatoon in 1912.

When men started enlisting to fight in Europe, the brothers decided they would flip a coin to see which of them would join up and which would stay behind and work the farms. After that fateful coin toss, Bill mustered at the Minto Street Barracks in Winnipeg, and Percy handled the home front. Bill's son Ted grew up knowing how different life would have been for him if the coin had fallen on the other side.

After his discharge from the army, with the door to farming slammed shut by his disability, Bill worked a couple of jobs, including Municipal Weed Inspector, before joining the staff of the Soldier Settlement Board in Saskatoon in 1919. The board had been set up in 1917 to help soldiers returning from Europe obtain farms by providing loans and training. It was a good fit. Bill got a durable job that carried his family through the Depression of the 1930s in relative comfort and supplied enough income to help his brother's family survive on the farm through some lean years.

Saskatchewan was among the hardest hit of all Canadian provinces during the 1930s. Average per capita income fell from $478 in 1930 to $135 in 1933, the lowest in the country. In the late 1920s, the province had essentially a single-crop economy. When the wheat crop was good and prices were high, as they were in the mid to late 1920s, the province prospered. Incomes in Saskatchewan were among the highest in the country. But the price of wheat started to fall even before the stock markets crashed in 1929. After the crash, the price of wheat plunged. Then came the drought. Saskatchewan was at the northern end of the dust bowl. Topsoil blew away in great black clouds.

When the rains returned, prices remained low. The dollar value of the wheat produced in Saskatchewan fell from about $247 million in 1928 to a low of less than $56 million in 1933. The net farm income for the province was a negative number for four straight years from 1931 to 1934. By 1932, two-thirds of rural residents were on relief.[1]

As Bill established himself in town, Percy remained on the homestead. Farming underwent significant change over the decades he tilled the rich prairie earth. Tractors replaced oxen and trucks took over from horse and wagon. But life on an isolated family farm still lacked many of the conveniences other Canadians took for granted. Percy married Myrtle Estelle Thomas in 1921, and a family history tells how, when they retired from farming in 1963 and moved to an apartment in Victoria, it was the first time they lived in a home with running water and electricity.

---

1 Information on Saskatchewan during the Depression is from Eric Strikwerda, *The Wages of Relief: Cities and the Unemployed in Prairie Canada, 1929–39*; Jeff O'Brien, *Saskatoon, The Great Depression, and the Civic Relief Board*; and John H. Archer, *Saskatchewan: A History*.

In 1922, still a bachelor at 38, Bill had married Florence "Florrie" King in Winnipeg, at his mother's urging. Florence was 30. She had known Bill's sister in England before they emigrated to Canada, and they kept in touch. Florrie came to Canada from London with her mother and brother after her father died in 1912. She was working at Eaton's on Portage Avenue before she married Bill and moved to Saskatoon. They built a modest two-bedroom frame house on 9th Avenue North, a couple of blocks from the South Saskatchewan River in a middle-class neighbourhood called City Park. It would be their home until they retired to Victoria almost 30 years later. The house and the two blue spruce trees they planted in front were still standing when Ted went back to visit more than 80 years later.

Their first son, William James, also called Bill, was born in 1925. Ted followed on June 12, 1927. Edward was a family name, one carried through five generations at last count, and Norman, his middle name, came from the mayor of Saskatoon at that time, George Wesley Norman, who ran a printing business and with his brother started The *Saskatoon Phenix*, a precursor to the *Star-Phoenix*. George Norman later became a Liberal member of the provincial legislature.

In the manner of the time, Florrie's mother, Mary King, moved in soon after, and eventually every fall the country cousins—Percy's daughters—moved to town so they could attend high school.[2] To accommodate the overflow, two bedrooms were added in the attic, reached through a downstairs bedroom. Ted shared a room with his brother until Bill left home to join the navy.

---

2 One of Percy's daughters who stayed with Ted's family, Catherine May Hughes, married Neil Crawford, who hired Ted, then a young lawyer, to chase a man who bought his trumpet but didn't pay for it. Crawford had sold the trumpet to pay for a diamond engagement ring. Crawford became a lawyer himself and worked as an executive assistant to John Diefenbaker when he was prime minister. He later became a cabinet minister in Alberta.

Mary Hughes, Bill Sr.'s mother, moved in with the Pritchards, one of three branches of the Hughes family in Saskatoon along with the Hugheses and the Arscotts. Her presence reinforced the influence of the Anglican church in all their lives. On Saturday nights she hid the colour comics from the *Star-Phoenix* so that her grandchildren couldn't read them on Sunday morning and break the Sabbath. When Ted or his brother and their father stopped by to see her on Sunday evenings, they would always end the visit by singing "Now the day is over—night is drawing nigh."

With farm income drying up with the crops, farmers had little to spend in town, and the hard times spread into Saskatoon. Until the Depression hit, the "Hub City" of the northern prairies had been a thriving commercial and cultural centre, which grew from its origin as a temperance colony in the 1880s to a population of about 40,000. By the height of the Depression, however, one in five people in Saskatoon was drawing relief.

With an extended family in one house and a single bathroom, life was spartan by modern middle-class standards, but with his steady government job, Bill was able to provide a relatively good living for his family. As a child growing up in the Depression, Ted was aware he was living in lean times, but had little to compare them with. "We didn't think anything of it in those days, that's just the way it was," he recalls. Compared to many others, his family was relatively well off, but they were not isolated from the poverty that followed the drought into Saskatchewan. Ted remembers men coming by from the nearby CPR tracks. "Fellows who rode the trains, rode the rods as it was called, seemed to know that our house was a place they could come to get a smoke."

Life was a lot tougher out on the farm, where Ted recalls Percy's wife, Myrtle, making dresses for their four daughters out of flour sacks. "The farm was without running water. You went to the outhouse down the trail. They used coal oil lamps in the evening," he says.

Still, while it may seem primitive and harsh by modern standards, the girls remember the farm fondly. When it was Catherine's turn to move in with her uncle's family for high school, she was desperately homesick for the first few months. She kept the malady to herself, though, and soon succumbed to the relative comforts of life in town. "It was a lovely home and Auntie Florrie was always a sweet lady and always treated me like one of their children, and Uncle Bill the same. They just made life very comfortable."

Ted remembers the house on 9th Avenue North as a happy place with regular routines. "I couldn't have asked to grow up in a more positive environment, both in the home and around the home," he says.

Monday was washday, with clothes hanging on lines all through the neighbourhood; Tuesday was for ironing, and one day a week Florrie and her friends would go downtown to shop or at least wander through the department stores. Groceries came from a small store where families ran an account, and dry goods were sold in bulk from behind the counter.

Dinner was at noon. On a 90-minute break, Bill and the children walked home for the main meal of the day and went back to work and school in the afternoon.

Every few weeks the family would go to a movie together at one of the four theatres in town, the Capital, the Daylight, the Roxy or the Tivoli. There were swimming and gym classes at the YMCA, and mandatory piano lessons. The teacher came to the house on the streetcar.

Ted didn't play much hockey, but the whole town paid attention to the crosstown rivalry that played out in the annual Eastside–Westside game, where a young Gordie Howe was catching the attention of scouts.

Bill and Florrie were ardent readers and made a weekly trip to the library. For a special treat the family would go to the cafeteria at the Bessborough, a monumental railway hotel that opened in 1935. "Today buffets are everywhere, but then it was a very novel thing to be able to go and walk through the line with a tray and pick up what you wanted,"

Ted remembers. "As a kid, that was just a real treat, it was an absolute highlight."

Sunday was for church. The family attended nearby St. John's Anglican Cathedral, where Bill Sr. was the People's Warden and served on the vestry. Florrie taught Sunday School, which Ted and his brother attended regularly. They also went through Cubs and Scouts at the church. The Anglican cathedral took on new significance in 1950, when a new dean, Norman Douglas Beer Larmonth, arrived from Vancouver with his wife, Muriel, and their bright and attractive 18-year-old daughter, Helen.

Ted remembers the neighbourhood of his youth as a place where safety was just assumed. Parents never worried about where their kids were or what they were doing. "If you left on your bike on a Saturday, whether you were going to the park or to explore the riverbank, you never reported in when you were going or when you would be back," Ted recalls. "It was a lifestyle that was very free and open and very different, I suspect, from the concerns that parents have today."

Bill and Florrie always found enough money for a summer holiday, often with cousins and their families, at Meota on Jackfish Lake near North Battleford. For Ted it was the beginning of an enduring love of cottage life and the simple pleasures of hanging out at a lake.

The family got their first car in 1935 when Ted was eight, a used Frontenac that they put up on blocks every winter and rolled out again in the spring. Few cars other than taxis ran all through the bitter Saskatoon winter at that time. It was a big day in the spring when the car was put back on the road.

By the time Ted entered his teens in 1940, Canada was at war again. While the fighting was far away, the spectre of the conflict dominated life in Saskatoon, where the progress of the fighting and the fate of family and friends overseas was followed closely. "You always gathered around the radio to find out what the latest had been," Ted says.

Ted's father served on the Dependents' Allowance Board, which allotted money to veterans' families who needed extra help. After the war, Bill Hughes was awarded the MBE for his work, presented to him by the Governor General. He was also the neighbourhood air-raid warden, checking for light leaking out of houses during blackout drills.

With other mothers, Florrie knitted socks and packed parcels for the boys overseas as part of the Navy Mothers' Association.

Ted's brother, Bill, joined the navy when he finished high school in 1943 and became a wireless operator on a frigate in the North Atlantic. "It was the expectation of any young man coming out of high school in those days, that's what you did. You picked your service, air force, army or navy, and away you went. My expectation in Grade 11 and 12 was that I would be going to war too," Ted says.

High school boys had to pick a cadet unit to join. Ted was an air cadet and drilled a couple of times a week. Male teachers at Ted's high school, the City Park Collegiate Institute, wore uniforms and taught extra classes in aircraft recognition and meteorology. They sang patriotic songs in assemblies, including "There will always be an England." When troop trains were leaving town, children were taken down to the tracks to wave farewell. "I have vivid recollections of waving to the soldiers in uniform as they were hanging out the windows, heading east to embark for overseas," Ted recalls. "I don't know whether as kids you really appreciate the severity of what was happening, that some of them might not come back."

Starting in 1940, City Park kept an honour roll of students who joined the forces after leaving school. By the war's end it had 700 names. Fifty-two boys on the list were killed.

Fortunately for Ted, the war was winding down in his final year of high school, so the Latin classes he took to ensure his eligibility for law school were more useful than the afternoons spent marching on the football field.

University and a Growing Interest in Politics

UNIVERSITY MEANT A change of venue more than a new way of life. Ted still lived at home. He walked to the University of Saskatchewan—down to the end of the street and across the frozen South Saskatchewan River in the winter, and farther along to the 25th Street Bridge in the spring and fall.

The tall, thin freshman with an eager smile fell easily into the academic life, attending classes in the distinctive buildings of locally quarried greystone spread around the large campus.

Hughes describes himself as an unexceptional student. He failed French one year and had to go to summer school to make it up. Fortunately, in the years after the war the threshold for getting into law school was fairly low. "If you had two years of Arts, you showed up and you enrolled and went in." In retrospect, Ted says that many of his classmates, who wouldn't make the grade to get into law school today, went on to become fine lawyers and judges. What they lacked in academic prowess or background, they more than compensated for with their life experience.

Regardless of how he was doing in the classroom, Ted revelled in the university's social life and extracurricular activities. He wrote for the school newspaper and bowled on the intramural team. But he found his passion in debating and the parliamentary forum. By the time he graduated, he was the president of the Debating Directorate (club) and a member of the Student Representative Council. He also was the co-chair of "Freshie" week, welcoming new students.

He completed the prerequisite two years toward an arts degree and started law school in 1947, finishing his BA in 1947. He still remembers how excited his parents were as they got ready to attend his convocation at the University of Saskatchewan. He was the first in his family to receive a degree. In law school, he says, he was still far from the top of the class. "I didn't excel in marks in law college but I made my way through."

Hughes may have been overly modest about his academic standing. In a letter of reference written the year after he graduated, Fred Cronkite, the dean of the law school, said Hughes was "a much better than average student" who "has been recognized as having high qualities of leadership." When the dean's kids got in a minor scrape with the law a short time after Ted started in practice, Cronkite hired the young lawyer to represent them, which Hughes took as an affirmation that he was doing all right.

In law school, Ted was in a class of 49 men and one woman. About 40 of the men were veterans, many of whom had families. Ted was among the small minority that had been too young to go to war. The returning veterans, including two who were in the Battle of Dunkirk, were generous with their wide-eyed younger classmates. "They treated us kids with the utmost care and respect, almost as though they were looking after us," says Hughes. "Like my dad from the First World War, those fellows never talked a lot about their war experience. They were far more interested in getting through their law degree."

And partying.

"I had my eyes opened. It was just hard drinking and those guys were well entitled to it after what they had been through," says Hughes.

"I was still naïve enough to go home and tell my mother what went on at a party."

His parents were surprised but encouraging when their bookish son chose a path that took him into more new territory for the Hughes family: public speaking and debating, a direction that also led to party politics. "I just enjoyed the opportunity of participating in public debating affairs," Ted says, adding, "It just was natural that that moved me into the political realm."

Politics beyond the municipal level were never discussed at the Hughes dinner table, perhaps because of his father's role as a civil servant. "When I became a young Progressive Conservative, that was a new thing for our family to have someone go out and identify in political life. But I found my mother and dad quite supportive and I always thought that, because they were supportive, that their own political views that I never heard them express probably must have aligned with the affiliation I had taken on."

He was soon one of the top debaters at the university and travelled to intercollegiate events. In 1949, he and his partner, fellow law student Hal Sissons, defeated a team from the U of S College of Education to win the Hill Cup, a symbol of intercollege supremacy. Hughes and Sissons argued in favour of the proposition "Resolved, that science has hindered the progress of Christianity."[1] The *Saskatoon Star-Phoenix*

---

1 William "Hal" Sissons wrote his own obituary, which appeared after he died in 2009. Despite his arguments in favour of religion in university, he described himself as a "dead atheist... I did not belong to any of the innumerable, fear-mongering, holier-than-thou religions plaguing our planet and causing the majority of society's problems." Sissons practised in Peace River, Alberta, for nearly 40 years before retiring to Victoria in 1990. In Peace River he wrote and starred in amateur theatre productions and stand-up comedy. He wrote several books after retiring from law, including novels, a history of burlesque and a novel based on his version of what he believed really happened to the twin towers of the World Trade Center on 9/11.

of February 3, 1949, reported on the competition, noting Hughes argued that science had obliterated 200 years of Christian missionary work in Japan with the atomic bomb.

In the 1949 competition for the McGoun Cup, a debating trophy awarded to the top school in Western Canada, Hughes was on the University of Saskatchewan team that was defeated by a team from the University of Manitoba. Ted and his team argued for the inclusion of a bill of rights in the Canadian constitution.[2]

Later he joined the student parliament as the member for Lake Centre, the riding of his political hero, John Diefenbaker, who, coincidentally, brought in the first Canadian Bill of Rights in 1960, when he was prime minister.

"In the days when Saskatchewan had Tommy Douglas and John Diefenbaker, they had the best two orators in the country," says Hughes, who, as president of the Debating Directorate, persuaded Premier Douglas to donate a trophy to the university in his name.

From a strategic point of view, the Progressive Conservatives were a curious choice for a young man with political and career aspirations in a province and country where the party had limited electoral success at that time. But Ted was enchanted by Diefenbaker's powerful speeches and his brand of prairie populism.

"That was a brand far different than what is the Conservative brand of today.[3] [Diefenbaker's] was a progressive Conservative brand. There wasn't a great difference between where John Diefenbaker and Tommy Douglas would stand on issues. They were both progressives—Dief more of a populist and Douglas perhaps more of a theorist, grounded in philosophy. I think I was influenced by Dief,

---

2 Hughes found his debating skills to be an asset in the courtroom when he was a lawyer but less useful after he became a judge because, he says, a judge who has too much to say on the bench is not a good judge.

3 Referring to the Conservative Party under the leadership of Stephen Harper.

who was such a compelling public speaker, and I was interested in public speaking."

In April 1951 Hughes won a province-wide radio speaking contest conducted by the Young Progressive Conservative Association. The prize was a trip to Ottawa to attend Question Period in the House of Commons, with a chance to have lunch with the PC leader, George Drew.

He made that trip in May, on his way to the national public speaking finals in Quebec, held by the Junior Chamber of Commerce, where he won the bronze beaver for placing first. The assigned topic was "Good Civic Government is the Cornerstone of Democracy." His speech reflected his politics at the time and what became a lifelong belief in the value of local government. He cited statistics he had gathered on the low turnout in municipal elections across the country—as low as 21 per cent in Saskatoon—and warned that such apathy was playing into the hands of Communists "within and without our Dominion."

"It is no secret that in our very midst there are those who, if they thought they had the least possible chance of success, would attempt at this very time to overthrow our government by force and establish in Canada a Godless Dictatorship ruled from far behind the Iron Curtain."

By then he had graduated from law school and was articling at a Saskatoon law firm. But Ted was interested in more than pursuing his career at that point. He had his eyes on romance.

Helen

REV. NORMAN DOUGLAS Beer Larmonth always felt he had too many names. So when he and his wife, Muriel, started having children, they gave their two daughters only one each.

Helen was the second, born on September 6, 1932, four years after her sister, Mary. The Larmonths were living in the rectory at St. John the Divine Anglican Church in Burnaby, the first of a string of postings that Helen remembers seemed to each last about five years.

Larmonth was born in Winnipeg and raised primarily by his aunt and uncle in Kaslo, a small town nestled in the mountains on the west side of Kootenay Lake in the southern Interior of British Columbia. His uncle, Henry Beer, was the rector at St. Mark's Anglican Church and later Archdeacon for the Kootenays. Norman's mother, J.L. Trone, had been living in northeastern Washington State, but Helen doesn't know much more about her. His father was never mentioned. Reverend Larmonth did not speak of his parents when Helen was growing up.

Years later, at a celebration of his 50 years in the clergy, Larmonth talked about being raised in a rough manner by his uncle, who roused him at 5:15 each morning with the shout, "You'll sleep your brains away!"

Helen's father followed his uncle's trade, taking his training at St. Mark's Hall, a theological college in Vancouver that is now part of the University of British Columbia. After graduation, one of his first assignments as an assistant took him to Toronto, where he met Helen's mother, Muriel Elizabeth Ewan.

Muriel was a rarity for her time. She completed a BA at the University of Toronto after graduating from Havergal College, a prestigious Toronto school for girls. Muriel's father, John Alexander Ewan, who had immigrated to Canada from Scotland, was an editor at the Toronto *Globe* and a correspondent for the newspaper in the Spanish American and Boer Wars.

The newlyweds' first assignments took them back to the Kootenays, first to the lakeside city of Nelson, 70 kilometres from Uncle Norman's church in Kaslo. Then they moved to Trail, a small town on the Columbia River that was home to a large lead-zinc smelter. At that time the smelter was spewing enough toxic sulphur dioxide to spark complaints from Washington State and inspire ground-breaking law on trans-border pollution. The local hockey team was proudly known as the Smoke Eaters.

Helen's sister, Mary, was born into this environment in 1928. "My mother said she put out the diapers and they came in black," Helen recalls. "And this girl from Toronto, this young woman from Toronto who had been sent to this place, I'm sure she wondered, What the heck?"

By the time Helen came along, the Larmonths had moved to the rectory in Burnaby, the first of three homes in Vancouver. A move to Holy Trinity Anglican Church in the comfortable Fairview neighbourhood followed, and then they were called to St. John's Shaughnessy in 1941.

Helen remembers a generally happy home. The age gap meant that she was often more of a plaything than a companion to her older sister. Mary would stage plays and Helen would be her cast.

Helen's mother was part of a team with her father, serving the parish in addition to running the home. "He was out most evenings visiting people, and she would go in the afternoon and do the visiting. You got two for the price of one," Helen says.

The Larmonth home was a house of service to the Lord and the community. Service was an ethic that Helen absorbed. And like many of her generation, the Depression shaped her approach to life. At the time, churches filled many of the roles now covered by government and non-profit agencies. People in need would come to the rectory looking for help or something to eat.

Helen was only eight at the beginning of the Second World War. Mobilization in Canada brought an end to the Depression, but it didn't bring an end to poverty in Vancouver or to the stream of indigent people who showed up at the door of the house next to the church.

"As a small child, I saw men—not many women—come to our door for help because they didn't have the money for a meal or a place to stay," Helen wrote in a reminiscence for the 75th Birthday Book of her high school, York House. That experience helped shape the direction of much of her later life's work. "I always felt so sorry for these people and I guess that's where my emphasis sort of became."

Norman Larmonth's emphasis seemed to be taking on churches with relatively large debts and putting them back on their feet. He never spent money that wasn't already in hand in a diocese, even when that meant the rectory traditionally supplied for the minister and his family was inadequate (or nonexistent, as it was when the family moved to Saskatoon a few years later).

"I'm a cash man. I won't have a church in debt," he once told a committee at St. John's Shaughnessy when they had only $130,000 and wanted to go ahead with the construction of a new $200,000 church by borrowing the rest.

"I was very good at keeping money," says Helen. "It was probably my Dad's influence. You don't buy anything unless you have the money, sort of thing. My sister, when she was in Pasadena, used to phone on the QT every so often and say, 'Helen, I need some money,' so I would sneak out and get some money and send it to her because she knew I had money because I wasn't a spender. Dad's influence was very deep."

Reverend Larmonth taught Helen thrift but also a skill that would prove useful when she started needing funds for community service projects of her own: the ability to shamelessly and tenaciously ask for money or other support for a good cause.

Even in the 1940s there was a lot of money in Vancouver's relatively affluent west-side neighbourhood of Shaughnessy. Yet when Larmonth took over St. John's Shaughnessy, it had a debt of $4,400, "which at that time was a terrible amount," Helen says. The Reverend loved to play golf, so he took a membership at the Shaughnessy Golf Club, which, she says, "he used to serve God." He did so by shaking down the other members to donate, regardless of whether they were part of the church or even Protestants. Putter in hand, he laid the debt to rest and was at the heart of the fundraising campaign to build a new church.[1]

Many years later, Kathryn "Kate" Waygood, who served on Saskatoon city council with Helen, testified to the lessons Larmonth's daughter had learned from her father: "She is a persistent persuader," Waygood said. "She's relentless."

One of the perks for the family of the minister of St. John's was that one of his daughters could go to York House, a private school for girls in Shaughnessy. Mary went for two years, Helen for three after Mary left.

---

1 "He has the face of a saint and the tough soul of a shortstop going into the hole behind third. Such is his fame as a fund-raiser who has startled the moths in the billfolds of half the tycoons in town, 200 men arrived to pay obeisance to a man who christens their grand-daughters and then arrives in their offices next with a smile, a cheque book and a sub-machine gun under his cassock." From an account of the celebration of the 50th anniversary of Norman Larmonth's ordination, held at Shaughnessy Golf Club, in the *Vancouver Sun*, October 9, 1969.

Helen, or "Larmie" as she was known, made the most of her time at York House. In her senior year she was everywhere, editor-in-chief of the yearbook, secretary of the student council, one of the five prefects, captain of Algonquin House, president of the glee club, on the school basketball team and on the honour roll for her "exceptional organizing ability."

"Here's to Larm," one of her classmates wrote in her school yearbook.

True to her house and true to me,
May her college days at Saskatoon
Be wild and wonderful—really "boom"
May she learn to cook,
May she learn to sew
So she'll make a good wife for some poor Joe!

By the time Helen started high school, her sister had already left home. Mary was following her dream of becoming an actress at the Pasadena Playhouse, an innovative theatre school founded in the 1920s that trained many notable actors, including Canadian Raymond Burr.

However, Mary's dream of making the big time as an actor fizzled. After graduation she worked in summer stock near Chicago and got some parts in off-Broadway productions in New York. Along the way she met Charles Ulick de Burgh Daly, whose aunt was a patron of a summer stock company she was appearing in near Chicago. Daly was going to Yale, and they kept seeing each other when she went to New York. They married in 1949. Daly went on to work with the American politician Stewart Udall and later served as a speech writer for the Kennedys. In the manner of the time, Mary became a society wife and mother, and her acting fell by the wayside.

Helen gives her parents full marks for allowing a 16-year-old girl from a deeply religious family to go to a theatre school far from home. But when it came time for their younger daughter to follow her childhood dream of becoming an opera star ("As a girl, eight years old, I was going to be Carmen. That was the dramatic part of me. I used to go to King Edward School at night and take classes in Italian and Spanish"), they gently but firmly steered her down a more practical path, swayed, she believes, by her sister's failure to achieve the goal she put her heart and soul into. Helen's youthful dream of singing Carmen on the great stages of the world yielded to preparations for university and a serviceable degree in Home Economics.

With no siblings at home, Helen had formed strong friendships with the York House girls, so when the call came in 1950, the year she graduated, for her father to move to Saskatoon to become dean of the cathedral, she says, "I was highly annoyed. My friends were all going to UBC."

Staying in Vancouver, however, was not an option.

"Today I would never have gone, but in those days you went with your mum and dad. They didn't have a lot of money to hand out for another room and board. So no, it wasn't even contemplated. It was just 'we're moving and you're coming.'"

One of shocks was that she would need Grade 13 to get into university in Saskatchewan. Rather than spend another year in high school in Saskatoon, Helen took an intensive course in the summer before she left Vancouver to complete the requirement.

She was impatient to move on from high school, but as with Ted, that didn't mean leaving home. And home in Saskatoon for the first year and a half was the Bessborough, the monumental hotel opened in the 1930s by the CNR. The Larmonths lived there because the massive, Gothic-style, red-brick St. John the Evangelist Cathedral on the banks of the South Saskatchewan River, to which Norman had been promoted, had no suitable accommodation. So while he raised money to build a deanery, he and his family lived in one of the sample rooms at the Bessborough, a large L-shaped space with a small room where Helen slept and a larger room that travelling salesmen had used to display their wares, which her parents used for a bedroom. The same cafeteria that had been such a treat for Ted as a child was the everyday kitchen for the Larmonth family.

Helen met Ted two weeks after arriving in Saskatoon at a reception for the new minister at her father's new church. In an interview with the *Globe and Mail* 57 years later, Ted said he would never forget the day they met; Helen couldn't remember their first meeting. Even so, the encounter sparked a courtship that went on for four years while Helen completed her degree at the University of Saskatchewan and Ted finished articling and finally got a job in Saskatoon.

Ted wasn't her only suitor. An American Helen met at her sister's wedding in New York came up for a visit. While Ted considered him a rival, Helen quickly realized he wasn't serious competition.

The long courtship was more a function of the times than the result of any real doubt on their part about where it was going. Ted proposed in the living room of the deanery on Christmas Eve in 1952. Helen said yes, but it would be another two years before they exchanged vows. Helen's parents wanted her to wait to get married until she had her degree.

"They were probably sensible because Ted was just getting going. They wanted us to be started out on a firm footing. There weren't the women working and going to school as there are now." she says.

The classes for Home Economics, or Household Science, as it was also called, were held in huts used by the air force during the war. The program offered three streams: a general degree, a teaching degree that took an extra year, and a course that allowed graduates to work as nutritionists in hospitals and other settings, which also took an extra year.

By the time Helen graduated with her general degree in 1954, she was focused more on marrying Ted than a career, so that was enough. "He seemed very kind and he seemed to like me a lot. I wanted somebody who was kind and who cared about other people too. I thought it was really important that there be the same concern that I had about what was going on in the world."

Helen did work between terms and for a few months after graduating and before marrying Ted. The dean of the Home Economics College asked her to help out with a Saskatchewan Research Council grant testing laundry detergent. She spent her time washing pre-soiled pieces of cotton in varying concentrations of detergent in water collected from Saskatoon, Regina and Moose Jaw to determine the ideal concentration for the best results.

Soon after, she recalls, the detergent manufacturers changed their formulas.

"At least I had a job."

Country Lawyer and Budding Politician

AFTER GRADUATING FROM law school in 1950, Hughes landed an articling position with one of the top firms in Saskatoon, Moxon, Schmitt, Estey and Robertson, Barristers and Solicitors, a plum position for an ambitious young man. Arthur Moxon was a Rhodes Scholar who came to Saskatoon as a founding member and first dean of the law school at the fledgling University of Saskatchewan. James Wilfred Estey became attorney general for Saskatchewan and was on the Supreme Court of Canada when young Hughes did his articles.

For $50 a month, Hughes got to know the workaday side of lawyering and had his initial taste of a real courtroom. The first client he defended in a trial was described in the *Saskatoon Star-Phoenix* as "a small, dark complexioned youth of 19." The young man was charged with theft after helping himself to a truck parked outside a dance and taking some friends for a ride.

Hughes argued that his client shouldn't be convicted of theft because he intended to return the truck. As proof of that intent, the young lawyer argued he had only put 75 cents worth of gas in the vehicle and had still been driving around the city when he was stopped by police and arrested.

On consideration, the magistrate dismissed the charge and Ted's client then pleaded guilty to a lesser charge of joyriding. Hughes asked for a minimum fine because his client had been taking care of his four brothers and sisters since their mother had left home. The magistrate fined the young man $50, or about $340 in 2016 dollars.

When he finished articling, the bright, energetic young lawyer got a glowing letter of reference but no job at Moxon Schmitt or any other firm in Saskatoon. The law business was hardly booming in the decade after the war. In fact, many of the older lawyers bridled at the notion that they were running a business at all. Most of the commercial business in the province was in Regina, and many lawyers in Saskatoon were on their own and barely had enough paying clients to keep their doors open. Only a few firms had more than a couple of lawyers, and many worked in antiquated offices with little or no staff.[1]

Hughes never seriously considered going out on his own. He had no money for a law library and, as he would later discover, not much of an appetite for the business end of law. But he did consider going to work for the growing oil industry. He applied for a job with the Albercan Oil Corporation in Calgary. When the company offered him a position starting at $250 a month, though, he turned it down. He wanted to stay in Saskatoon.

In July 1951 he took a position paying $200 a month in North Battleford with a more entrepreneurial-minded lawyer who was looking for a young associate. Ariel Sallows was a prominent local solicitor who also owned the only funeral parlour in town, a business he had inherited from his father. "Every morning when he came to the office you would hear him dial a number and say 'how many?'" Ted recalls.

---

1 In his book *Prairie Lawyer, Country Judge*, David Beaubier described looking for work as a recently graduated lawyer in 1961: "I believe I visited every law office except one in Saskatoon. The visits . . . to the offices of lawyers over 65 were amazing to me. It was like walking into a Charles Dickens novel . . . the whole effect was cramped, dismal and tired. The fact was that most of them had not received a new client since the depression started in 1932."

Sallows expected Ted to go out and find work. One source was fowl suppers, which were community events held in church halls in the towns around North Battleford. Sallows told him: "I'll get you the calendar, and I expect you to be at every one of those fowl suppers. That's where you meet the farmers. That's where you get your clients. I want you there, and I'll be at some of them."

"So that fall I made the rounds to several fowl suppers," Ted says, "and I really did enjoy meeting the farm community."

Like other lawyers in Saskatchewan at the time, Hughes took on whatever came along. "There was absolutely no specialization, because everybody was anxious to do everything to earn a living," he says. The work he found was mainly conveyancing and wills. "Crop-share agreements, leases, were very common, where a farm property would be leased on the basis of not so many dollars for the year, but on a share of the crop. Generally, one-third went to the owner of the land and two-thirds to the renter, who had to bear all the expense for putting in and reaping the crop. If it was a good year, the landlord did very well. If it was a drought, then the landlord suffered along with the tenant."

He also helped farmers buying equipment. "The farmer would be buying a tractor, payable on time, and would want legal advice on the terms of the contract and that kind of thing.

"In those days there was not much family or matrimonial law. Families just stuck together through those days, more so than is the case today."

Hughes also got valuable experience in court as a prosecutor. North Battleford did not have in-house lawyers, so to enforce its bylaws it contracted that work out to Sallows.

Another lesson he learned early was that while he loved the practice, he only reluctantly shouldered the business side of law, especially when it came to charging less wealthy clients for his services, whether it was a sharecropper for a lease or a widow for a will. "That was one reason, and the principal reason, why I wasn't happy in private practice. I hated the billing part of it and rendering accounts."

Most weekends he worked until noon on Saturday and then hitchhiked the 140 kilometres to Saskatoon for church on Sunday and a chance to see Helen. Then it was a bus ride back to North Battleford Sunday evening for work on Monday.

Before the year was out, he heard about an opening at a law firm in Saskatoon, which would allow him to move back home and be closer to Helen. He promised Sallows that he wouldn't leave him in the lurch and persuaded a friend from law school to take his place. That friend, H. Albert "Al" Osborn, stayed with Sallows and became a partner in his firm. Sallows became a lifelong friend, visiting Ted and Helen in Victoria more than a dozen times before his death in 1984.[2]

Ted went to work for Francis, Woods and Gauley, a well-established Saskatoon firm that had recently lost a partner. The firm represented more than just an opportunity to be closer to Helen; it was an extraordinary group of lawyers with an eclectic mix of politically conservative and socially progressive views. In addition to their legal training, the partners brought to the practice their experience of

---

2 Sallows was unusual in his time as a lifelong bachelor who travelled extensively, including trips to China in the 1960s before many Westerners were admitted to the country. He gave parties on his return every year, which became major events on Ted's social calendar. Later he endowed a chair in Human Rights at the University of Saskatchewan law school and was presented with an honorary doctorate.

Two decades later, Al Osborn, the friend Ted found to take his place, had become the president of the Law Society of Saskatchewan. He included Ted, with a glowing recommendation, in a confidential report on Saskatchewan lawyers and judges that he submitted to Ed Ratushny, a special advisor to the federal justice minister, Otto Lang. Osborn recommended Ted for the Court of Appeal. Three months later, Lang appointed Ted to the Court of Queen's Bench. Osborn was appointed to the Court of Queen's Bench himself in 1984.

living through the Depression in Saskatchewan and their service in two world wars.

In 1953 the firm became Francis, Woods, Gauley and Hughes when Ted signed on as a non-equity partner. The partnership agreement reflects a time when becoming a partner in a law firm was not the major step that it is now. It also reflected the values of W.B. Francis, who was a lead solicitor for the co-op movement in Saskatchewan. The contract called for all partners to draw a minimum salary of $250 a month. Partners with wives were to receive an extra $50, and an extra $25 for each dependent under the age of 25.

"That would be unique to that firm, under the leadership of W.B. Francis," Ted recalls. "He was just that kind of person who would see the need, and the kind of people who were there would quickly subscribe to that philosophy. He was really a very forward-thinking person."

The other partners were also on distinguished career tracks. Mervyn J. Woods was president of Saskatchewan's Progressive Conservative Party. He taught law at the university and was appointed to the Saskatchewan Court of Appeal in 1961. David Eldon "Tom" Gauley was appointed Queen's Counsel in 1956 and was made a Member of the Order of Canada in 2003 in recognition of his service to the University of Saskatchewan and the legal profession.

Over the next few years, Hughes gradually became a full partner, building up equity by forgoing part of his annual salary. When he left to become a district court judge, he sold his equity share to a new partner for the equivalent of $4,000.[3]

Although there were no longer any fowl suppers, work in the new firm was as diverse as it had been with Sallows. Ted's practice now ranged from drafting wills to defending murderers facing the noose.

3 The new partner paid Hughes $3,000. The other $1,000 reflected a debt to another partner that was settled as part of the deal.

He was quickly proving himself to be an able courtroom lawyer, but there were some bumps.

While he was still living at home, he represented a young man who had been fired from the post office. The case was heard in Saskatoon in the Exchequer Court of Canada, the forerunner to the current Federal Court, that travelled around the country. The judge was Joe Thorson, a former Member of Parliament from Manitoba who was minister of war services in 1941 and '42.[4]

"It was in my early days," Ted recalls. "I was very nervous. I was called upon to present my closing submission, and I opened my statement with 'May it please your Lordship,' and Joe Thorson leaned over the bench, and he said: 'Young man, you're here to present your argument whether you please me or not. Get on with it!' It completely unnerved me."

According to Ted, some judges saw hazing as a rite of passage for young lawyers. "In those days there was a theory, obviously, on the bench that giving the young lawyers a rough ride was probably going to make them better lawyers at the end of the road."

A few months after Ted started his new job in Saskatoon, he was on the move again. The firm opened a branch in Regina to serve some of the co-op clients that were headquartered there. "We were lawyers for Federated Co-op, which is the big wholesale distribution facility, and we incorporated the Co-operative Trust Company, which is a very thriving entity today."[5] As the junior partner, Ted was sent to run the office. He commuted every week for more than a year, taking

---

4 Thorson was a veteran of the First World War, from which he emerged unscathed. He was wounded in both legs, however, while fighting off muggers during a holiday to Rio de Janeiro in 1962.

5 In 2005, Co-operative Trust was reorganized as Concentra Financial Services, with over $7 billion in assets. By 2015 it had over $34 billion in assets under administration.

the train that left Saskatoon at midnight on Sunday and pulled into Regina early Monday morning. Sleep was not the first priority, and Ted learned he could get by on six hours a night, an important advantage for a man with such a prodigious appetite for work.

Ted was also expected to find new clients.

One of his early acquisitions was a used-car salesman. Ted was hired to collect overdue payments, a job that lawyers commonly did then. But when it came time for the salesman to pay Ted, he couldn't raise the cash. So he invited Ted to pick a set of wheels off his lot. Ted chose a used red and white Austin with a comatose heater that offered no comfort on cold winter days. It was his first car.

A client who bartered for legal services was an exception, however. "I wasn't like the country doctor, who got the chickens and the eggs," he says. But indigent clients did get served. "There was no such thing as billable hours. If someone couldn't afford to pay, you probably didn't charge them anything.

"I was never in a law firm where money was the driving force. The fellows I was with were very community and socially minded. W.B. Francis, who was really the chief solicitor for the cooperative movement of Canada, as you might expect, had that ilk about him and he seemed to attract people who were of that frame of thought."

One of Ted's political connections turned out to be a major catch for the firm. In 1958, Hughes was the president of the Saskatoon Progressive Conservative Association and managed the campaign of Gilbert "Gib" Eamer when he ran for the leadership of the Saskatchewan Progressive Conservative Party. Eamer lost in two ballots to Martin Pederson, a farmer who harvested the farm vote and swung the convention. Eamer was the general secretary of the Saskatchewan Teachers' Federation, and Ted was able to reel in its legal business.

Pederson later persuaded Ted to run for the provincial legislature in 1960, in a similarly futile campaign to the one he managed for Eamer. Hughes, then 32, ran in the three-member constituency of Saskatoon City on a platform that was more progressive than conservative, promising a raft of measures to aid farmers, more money for pensioners, increased health insurance and more money for roads and schools. He finished a respectable second among the three Progressive Conservatives in the riding. But they all finished behind the Liberals and even farther behind the Co-operative Commonwealth Federation candidates, who were elected along with their leader, Tommy Douglas. Douglas was running on a platform that included the radical notion of government-funded health insurance. The Progressive Conservatives didn't win a single seat in the province.

"I knew at the time it wouldn't interfere greatly with my law practice, because I knew there was no chance of getting elected," says Hughes.

Part of the work for the Teachers' Federation involved representing teachers whose contracts were not being renewed by local school boards. They would get a hearing that usually attracted a large crowd. One such hearing took place in a community hall in Redvers, a small town just shy of the Manitoba border, in the southeast corner of Saskatchewan. The lawyers were on the stage and the hall was full. Ted was acting for a teacher. Another lawyer, George J. Tkach, represented the school board. Tkach, like Ted, had recently been defeated in the provincial election, a point he seemed to have forgotten in his attempt to undermine the credibility of the witness he was cross-examining, a former trustee named Funk.

"I put it to you, Mr. Funk, that on your last time out you were defeated in your bid to be returned to the school board."

Funk sat back and considered his reply. "Yes, Mr. Tkach, the same thing happened to me as happened to you on June the 8th," he finally said, a response that brought down the house.

"That was 45 years ago, but I well remember," Ted says. "I think we adjourned for lunch. The whole hall just broke up."

It wasn't all good fun. Teachers' careers were at stake, and sometimes they were on trial for assault or other serious allegations.

In his wider practice, Ted was called on twice to defend men whose lives were on the line. Both were charged with murder. In a city where murder was still a rarity, such cases were seen as real opportunities for a young lawyer, but there was no mistaking the severity of the potential consequences.

"With both those guys I was down in the cells waiting for the jury to come in, because it was a very emotional time," Ted says.

The first case was tried in 1958. His client, Robert Yund, had shot and killed his wife, Caroline Yund, and her lover, Jake Friesen.

"In those days there was no degree of murder," Ted recalls. "It was the noose if you were found guilty."

Ted argued that his client should be treated more leniently because of the circumstances of the case. He told the jury that Friesen was a "homewrecker... I ask you to picture this distraught man who had lost the love and affection of his wife and was driven from his home by his best friend."

The jury brought back a verdict of manslaughter, sparing his life. Speaking to the sentence, Ted told the judge his client should be considered to have diminished mental capacity, as demonstrated by the fact he had been placed in a special class when he was in school. Unlike the jury, Judge Harold F. Thomson was unmoved by Ted's arguments. He sentenced Yund to spend the next 20 years in prison, an unusually long sentence for manslaughter at the time.

By the time Hughes represented his second client charged with murder, the law had been amended so that the death penalty was only applied in cases of "capital murder," which included the killing of a police officer, premeditated murder and some other special circumstances.

Ted's client, Stephen Kozaruk, was accused of attempted rape and murder of 34-year-old Rose Whitehead, a case in which the death penalty could have applied. Kozaruk was a 35-year-old construction worker. Rose Whitehead was an Indigenous woman from Calgary with at least three children.

With the jury absent, Ted persuaded the judge that there was no evidence of any attempt to rape the victim. While there was very little about her in newspaper accounts, the inference was that she had been paid for sex. Mr. Justice D.C. Disbery then instructed the jury that it was no longer a case of capital murder, so the death penalty was off the table. The jury found Ted's client guilty of manslaughter, and Judge Disbery sentenced him to six years. After the trial, Kozaruk was taken to Winnipeg to face another murder charge. He pleaded guilty to non-capital murder and was sentenced to life in prison.

Ted was often on the road. District court cases that were heard outside one of the judicial centres in Saskatchewan were handled by a circuit court.[6] The judge, Crown prosecutor, defence lawyer and court clerk would often travel together in the same car, then resume their disparate roles once they arrived at their destination.

Ted also spent a couple of days a week in the offices of the Federated Co-operatives, a major wholesaler for co-ops across Western Canada, where he would either give advice on the spot or take issues back to his office for further study. He worked for rural credit unions as well. "Credit unions in those days were very different than the credit unions of today, which are in themselves very commercial operations. The credit unions in those days adhered to what was known as the Rochdale Principles. They were based upon resident helping resident, rather than going out and looking for commercial transactions."

And a lot of his business was still estates and wills.

---

6 District courts tried mostly criminal cases, and only those that were heard by judge without a jury. Prior to 1958 there were 21 separate districts, but in that year they were combined into a single district with 21 judicial centres. In 1981 the district courts were merged with the Court of Queen's Bench.

"We did everything. You had to make a living. It was an entirely different climate as to how you dealt with clients. You know, the offices were—let me tell you—very spartan, compared to what exists today. But I was appreciative of the opportunity to join that practice, and my partners were very compatible people."

However, when, at the relatively young age of 35, he sensed an opportunity to become a judge, he jumped at it.[7]

7 The descendent of Ted's firm is McDougall Gauley, which in 2017 advertised itself as a Saskatchewan law firm with global reach, offering the services of more than 80 lawyers.

A Powerful Patron

THE SASKATOON OFFICES of Francis, Woods, Gauley and Hughes were located behind the stone columns of the neoclassical Royal Bank building on 2nd Avenue South. The provincial Progressive Conservative Party had an office next door. For Hughes, it was an auspicious coincidence.

After years of admiring John Diefenbaker from afar, the young lawyer got to know "Dief" as a friend during his visits to the office in Saskatoon. Ted was heavily involved with the PC party as a young lawyer, building on connections he made in university. He was the president of the Saskatoon PCs in 1957 and 1958 when Diefenbaker was winning over the country, and later made his own run under the party flag for a seat in the provincial legislature.

The mid-1950s were exciting times for Progressive Conservatives in Saskatchewan. After years on the fringes, not only was the party's national leader from their province, but for the first time in decades that leader also had a fighting chance of becoming the prime minister of Canada.

Provincially, Tommy Douglas and his CCF were still the dominant force, with the Liberals not far behind. But Diefenbaker's populist oratory was starting to catch fire across the country, and people in Saskatchewan saw no contradiction in voting for a socialist party provincially and sending conservatives to Ottawa.

Diefenbaker's surprise victory led to a minority PC government in 1957, and his landslide win in 1958 brought a new regime to Ottawa. It also created a new world of opportunity for Progressive Conservative lawyers in Saskatchewan, who had been effectively shut out of federal appointments under the patronage system that operated, largely without question, at the time.

For the previous two decades under Prime Ministers William Lyon Mackenzie King and Louis St. Laurent, Liberals ran Ottawa and were able to appoint judges who had supported them to Saskatchewan courts. For the six years that Diefenbaker was prime minister, lawyers with a PC stripe were first in line for most of the appointments. At the time, the court system in Saskatchewan consisted of individual magistrates, district courts, the Court of Queen's Bench and the Court of Appeal. Magistrates were appointed by the province.[1] Judges for all other courts were appointed by the federal government.

"There was a whole group of prominent and active lawyers who had ties to the Progressive Conservative Party who, all in turn, got appointments to either the Queen's Bench or the district court," says Hughes. "Dief's first appointment was Emmett Hall to the Chief Justice of the Queen's Bench, and then when Emmett was moved up to be Chief Justice of the Court of Appeal, Chief Justice of Saskatchewan, Alf Bence became the Chief Justice of the Queen's Bench.[2] It got to the point where anyone who had impressive Progressive Conservative

1 In 1964, a Magistrates Court was created as opposed to individual magistrates sitting on their own. It later became the Provincial Court.

2 Alfred "Alf" Bence had been a Progressive Conservative MP from 1940 to 1945. Emmett Hall went to law school at the University of Saskatchewan with Diefenbaker and ran unsuccessfully for the provincial legislature after the war as a Progressive Conservative. While Hughes scrupulously avoided partisan connections after he was appointed a judge, Hall continued to publicly promote Diefenbaker after being appointed Chief Justice of the Court of Queen's Bench and later the Court of Appeal.

credentials, and was seen to be competent, was on the bench by 1961, '62. Rumours were always flying around about who was being considered for what appointment, and I began to hear of names being suggested who were contemporaries of mine."

The procedure for becoming a judge in the early 1960s was not straightforward. There was no application form to fill out or office to apply to. "In those days," Hughes says, "judicial appointments very much revolved around political association. I honestly don't believe that competence was sacrificed, but if you weren't close to the governing federal party, you had a difficult row to hoe to get a judicial appointment. I'm not proud of that fact that I got appointed under that system. But that's just factual. In those days there was no committee to which you applied, which exists today."[3]

Ted knew by then he didn't want to stay in private practice forever. Through his party connections, Ted also knew whom to approach. In addition to being politically allied as a Progressive Conservative, he had influential neighbours. The Hnatyshyns lived a few houses away.

"I said to my very close friend and neighbour John Hnatyshyn, who was by then a senator and probably closer to the prime minister than anybody else—that's the father of Ramon, who ultimately became the Governor General—I said to John, 'Listen, if they're considering X, Y and Z, might as well put my name in the hat for appointment to the district court.' So John Hnatyshyn said, 'Well, I'll pass that on to the boss.'"[4]

Hnatyshyn floated Ted's name to Diefenbaker on a trip to the West Coast. Diefenbaker liked Hughes but thought that at 35 he might be too young to become a judge. When he got back to Saskatchewan,

3 In 1967, when Pierre Trudeau was justice minister, he agreed to a proposal to have committees set up by provincial bar associations vet potential judges.

4 Ted and Helen's son David later worked as an aide to Ramon "Ray" Hnatyshyn when he was the minister of energy in Joe Clark's Progressive Conservative cabinet in 1979–80.

Hnatyshyn wrote Diefenbaker and reminded him that the Liberals had appointed Judge Alfred Monnin to the bench in Manitoba in 1957, when he was only 36 or 37, and he had recently been elevated to the Court of Appeal.[5] "Ted will be 36 on his next birthday and is in his 12th year at the bar," wrote Hnatyshyn.

Ted wanted to be a judge, but not so desperately that he was prepared to take any posting that came along. In the fall of 1962 he knew of three district court positions that needed to be filled, two in Regina and one in Melfort, a small town about 170 kilometres northeast of Saskatoon. Ted had always lived in Saskatoon, but if he were to be offered a Regina posting, he was ready to move. His children were still young, and he and Helen felt it wouldn't be too much of an upheaval. But Melfort was another matter.

"I talked a little with Helen, and we decided that if I was offered the district court in Melfort, I would decline with thanks, because it was a known fact that there was very little work up there to be done, and the retiring judge had kept busy as the president of the local horticultural society and fulfilling such activities. At 35 years of age, I wasn't prepared to spend my life in that way."

In the fall of 1962 he was sent to Vancouver to negotiate the purchase of a sawmill in Canoe, BC, for Federated Co-operatives. He flew back to Saskatoon on Friday, October 12, and went into the office, where he found a message to call the prime minister.

Ted considered himself a friend of Diefenbaker, but at that point he thought the message might just be someone pulling his leg.

The office manager assured him that the message had been left by the prime minister. "So I phoned that number, and got Dief, and he was obviously not in for a long conversation. It just exactly went like this: 'I hear you want to be a judge.' My response was 'Sir, I'd be highly

---

5 Monnin later served on the Court of Appeal and became the Chief Justice for Manitoba.

honoured to take on an appointment of that kind,' waiting anxiously to hear whether I was going to get a call to go to Regina."

Without giving him time to respond further, the prime minister told him that the appointment would be confirmed the following week and the posting would likely be to Melfort.

In a memo to file written in 1963, Hughes detailed how, after not hearing any more over the next couple of days, and still worried he might be appointed to Melfort, he decided to take the midnight flight to Ottawa to see the prime minister. On Wednesday morning he went to see Senator Hnatyshyn. That afternoon the senator took him to Diefenbaker's office behind the House of Commons, where the prime minister routinely went after Question Period. Hughes was able to see him for a couple of minutes, and he told Diefenbaker that if the posting was Melfort, he would turn it down if it wasn't too late.

Hughes wrote: "He told me that he thought I was making a mistake and to come and see him next morning in the East Block office at 8 AM."

Ted had planned to go back to Saskatoon that night. But he booked a room at the Lord Elgin Hotel and had dinner in the parliamentary restaurant with Hnatyshyn and some MPs from Saskatchewan.

The next morning he met with the prime minister and told him again why he did not want to go to Melfort. Diefenbaker phoned Robert Harold McClelland in Swift Current, another patronage appointee, getting him out of bed to ask if he would consider the Melfort appointment, but McClelland also only wanted to go to a larger centre. Diefenbaker told Hughes that he would have liked to be able to appoint him to Regina, but that wouldn't be possible. He asked Ted to think it over carefully and come back to see him that afternoon.

At four, Ted told the prime minister again that he appreciated his kindness in making the appointment, but that his "final decision was to decline as [he] was not prepared to go to a rural area and work half a day a week."

Diefenbaker called in the secretary to the cabinet and asked him to show Hughes a copy of the order-in-council that would have gone to cabinet. He said he would send Ted a copy as a souvenir, so he would always know how close he had been to becoming a judge. He also asked Ted when he was leaving town, and where he could be reached later in the day.

Hughes planned to catch a plane back to Saskatoon around midnight. He was going to have dinner with Dinny Hanbidge, the MP for Kindersley, who later became lieutenant-governor of Saskatchewan.

Hughes arrived at Hanbidge's office about 6 PM and found his friend "greatly worked up. The minister of justice, the Hon. Donald Fleming had been trying to reach me."

Diefenbaker had not taken Ted's second "no" as a final answer. He told the justice minister to call Alf Bence, the Chief Justice of Saskatchewan's Court of Queen's Bench, and see if some arrangement could be made to keep Hughes busy. When Fleming got through to Bence he was in the middle of a charge to a jury, but he came out of court to talk to the minister. Bence assured Fleming that something could be worked out if Hughes would take the appointment.

Ted met Fleming that night about 10, after passing some time watching the minister of agriculture, Alvin Hamilton, another MP from Saskatchewan, speak in the House. After all the trouble that Diefenbaker and Fleming had gone to, Ted was ready to sign on immediately, but the justice minister advised him to wait until he had a chance to talk to Bence before committing himself.

Back in Saskatoon, Bence and Senator Hnatyshyn came to see Hughes at his home on University Drive on Saturday. Bence said he would do everything he could to keep Ted busy in Saskatoon most of the time, even though the appointment would be to Melfort. After they met, Hughes phoned Fleming at home in Ottawa to confirm that everything was set.

Hughes was sworn in as a judge of the district court of Saskatchewan on Monday, October 29, 1962, at the age of 35.

The next year, Diefenbaker led his party to defeat in the general election, but stayed on as leader of the opposition. Over the next decade, Ted became better friends with John and Olive as the former prime minister became increasingly embittered about political allies who had turned against him. When Diefenbaker died in 1979, Ted was one of four executors of his will.

By that time, the political connections that led to his first appointment were no longer standing him in such good stead.

Family

TED AND HELEN were married on October 16, 1954. The ceremony was performed by her father in his church, St. John the Evangelist. She wore a dress she had sewed during her lunch hours while testing laundry detergent. For their honeymoon, Ted and Helen drove his parents' Morris through Yellowstone National Park out to British Columbia. Bill and Florrie had retired to Victoria earlier that year. This was the first of many such trips to visit relatives that became a twice-yearly routine for the Hughes family over the next quarter century before they moved to the Vancouver Island city in 1980. Helen's parents retired to Vancouver in 1955, adding another waypoint to the semi-annual odysseys.

Once they were back in Saskatoon, Ted and Helen borrowed $10,100 and hired a contractor to build a small bungalow south of the University of Saskatchewan on 13th Street. The lot was on the other side of the river but still just a couple of kilometres from where Ted had grown up. The total cost for the house, with extras that included clothesline posts for $26, a built-in ironing board for $25 and a milk delivery door for $6.50, was a little under $14,000. On the loan application, Hughes listed his annual salary as $5,500.

David William, their first child, was born in 1956. Sheila Elizabeth followed three years later, and Keith Douglas came along in 1961.

The growing family moved to a larger home on University Drive, just down the street from another prominent Saskatoon family, the Hnatyshyns. John Hnatyshyn was then a senator; his son Ray later became a Progressive Conservative MP and, in 1990, the Governor General of Canada.

Brian Edward Hughes made his appearance just before the end of the year in 1963. By then Ted was a judge, and the family was well enough off to move to a riverfront house on Saskatchewan Crescent East, a few doors away from Ray Hnatyshyn's house.

Helen could see Ted's office in the courthouse across the river, and she could tell if he was there by whether the light was on. He was there a lot. He would often return to work after coming home for dinner, and even when he was home, he was usually working on something. Weekends were family time, but Sunday nights he was almost always back in the office, preparing for the coming workweek.

Ted and Helen had a traditional 1960s household to a point: Ted had a career job, and with his relatively good salary as a lawyer and a judge, he earned enough that Helen could stay home and look after the family. Helen quickly immersed herself in the community as a volunteer. They were fortunate to have neighbours on 13th Street, Joe and Lillian Schmidt, who would happily look after the children, even when they were infants, while Helen headed out for her community work. It was an early version of on-demand daycare, and the service continued after Ted and Helen moved farther away.

Helen started volunteering with the Consumers' Association of Canada, working on campaigns to get better labelling. At the time, products could be sold in packages that didn't indicate how much they contained. "That's something that we take for granted now," Helen says, "but if a company changed the amount of product within a package, nobody had to know or did know about it. It would have the same price but they would take out a little of it and give you a little less. That was one of the things as a home economist that I volunteered to help with."

The group was also concerned with what was in the packages and pressed for better labelling of ingredients. For Helen, that concern intensified when her son Keith developed strong allergies. Helen had been allergic as a child as well. She was never allowed a dog despite her pleadings with her parents. But Keith's allergies were more serious. His diet was reduced to bread made without milk or eggs, ground beef and potatoes. He slept at home in a hospital bed so Ted and Helen could prop him up when he had trouble breathing at night. They also occasionally rushed him to the hospital emergency ward with an acute reaction.

"I always say I spent a third of my childhood in the hospital. I don't know if that's true or not, but I spent a whack of my time in the hospital," says Keith, who still has to carefully manage his asthma as an adult.

In addition to the adjustments Helen made at home, she worked with some other concerned parents to create an allergy information association to spread the word about the dangers that could be posed by everyday substances.

She joined the board of the YWCA and was the president in 1975–76. She started the Big Sisters of Saskatoon, was one of the founders of Crisis Intervention Services and sat on numerous boards and committees connected to the Anglican church, the arts and community services.

"She was the original energy bunny," says Kate Waygood, who as a young mother joined Helen on Saskatoon city council in 1979. "It was a different kind of society, and they were just recognizing that you could have women participating here, and Helen, gosh, was the role model, to put it mildly. It just blew me away the amount of time that she spent. It was a bit scary, actually, because it was only supposed to be a half-time job. At that time Saskatoon wasn't that big, so we were all part-time."

Helen had run for city council in 1976 at Ted's urging. He suggested she should run after he was challenged by a man on trial for murder who appeared before him in 1974. He told Ted the courts were irrelevant to the lives of Indigenous people. The 20-year-old Indigenous man, Delbert Alexson, worked at a nursing home in Regina and was accused of kicking a senile 91-year-old resident to death. Alexson had been drinking heavily, but there was no real explanation for the attack, which occurred after he left a bar and went back to the nursing home to get his paycheque. Alexson testified that he had been drinking since he was 12. He said he had blacked out and couldn't remember what happened between the time he left the bar and when the police arrived at his sister's house to arrest him.

During his cross-examination, Alexson started arguing with the Crown prosecutor, and Judge Hughes asked him if he had something to say.

"Well, all courts are shit, let's put it that way. I don't believe in court," he replied.

While it was a clear case of contempt, Ted listened. When he came home, he told Helen she ought to run for city council so she could to try to do something about the problems being encountered by so many Indigenous people moving from the reserves into Saskatoon.

"That really moved him," she says. "He came home and he said, 'You should get into civic politics. Run for city council, because that's the only venue where you can make any difference.'"

Despite Ted's growing concerns about the societal roots of the case, when the jury found Alexson guilty of non-capital murder, Ted gave him the mandatory sentence of life in prison.[1] An appeal of the verdict was subsequently dismissed.

---

1 Hughes never had to decide as a judge whether to impose the death penalty. Although capital punishment was not abolished in Canada until 1976, the last executions were in 1962. In 1967 the death penalty was suspended for five years except in the case of the murder of peace officers or prison guards. The suspension was renewed in 1973 and made permanent in 1976.

Helen took up the challenge in the October 1976 election.

Saskatoon had a ward system for city council, which made it a little easier to campaign. The Hughes family was in Ward 9, in the southeast corner of the city, and Helen was already well known in the city for her volunteering. She launched her bid with the same organization and energy that she brought to other activities, and emerged after election night as Alderwoman Hughes.

It was a proud moment when, as a judge, Ted presided over the swearing-in of the new council.

Helen's first action as a councillor was to pursue Ted's agenda of trying to do something about the problems facing the growing number of Indigenous people in the city, especially teenagers. Saskatchewan has one of the highest concentrations of Indigenous people of any province in Canada. The Indigenous population of Saskatoon quadrupled during the 1960s, growing much faster than the overall population of the city.[2] That trend occurred in other Saskatchewan cities and has continued in the decades since, albeit at a slower pace.

Ward 9, in relatively affluent, suburban, southeast Saskatoon, was relatively unaffected by the influx, but the owners of downtown businesses and their customers, on the other side of the river, saw the young Indigenous people who were hanging around the streets as a nuisance.

While recognizing the street youth as a problem, Helen also saw the issue as a symptom of a lack of jobs and recreational opportunities, and of schools that made no provisions for Indigenous children despite the difficulties they were having. The attitude was "why don't these kids become like us," she says.

She pushed for a community liaison committee that would have representatives from the city, school boards, First Nations, Métis

---

2 According to an entry in the *Encyclopedia of Saskatchewan* by sociologist Alan Anderson.

and non-status Indigenous people, health care and housing interests. They met twice a month with a facilitator, Ron Fisher, who was a professor at the University of Saskatchewan and a specialist in conflict resolution.

The committee was partly an exercise in breaking down barriers. Helen says, "We had some downtown business people. Their idea of an Aboriginal person was just someone sitting on the sidewalk sort of thing. We had a lunch and we made sure that these business people sat with Indigenous people at the table, and it worked. They had to think, and it evolved to 'OK, you're not all so bad.'" Unfortunately, shortly after Helen left Saskatoon in 1980, infighting between factions in the Indigenous community caused the committee to implode. It was reformed as a race-relations committee.

Helen was working about 40 hours a week on the liaison committee alone, and another 30 hours on other council business. That didn't leave her much time to be a stay-at-home mom. Ted continued to log the long hours that he worked all his life, and he was often on the road, both as a judge and for the volunteer assignments he took on. Yet, looking back, none of the Hughes children felt they were being neglected.

"Helen and Ted were out a lot," says Keith, now a bank executive in Edmonton. "They were very busy, what with Ted with the hospital work and on the road as a judge; Helen with her committees and so on and so forth. But at the same time the house always felt like a home."

Despite the attractions of living on the river, the house on Saskatchewan Crescent turned out to be less than ideal for the Hughes family because it wasn't in a family neighbourhood. Keith's allergies meant he couldn't stray far from home to play with friends, and there weren't many children close by. He would lie on the floor, playing with his Lego, laboriously breathing in and out. So in 1968, Ted and Helen moved the family to a home a couple of kilometres to the east in a suburban development of looping streets within a short walk of an elementary school.

The new house was one of the larger ones on Kirk Crescent. It was on a double lot, but not out of scale with the neighbourhood. There was a park a couple of houses down, and the street and the sidewalks were also a playground. Son Brian remembers it as the kind of neighbourhood that doesn't exist anymore. Most houses had kids to play with and stay-at-home moms. "You would go in and out of people's houses and somebody's mom would have baked cookies and everybody would be invited in to have some."

Children entertained themselves. The Hughes house had a double driveway and a front walk that created a loop separated by a bed of flowers and junipers that served as a racetrack for the kids on their bikes. They played marbles, and when it rained they raced toothpicks in the gutters.

Much like Ted's parents, for most of their time in Saskatoon Ted and Helen did not worry about the safety of their children outside at play or when they set off by themselves for school.

Greystone Heights Elementary School was only a couple of blocks away along paths called kiddy walks that cut across the adjoining crescents. The children came home for a lunch made by Helen and the odd episode of the *Flintstones* before heading back to school. Lunch might be Libby's beans or soup and crackers, but Helen's specialty was a triple-decker sandwich that featured Prem, Miracle Whip and green hotdog relish in the top layer and Cheez Whiz on the bottom.

Keith remembers that the house was never locked, and he and his siblings could readily come and go with a freedom that was afforded not just by the times and the neighbourhood, but by the relaxed attitude Ted and Helen—the Hughes children always called them by their first names—had toward most of their activities.

"They always have been Helen and Ted. I think that was in big part because our house was very often a gathering spot for our friends. It was a very social household, and we were always introducing them to our friends, not as Mr. and Mrs. Hughes but as Helen and Ted. That's what they very much preferred to be called," Keith says.

When the children became teenagers, the house was still a gathering point, in part because they felt welcome and because the parents were often not home.

"Helen and Ted had a theory that they would rather have you in their basement doing your thing, whatever your thing was, rather than out on the streets doing your thing. So parties were always very welcomed," says Keith.

The Underhills lived around the corner on Kirk Crescent. Elizabeth Underhill, now Elizabeth Hughes (no relation) and a Court of Queen's Bench judge in Calgary, was David's age. She doesn't remember ever being in the basement, but she recalls listening to music in the living room and sampling Baby Duck.[3] "Ted and Helen were pretty easygoing," she says. "I'm sure that they knew at least some of the things that we did but would never come down on us. But when parents were out or away, that was usually the house that the group of us would go to. Not surprising."

"We were very fortunate kids growing up," says Keith. "They appreciated that we weren't that bad of kids, and they thought if they gave us lots of latitude to do what we did, we would be better people for it.

"Trust me, there was lots of discipline in the house," he adds. "However, if we got disciplined, we certainly deserved it. They were understanding of what life was like and they didn't have the expectation of us being perfect angels. At the same time, though, they certainly expected us to be accountable for our actions."

Ted and Helen weren't all work. They packed a lot of play into their lives. Saskatoon had an active social scene, even for parents, with

---

3 A sweetened, sparkling concoction that was the bestselling domestic wine in Canada in the 1970s.

after-nine parties that started after the kids went to bed. When Ted was elevated to the Court of Queen's Bench, he and Helen invited all the lawyers in Saskatoon to a party that went on in shifts over a weekend. Their social circle included the upper crust in Saskatoon, but not exclusively. Brian remembers the Diefenbakers coming for dinner but also many meals with family friends from church. "It wasn't for them about entertaining the right people to (climb) the social ladder, and I don't know that that was important to many people in Saskatchewan in the '60s and '70s. They probably weren't unique in that regard."

Ted and Helen bought a cottage at Pike Lake, about 30 kilometres out of town. Then, when the children got older and wanted to waterski, they bought a cottage at Blackstrap Lake, about 50 kilometres south of Saskatoon. They had a boat, and small motorcycles for the boys to roar around on. Ted would pile up the charcoal and put a beef roast on the barbecue.

But Ted and Helen rarely stayed the night. They usually had other engagements, and the cottage wasn't far from town. Often as teenagers the children were allowed to stay on their own on the weekends, and Ted or Helen would come back to pick them up. It was part of the trust they had in their children.

Sometimes, though, it was trust but verify. Keith remembers Ted occasionally driving home two hours from Melfort, where he was presiding in court, to make sure that mayhem didn't reign supreme, then getting up at five the next morning to go back.

Being a lawyer and later a judge in Saskatchewan meant being on the road a lot. And that meant driving long distances on long, usually straight roads with little traffic in all kinds of weather. Queen's Bench was a circuit court. Hughes estimates he was travelling about half the time to the various judicial centres. Even as a district court judge he was often on the road, either to Melfort or filling in for judges in other districts.

Hughes liked to drive and he was often in a hurry. "I had a few tickets. I recall one. A jury had come in on a murder trial in Moose Jaw. They'd come in about 10 in the evening. I had to get packed up and leave for Saskatoon. I was roaring up the highway at, I guess, 80 miles an hour or perhaps a little more at 1:30 in the morning, and the red cherry came on behind me. The police officer recognized me. It was awkward for both of us.

"After being told I was speeding, I asked, 'Did you stop me to give me a ticket?'"

"He said, 'Yes.' And I said, 'Well, I'll wait while you write it out.' No way was I going to have some policeman saying 'Those damn judges get a break.'

"On another occasion I got a ticket coming in from Biggar, Saskatchewan. I don't know why, but it had to get settled out there. So I had Helen go out to Biggar on the day this ticket was returnable, and the headline in the Biggar *Independent* was 'Judge's Wife Pleads Guilty to Judge's Speeding Ticket.'"

Through all the miles, in all conditions, he never had an accident in Saskatchewan, and he brought his blasé prairie outlook on snow to Victoria, a city where the word "blizzard" is usually associated with falling cherry blossoms.

"When I was deputy attorney general, I got a phone call about 2:30 one afternoon. I don't know who was calling, but it was someone in the ministry, who said, 'Are we closing early today?' And I said, 'Why would we close early?' And they said there was a storm warning out, there's going to be a snowstorm, and that some other ministries' deputies had given their staff the permission to go home. I looked out the window, and snowflakes were just beginning to come down, and I said, 'No, we're not closing today. There's a storm, but it won't keep anybody from getting home at the end of the day, as far as I can see. And we're carrying on with our work as usual, thanks very much.' I always remember that. On the prairies you worked your full day and went home, whether it snowed or not. I don't remember who called me, but I always remember sitting where I was when I got that call and how I thought: Holy Lord. Not a chance are we shutting down."

While Ted was never fazed by snow and ice, licorice allsorts almost did him in. Ted and Helen were on their way home after vising their son Brian and his family in California when Ted fell asleep at the wheel of their new white Ford Taurus near Bend, Oregon.

"I'd been eating these licorice allsorts, and I'm satisfied that the sugar put me to sleep," he says. "You know, it's one of my most fearful moments. I apparently crossed the centre line and went into the ditch on the other side of the road, turned upside down four times... one, two, three, four... and eventually was stopped by a tree."

Help was soon at hand and an ambulance summoned to take Ted and Helen to a hospital in Bend. "We rode in the ambulance side by side. One ambulance. Neither of us had ever had an ambulance ride before."

Several hours later they were discharged with no serious injuries. The car did not fare as well. "The ironic part about it was that I'd always wanted a white car, and this was a brand-new white 2002 Taurus, and it was a total writeoff. I decided that I wasn't going to have another white car."

Or another licorice allsort while driving.

"To this day I've never eaten another sweet in the car—never."

Road trips were a big part of growing up in the Hughes family. Twice a year Helen and Ted and the four kids piled into one of a series of big late-model Chrysler or Pontiac station wagons that populated the driveway on Kirk Crescent and headed west.

Ted always drove, usually at as brisk a clip as the weather would allow. Helen sat in the back to referee, and David, Sheila, Keith and Brian rotated through the seats. The usual destination was Vancouver to visit Helen's parents and across on the ferry to Victoria to spend a few days with Grandma and Grandpa Hughes.

Muench's Family Resort on the Detroit Lakes in Minnesota was another favourite destination. Ted rowed while the kids caught turtles to decorate for races held by the resort on weekends.

For a mid-winter break, the family would check into a motel with an indoor swimming pool in Minot, North Dakota, for a few days over New Year's. The kids hung out at the pool all day, and the parents socialized over drinks with another family from Saskatoon without having to drive anywhere.

Despite Helen's intervention, Ted had to stop the car occasionally to read the riot act. According to family lore, on one memorable trip from Chicago to Las Vegas, Ted pulled over and Sheila, needled to the breaking point, bolted off across the desert while David chanted "Let her go, let her go."

First David, then Sheila dropped out of the family pilgrimages, but more than once they were replaced with friends from their church, Ralph and Mabel Carter.

Ted and Helen were the opposite of helicopter parents. Despite their own prodigious appetite for work and their extraordinary achievements, their children say they weren't pressed to follow their parents' examples. They were expected to take some kind of post-secondary education, but Helen and Ted didn't prescribe the form it should take.

"I don't think they wanted us to push grocery carts for the rest of our lives, and I don't mean that demeaningly," Keith says. "That was more their belief and understanding that education will allow opportunities to not only better yourself but to give to the community and those sorts of things."

"They just never told us what to do," says Brian. "They just sort of let us do our thing, and they quietly instilled sort of a compass on each of us that we sort of knew what we should be doing without them pushing us to do it."

"They certainly, I presume, had their own ideas as to what success was," David says. "But they weren't dogmatic about what your success would be. Success for them was to give your best try, and completion was always important to them. You couldn't go in halfway and just give up."

David was the only one who went straight through university. He earned a master's from Queen's University, travelled extensively and worked as a political assistant in Ottawa to Ray Hnatyshyn. After a taste of law school, he dropped out to start a successful landscaping business in Caledon, Ontario, where he served two terms on the Caledon council. He retired at 49, got divorced and started spending most of his time in Laos.

Sheila went through nursing school. After stops in Prince Albert and Ponoka, she settled on Vancouver Island, where she provided care for many years in the nursing home where she met her second husband while he was visiting his grandmother.

Keith took a two-year business program at Camosun College in Victoria, which led to a career in banking.

After graduating from high school in Victoria, Brian stayed at home and worked for a year before going into a hospitality program at Camosun College. His path took him into hotel management and a degree at Cornell University.

There were a few requirements for the children, however. Brian remembers being forced to take confirmation in the Anglican church, which at the time he bitterly resented. "The only thing that they made me do that I was adamantly opposed to was being confirmed in the church. That was an absolute battle and they were relentless on it. I remember being taken to confirmation classes, which you did after school. I was so angry and pissed off and not wanting to do it. I was sitting in the front seat, and I can't remember if it was Ted or Helen driving, but it was definitely Ted's car. It was a red station wagon. Not a lot of cars had air conditioning as part of their standard equipment, so he had an air-conditioning system installed, which sat underneath the dashboard, and I kicked the shit out of it and broke it into pieces, and they kept driving and took me to the confirmation. That was the only thing that they, that first of all they insisted that I do, and that, when I expressed vehement opposition to it, it was like, 'tough nuts, you're going.' That was quite remarkable."

The children were also required to take swimming lessons at the YMCA and music lessons downtown. "It was busy," Keith says. "Saturday mornings the majority of us would head off to the YMCA and do our swimming classes and go buy our French fries for lunch and those kind of good things. We would take the number 8 bus, which used to go by half a block away, so we would bus. We were not chauffeured around, but then Helen and Ted were always quite busy, so they weren't available to chauffeur, per se."

Helen never got to sing in the opera, but she retained her love of music. She sang in choirs and choral groups in and out of church, and all of the children were expected to play an instrument, like it or not. David played trumpet, Keith had a saxophone, Sheila tackled the piano and Brian played drums. "While I don't think we were ecstatic about it, it's just very fortunate it was one of the things we got to do. I don't think we understood why they were doing what they were doing at the time, but it turned out pretty good," says Keith.

As teenagers, they all had jobs. They were not expected to save for their post-secondary education, but they were expected to pay for their own fun. "Ted obviously earned a comfortable income as a judge," says Keith. "Helen never earned much, she did so much volunteer work. She would have been paid a little bit for city council work. At the same time, because they knew Ted would have a comfortable pension from the federal government for being a judge, they weren't savers. They certainly spent it all, and that was for the benefit of us. Whether it was for trips to Hawaii before it was fashionable to go to Hawaii, whether it was for a motorboat before it was fashionable to have a motorboat, all those kind of things. We were very fortunate. If any of us kids wanted to play whatever sport or someone needed a musical instrument or anything like that, obviously we weren't privy to the conversations that went on in the bedroom, but my impression was that was never an issue. They just made it happen."

Judge Hughes

HUGHES' APPOINTMENT MAY have been pure patronage, but over the next decade he proved that it was not without merit. Despite his young age he quickly earned the respect of his fellow judges and the lawyers who appeared before him for his command of the courtroom, his attentiveness, his preparation and his even-handed decisions.

Prosecutors liked appearing before him because they knew it would be a good trial with no shenanigans. Hughes believed that, for a judge, listening was often more of a virtue than speaking, but he was a big man with a big voice that carried clearly to the far corners of a courtroom. When necessary, he used it to full effect to keep the lawyers, witnesses and occasionally the gallery in line and on track.

Marsha Erb covered the courts for the *Saskatoon Star-Phoenix* through much of the 1970s before going to law school and later becoming a judge on the Court of Queen's Bench in Alberta. She says Hughes dominated the courtroom without bullying. "He was very strong. He was very direct. He had a booming voice, not used in any aggressive way or anything. You could hear everything that he said."

He treated everyone who appeared before him with respect, accused, counsel and witnesses alike. At least, he did as long as they were prepared and not, in his opinion, playing games.

Silas Halyk was a Saskatoon lawyer who often acted for the Crown. "I can remember him being very unhappy with some police work on a particular issue and making it very well known that it was the worst job that he had ever seen done by the police. He let it be known if he was unhappy. He's always had a bit of that side to him."

But he didn't equate inexperience with incompetence.

Edward Ratushny, who later became a law professor and a key player in another chapter in Ted's life, argued a case before him as a young lawyer. The opposing lawyer was Victor Hnatyshyn, the younger brother of Ray, and Ratushny says, "I remember we—he was very young too, just out of law school—we worked like dogs because it was very competitive." Hughes delivered a compromise judgment, giving a bit to each side. "He said, 'It's incredible that I should have a case that is as well researched and presented and as thorough on a matter of this nature,' something like that to make us both feel good, but then he said, 'But I wonder whether this case should have been litigated at all.'

"He was teaching from the bench, and doing it in a nice, good, objective, judicial way. Those are the kinds of things that endeared him as a judge."

For Hughes, the choice was deliberate. "When I first started to practise there was one Queen's Bench judge who was a very miserable person and treated lawyers with a lack of respect, and there were others who, to young lawyers, gave the appearance of being very crusty and made the difficult job of being counsel more difficult than it needed to be. I was bound and determined that any lawyers that came into my court were going to feel comfortable, were going to be fairly dealt with. Not everybody was going to be satisfied with the result and usually half of them wouldn't be. Nonetheless, I wanted to be in a position where even those who were unsuccessful would at least feel they had a fair hearing."

The jurisdiction of district courts was limited to minor civil cases and criminal cases in which the defendants chose to be tried by judge without a jury. As he had been as a lawyer, Hughes the judge was faced with a range of misdeeds, from break-ins to bank robberies, bar fights to abduction and sexual assault.

Roy Romanow was an attorney general and the premier of Saskatchewan from 1991 to 2001. In the mid-1960s he was just getting started as a lawyer. He argued a few cases before Judge Hughes, but he also appeared in the witness box after his Chevrolet collided with another car at an intersection. He was being sued by the other driver, who alleged Romanow failed to stop at the stop sign. To Romanow's surprise, Judge Hughes agreed and found him at fault for his "Hollywood stop" (another name for a rolling stop, in which a vehicle slows but doesn't actually stop at a stop sign).

"I don't know why I should have been surprised at that, because it was a reasonable judgment," Romanow says now. "But I think buried way back in my mind was probably some misperception that since I was a member of the bar and he was a judge, there would be some sort of unspoken realization that a member of the bar like me would be dead honest in my testimony. I think I was dead honest in my testimony. But he was not having any of it."

In one bizarre case in 1968 that is as much a period piece as it is an example of Ted's judgment, a prominent surgeon and his wife were both charged with indecent assault. Halyk was brought in as a special prosecutor, primarily, he recalls, because the accused lived in the same prosperous neighbourhood as the chief Crown prosecutor. The accused were represented by Calvin Tallis, a top trial lawyer in Saskatoon, who later went on to become a Justice of the Saskatchewan Court of Appeal.

The trial was a sensation in Saskatoon. It was held in a large courtroom, but because of the phenomenal public interest in the case there was standing room only for onlookers. The victim was under police protection.

The surgeon had begun an affair with a nurse he worked with at the hospital. They got together three or four times a week. Then one day in June, his wife "confronted him with the facts of this outside association."[1] At 2:15 the next morning, the three of them met in a parking lot. The surgeon's wife called the nurse a slut and physically attacked her. The nurse ran off and the surgeon restrained his wife.

As Hughes described the events that unfolded over the following weeks in his written judgment, he said he believed the nurse's account beyond any reasonable doubt, along with her assertion that she realized the affair was over and wanted nothing more to do with the surgeon outside of work. She testified that the surgeon called her three days later. He told her to leave his wife alone. The wife was also on the line and asked her husband if he had anything else to say. So prompted, he called the nurse a whore.

"There was no suggestion as to how such a married man should be appropriately described," Hughes commented in his judgment.

Over the following weeks, the surgeon tried a couple of times to persuade the nurse to meet him, once at a motel and once in a parking lot. Both times his wife was with him. The nurse wisely refused.

Then one morning while walking from her boarding house to the hospital, the nurse was met by the surgeon and his wife. He pulled her into a car. His wife drove to an isolated spot on the prairie five kilometres out of town. There he held the nurse down, verbally abused her, spat in her face and stuck two fingers in her vagina while she struggled and his wife stood by.

---

1 The account of this case is entirely from the oral judgment rendered by Hughes, a copy of which he retained in his personal papers.

The surgeon admitted to the verbal abuse and the encounter, but denied forcing the nurse into the car and the physical attack. Witnesses testified that when the nurse got out of the car, she had scrapes on her face, she had been crying and her hair was mussed. A doctor found blood on her underwear.

In his judgment, Hughes found that the corroborating evidence on its own was too weak to support a conviction of the surgeon for sexual assault. But because he believed the nurse's testimony beyond any reasonable doubt, he said, "I am entitled to find him guilty."

His assessment of her credibility as a witness was based partly on how she described the role the surgeon's wife played in the assault. Despite the animosity the nurse obviously felt toward the woman, who must have been the motivating force behind the surgeon's attack, she said the wife did not physically assist him in any way. That testimony empowered Hughes to find the husband guilty of sexual assault but it also saved the wife. Hughes found that her presence alone was not enough to attach criminal liability to her actions, even though she had asked her husband "Did you get in?" when he stuck his fingers in the nurse's vagina. When he said he had, she said, "You have proved you don't love her."

But the nurse also testified that the surgeon was furious during the attack. Hughes found that his level of anger raised a reasonable doubt as to whether the wife was aware of his full intent in assaulting the nurse. As a result, he found the wife not guilty of the charge of indecent assault.

On sentencing, Hughes noted that in previous cases of indecent assault his sentences ranged from a fine of $35 to nine months in jail. For the surgeon, he took into account his "clear and unblemished background." He also found the surgeon had become a victim of his wife's uncontrollable emotions. "I do appreciate, and accordingly weigh in your favour, the known fact that in situations of extreme emotion, reason slips into second place—and I have no doubt at all that this is what happened here throughout."

Hughes fined the surgeon $500 (about $3,400 in 2016 dollars) and expressed the hope that "in the interests of everyone including yourself, your family, you and those with whom you associate professionally and socially will recognize that the debt you incurred to society for your wrongdoing has been paid."

In the context of how these issues are viewed now, nearly 50 years later, one suspects that, at the very least, the nurse was not happy with this result.

But the fine wasn't the only penalty for the surgeon and his wife. Their comfortable life in Saskatoon was over. He had to leave his practice and moved with his family to a small community west of Saskatoon. When he died a couple of years later, his wife and children returned to Saskatoon, where she went back to work as a nurse.

In another case, Hughes recalls giving a much stiffer sentence that was not received in the way he expected. "There was an old branch of the Canadian Imperial Bank of Commerce up on 33rd Street in the Mayfair district of Saskatoon, and this guy jumped up on the counter with a gun or a replica and scared the living daylights out of the teller and demanded money.

"When it came time to sentence, I guess I said, 'You know you are going to get a very severe sentence, and it disturbs me to put someone of your age and potential away for this period of time, but you deserve it for what you did and I give you 11 years.'

"And the guy got up and said, 'Judge, don't feel sorry for me. If you knew all that I've gotten away with, you would know that that was probably a very fair thing that you've just done.'"

In Windrem v. Hamill, Hughes found a farmer at fault when one of his cows was hit by a motorist one winter night. The cow was part of a herd that escaped earlier in the day and was missed by the farmer when he chased them back into a fenced field with his snowmobile. Hughes found the farmer negligent and awarded the driver $10,000 for his injuries and damage to his truck. The farmer appealed, and the Court of Appeal reduced the award to $4,000.

Ted's judgment in Canadian Industrial Gas and Oil Ltd. (CIGOL) v. Saskatchewan, one of the first cases he heard after being elevated to the Court of Queen's Bench in 1974, was appealed to the Supreme Court of Canada. The oil company was challenging legislation brought in by the province the previous year, which aimed to harvest the lion's share of the enormous increase in the global price for petroleum following the 1973 Arab–Israeli War.

CIGOL argued that the new royalties were unconstitutional because they were effectively an indirect tax of a type that provinces are not allowed to impose. The company also claimed it was an attempt to regulate interprovincial trade, which would have been the exclusive purview of the federal government.

In his 160-page judgment, Hughes described the new fee regime as a 100-per cent levy on the increased value of oil produced in Saskatchewan, but he found that the province was within its rights to impose it.

CIGOL appealed, and all five judges of the Saskatchewan Court of Appeal backed Ted's interpretation of the law. At the Supreme Court, however, his judgment was overturned, with two of the nine judges dissenting from the majority opinion.

The Supreme Court judgment could have been a huge blow for the province. In November 1977 the *Globe and Mail* reported that by the time Saskatchewan was ordered to repay the oil companies, the bill would have been more than $500 million, half the provincial budget and $500 for every resident of Saskatchewan. The province was able to sidestep the impact of the decision by changing the way it raised revenue from oil production. And within a few years, by the early 1980s, the focus in Saskatchewan had shifted to easing the burden on oil companies to stimulate investment.

While Hughes always respected the authority of the higher courts, he did not always agree with their verdicts. In 1972 he heard an appeal of a ruling by a magistrate that a film, *The Stewardesses*, was obscene. The magistrate found it offended community standards and fined the Daylight Theatre Co. Ltd. for screening it.

The company appealed on the grounds that the film had already been approved for viewing by the Saskatchewan Film Classification Board. Hughes agreed and overturned the conviction. He said the government was talking out of both sides of its mouth by having one group of civil servants allowing the film while another pursued it for being obscene as defined by the Criminal Code. Hughes ruled on the basis of what he would later describe as an attempt "to give to a never-used statutory anachronism, with its roots in the 17th century and adopted in Canada some 80 years ago, a 20th-century interpretation that would have kept law and justice travelling on the same road."

Hughes' ruling was quashed by the Court of Appeal, which sent the case back to Hughes to try again on its merits.

In his ruling on whether the film met the community standards test for obscenity, Hughes said he of course respected the superior court's authority, but commented, "I must say, my ideal of law and justice as constant handmaidens has indeed received a bit of a knock."

As for the film itself, Hughes faced the difficult task of determining what the community standards were in Saskatoon at the time. With no guidance from the evidence presented at trial, he ruled that sex that flows from the plot was acceptable, while sex for the sake of sex was not. In *The Stewardesses*, "there was little there but a preoccupation with sex," he said, while rejecting the argument that this distinction shouldn't matter because the sex acts were simulated by actors rather than being real.

"If the scenes of fornication in 'The Stewardesses' were 'play acting,'" he wrote, "then if and when the smut wing of the movie industry holds an Oscar night, the participants in 'The Stewardesses,' air hostesses, air crew and passengers alike, have every right to anticipate a call from the stage to come forward to receive a deserving reward."

Hughes ruled the film obscene and fined the theatre company $250. But he went on to stress that while *The Stewardessess* offended community standards, there was a place for sex in the cinema. "The very epitome of or essence of decency can be found in nudity, love and sexual fulfillment when portrayed with dignity, warmth and, above all, the presence of mutual respect for one another."

Hughes was a confident judge. He thrived on difficult decisions and never second-guessed himself in spite of the stakes for those appearing before him. "In civil cases I always found a way to reach the result that I thought was fair and just. Precedent is a great resource for judicial work, but in civil matters, I always rationalized in my mind what was the right result—what should it be, based upon what I heard. I don't think I ever turned out a civil judgment that I didn't think was the result that should be arrived at.

"On the criminal side, in a sense it was the same, but you are dealing with an individual's life. You are sitting there with the power to take away the freedom of your fellow man or woman. That is a very, very onerous responsibility. Of course, you have to not only look at the future of that young person and what you can do to try to straighten out their life. You've also got to look at society that has been injured by what he or she has done. Determining guilt and sentencing, these are serious matters requiring very thoughtful attention.

"On the guilt issue, we do have the standard of guilt beyond a reasonable doubt being required. I think it works well. For the individual, what you can do for her or him relates more to the sentencing."

Hughes found sentencing more challenging because of all the variables. "But when you weighed all that, you make your decision and I never second-guessed myself. That is, when I made my decision, I was content with it, and I don't think there was ever a case when I said the next day, 'I should have done such and such.' I felt I gave it the consideration that was required, but I was always very gratified to know that there was a court of appeal sitting above me, who, if I had been wrong, could correct it. I never, ever, took offence to appeals of my judgments being taken. I don't think I was appealed a lot, but it happened. I think it happened to every trial judge. I always was grateful that if I made a mistake involving someone's livelihood or life, there was a court to say, indeed you were wrong, and the right thing was ultimately done."

Ted learned one valuable lesson about potential weaknesses in the justice system outside the courtroom. He had picked up a babysitter and taken her to the Hughes home on Saskatchewan Crescent. He was sitting in the car, waiting for Helen to come out, when he noticed a strange man coming out of the house four doors down where Ray and Gerda Hnatyshyn lived.

The man appeared to be drunk. He left the veranda door open when he left the house. After he wobbled by Ted's car, Ted went to the Hnatyshyns' house to investigate. They were out. "The guy had messed things up and taken a Texas Mickey and poured this rye all over the plants and so on. So I quickly got back in my car and followed the guy. It wasn't hard to know which route he was going to take, and sure enough, he was just stumbling into a service station at Five Corners. Anyone who knows Saskatoon knows where that is. And he gets a taxi called for him. The taxi comes, and I'm sitting in my car watching all this, and the guy gets in the taxi. The number was such-and-such, the licence number was such-and-such. Then I go in and I phone the police and tell them of this guy, who it appears had broken into the house, and right now he's in taxi number such-and-such, with licence number such-and-such, and that they'd better find out who he is and get him.

"I went back to the Hnatyshyn house and found that it was all roughed up and so on, and Gerda and Ray—he was a Kinsman in those days—were down at the arena at a charity bingo. So this guy gets arrested. Very, very foolishly on my part, I agree to try to pick him out of a lineup. It was a very foolish thing for me to do, because I'd never really got a good look at the guy's face. Anyway, I go in and I pick the wrong guy, and as a result of it they had no case, and there were never any charges laid. That's just a little fun story."

Life Means Life

"My Lord, I submit that this accused is the most dangerous individual this city has ever seen. In fact, probably the most dangerous individual the province has ever seen."

CROWN COUNSEL IN R. V. THREINEN

SECURITY WAS TIGHT at the Saskatoon courthouse in February 1976, on the first day of the trial of David William Threinen. Spectators, witnesses, prospective jurors and journalists were searched with metal detectors and asked for identification.

Emotions had been running high in the city since two children, 12-year-old Dahrlyne Cranfield and 9-year-old Robert Grubesic, rode off on their bicycles in the middle of June and disappeared. About a month later, two more children, 8-year-old Samantha Turner and 7-year-old Cathy Scott, did not make it home. Their bodies were not found until the second week in August, when Threinen, a 27-year-old truck driver with a long criminal record, took police to the shallow graves he had placed them in and described how he killed them all and sexually assaulted one of them.

If there had been an age of innocence in Saskatoon, it came crashing to an end. Parents like Ted and Helen, and Ted's parents before them, who had never had cause to worry about where their children were when they were out playing, were shocked and terrified. "There was a great fear, and parents were very rigid with their control of their kids over that period until he was caught," says Hughes.

In the weeks leading up to the preliminary hearing and trial, outraged parents campaigned for a return of the death penalty.[1] There were protests outside the preliminary hearing, and police said they were aware of threats, but they would not specify who had been threatened.

Brian Hughes, who was 12 at the time, remembers unmarked police cars sitting outside their home on Kirk Crescent, and his father being picked up by police and driven to the courthouse. Every day they took a different route.

Ted's biggest fear wasn't for his own safety; it was that he might not be able to keep Threinen locked up forever. "I just felt that someone who killed four kids in our town should never, ever have his freedom again, it was so heinous a crime," Hughes says.

In the end, he didn't have to rule on guilt or innocence. Threinen pled guilty to four counts of non-capital murder. After the plea, Crown counsel revealed that Threinen had a record of a long series of attacks on children going back a decade. He had been arrested in the death of a 16-year-old girl in Lethbridge three years earlier, but was released when police could not determine how she died. At the time he killed the four children in Saskatoon, he was on parole from previous offences.

Before sentencing, Hughes asked the Crown and defence to comment on two questions regarding whether someone who commits

---

1 At the time, the death penalty was only available for the murder of police officers or prison guards. By coincidence, two weeks after the Threinen sentencing, the federal government brought in Bill C-84, which eliminated the death penalty for all criminal code offences and created the categories of first- and second-degree murder.

multiple murders can face consequences for each additional murder after the first. He wanted to find a way to ensure that a life sentence would mean life in prison with no parole. Ever. He wasn't persuaded he was going to be able to ensure, as he told Threinen, that he would "never again be on the streets and roadways of our country, but rather a life under surveillance must be yours until death do arrive. No one's child, grandchild nor great-grandchild must ever again be subject to your presence in their midst."

Under the law at the time, the sentence for non-capital murder was life with no eligibility for parole for 10 years. Hughes had the discretion to increase the period before parole could be considered to 20 years, which he did, but an early release still remained a distant possibility.

The Crown wanted consecutive life sentences for the four murders. After considering the submissions, Hughes ruled that would be pointless, because a second life sentence would only take effect after the completion of the first. The first would not be finished, as he told Threinen on sentencing, "until the last breath leaves your body, and on the occasion of that event there will be no David William Threinen on whose person a consecutive life sentence can then become operative."[2]

Having determined the futility of prescribing consecutive life terms, he gave Threinen four life sentences to be carried out concurrently, but not before experiencing "moments of extreme anxiety" over the possibility that a man who had killed four children might someday be out. "My questions to counsel on Monday almost certainly showed anxiety, if not some panic on my part," he said. But he took solace in his belief in the honour of the individuals behind the institutions in Canada.

---

2 A life sentence remains in effect even if a convicted offender is out on parole. In 2011 the Criminal Code was amended to allow for consecutive life sentences with longer periods before parole can be considered. Sentences of life with no possibility of parole for 75 years have since been imposed.

Under the law at the time, the federal cabinet had to give final approval to any decision to release a prisoner serving a life sentence of murder, regardless of the mandatory period of incarceration. After researching their oath of office, Hughes was calmed by his abiding faith that the members of both the Parole Board and the Privy Council would behave responsibly when it came their time to act.

"I am satisfied that Cabinet Ministers from 1867 onwards have always had the safety of the citizenry of this country as their constant concern," he remarked. "How then on the facts of this case there could ever be a favorable decision for your parole, I cannot imagine. I am totally comfortable in the belief that as long as we have responsible government, you will never be released from custody, and accordingly the term of life that I impose upon you today is exactly that."

Hughes didn't rely entirely on his faith in the honour of officials in his quest to ensure that a life sentence for Threinen meant life in prison. He wrote a letter to the Parole Board and the Privy Council in the hope they would keep it on file: "Let it be clearly understood by those who read this letter in your offices 20 years from now, to the extent that the opinion of the trial judge is deemed worthy, that I am firm, definite and emphatic in the view that the safety of the public and in particular that of children demands that the prisoner, Threinen, forever be prevented from release of any kind."

When Threinen first came up for full parole in 1995, Hughes' recommendation was part of the review in which his application was denied. In 2000, the second time he came up for a parole hearing, Threinen told the board he did not want to be released and that he expected to spend the rest of his life in prison.

In a postscript to the horrific affair, Hughes later heard a case of criminal contempt against Daye Cranfield, the father of one of the murdered children.

After his daughter Dahrlyne was abducted and murdered, Cranfield raged against politicians, holding them responsible for allowing

Threinen to be free to harm other children long after he came to the attention of the criminal justice system. In 1979 Cranfield was producing and hosting a twice-weekly commentary, *D.D. Cranfield's Viewpoints*, on a community cable channel owned by Saskatoon Telecable Ltd. The company knew that Cranfield was prone to voicing strong opinions on politicians and the judiciary, verging on libel, and had cautioned him in the past. It had even pulled one episode off the air.

But Episode 23 was not reviewed by anyone at the station, despite being recorded 16 days before it aired. On that episode, Cranfield read a letter from someone he identified only as Mr. Bold. The letter named four judges and concluded with: "Thus it is a little confusing whether our judges are suffering from a condition known as 'alcoholism' or whether they are involved in one of the huge conspiracies involving themselves, the Attorney General, and the complete justice system as a whole." In his introduction to the letter, Cranfield described the justice system as corrupt, a racket and a mockery.

Hughes had no trouble finding the entire broadcast "shocking, outrageous and scurrilous." He found Cranfield and the station guilty of criminal contempt. He explained that courts and judges are not immune from public scrutiny and comment: "It is the inalienable right of every citizen provided that he or she stops short of scurrilous abuse."

Cranfield's crime was therefore not that he was critical, but that his criticism was maliciously intended to undermine the reputation and therefore the authority of the judges, which in turn would serve to undermine the authority and effectiveness of the court.

Hughes made no explicit mention of the loss Cranfield had experienced and how it might have coloured his outlook on the judicial system. But he may have considered this factor in his decision not to impose either a fine or time in prison. Instead, he put Cranfield on probation for a year, with the conditions that he immediately write letters of apology to the four judges, and that he undertake to henceforth restrict his comments on judges and courts to "fair, reasonable and respectful criticism."

As for the station, while commending the management for allowing wide-ranging commentary on the community channel, Hughes rejected the argument that it had no responsibility for the content of community productions. He also noted that the station had undermined that argument with its previous meddling with Cranfield's commentaries. Nevertheless, since the station had already issued individual apologies to the judges, he meted out no further punishment beyond the "sharp reprimand" that the conviction represented.

"Commenting on judgments is fair ball," says Hughes. "I think there is more of that today and it's more acceptable today than it once was. But included in that acceptability is not attacking the character of the judge unless there is evidence of that character flaw."

Cranfield's radio career was sidetracked by the ruling, but he continued to butt heads with the government. He later spent time in jail and went on a hunger strike in a fight over income taxes.

And as of late 2017, David Threinen is still in prison, 40 years after Hughes sentenced him to life.

Marriage

WHEN HUGHES WAS a district court judge in Saskatchewan, one of his happier duties was performing marriages. "I used to marry two or three a week. Valentine's Day was just as busy as you could get. Often they wouldn't have an attendant and I would have to round up Helen or neighbours to be a witness to the wedding.

"Weddings were in the courthouse. They frowned upon you doing it anywhere else, but I did marry friends in some other locations on occasion."

Only 15 people in Saskatchewan could perform civil weddings at that time, he says. "That just shows how things have changed. If you lived in Lac la Ronge or Kindersley, you had to drive. From Kindersley you had to come into Saskatoon for a civil marriage, whereas today I'm sure marriage commissioners are spread all over the province."

After he moved to British Columbia, Hughes had to apply for a special licence to officiate at weddings, which he did occasionally for relatives and friends.

Isabel Lloyd, a friend and colleague, was among them. "We wanted just a quiet ceremony," she says, "and to include a dear friend, an Anglican priest who was dying of cancer, who was also a friend of Ted's. In the end, among eight witnesses at our ceremony were a former judge, a priest, a bishop, a human rights council member and a lawyer. After the ceremony, which was a third for each of Tony and I, Ted turned to us with a smile and said, 'Now then, try to get out of this one!'"

Hughes believed strongly in the importance of keeping marriage vows. It saddened him when two of his children's marriages ended. But he didn't try to interfere. "I realize it doesn't always work," he says. "I'm not so hell-bent that you stick it out through thick and thin."

At the time of writing, Helen and Ted have been married 62 years. "It's a way of life. It's for keeps and it works. You take the good and the bad. It's met my expectations and they have been good years."

Hospitals

"Can there really be any greater satisfaction in this life than serving others? I think not."

TED HUGHES SPEAKING TO A GRADUATING CLASS OF NURSES IN YORKTON, SASKATCHEWAN, JUNE 13, 1968

THE BATTLE OF Saskatchewan that marked the beginning of universal health care in Canada was just over the horizon in 1961 when the mayor of Saskatoon asked Ted to sit on the board of the Saskatoon City Hospital.

Hughes was by then an established lawyer, and his childhood roots in the community were spreading as a result of both his legal career and his volunteer work. Naturally social, over time Hughes joined the Rotary Club, the Kinsmen and the Junior Chamber of Commerce, and volunteered for the Red Cross and the Heart and Stroke Foundation, among other outside activities.

His appointment to the hospital board led to what became a second, voluntary, career that immediately drew him into the fight between Saskatchewan doctors and a government determined to bring affordable health care to people across the province.

Volunteer hospital boards were caught in the middle when doctors went on strike. A group of citizens set up a clinic in Saskatoon, and foreign physicians (many of them from Great Britain) were brought in as replacements. Hospital boards were responsible for issuing hospital privileges, which at the time were crucial to the way most doctors treated their patients.

Many Saskatchewan doctors viewed the newcomers as scabs. With the financial backing of doctors from outside the province through the Canadian and American Medical Associations, the Saskatchewan MDs put enormous pressure on locally based volunteers like Ted to keep the imports out.[1] Many doctors who were heads of departments in the hospitals also wanted to keep them out.

It was a crucial campaign in the doctors' fight to put a stop to what they called socialized medicine before it could get a toehold in Canada. But Hughes and the other community volunteers who comprised the Saskatoon City Hospital board were not willing to be used that way.

"It was a delicate time," says Hughes. "But if those doctors involved with the community clinic were qualified, they got their privileges."

The doctors eventually came to an agreement with the government and ended their strike. Over the next decade, publicly financed health care spread across the country. But along with it came the issue that has overshadowed all others in the past 50 years as Hughes continued to work in health care: ballooning costs.

From his start as a member of the board, Hughes went on to become chairman of the board of governors for the Saskatoon City Hospital, president of the Saskatchewan Health Care Association, and president of the Canadian Hospital Association, all the while continuing as a judge and a father of four children.

As usual, he was not just carrying out the day-to-day duties of a trustee. Rather, he was looking at how volunteer trustees fit into the health care system, first in relation to professional administrators in

---

1 Frederick Vaughn describes the Saskatchewan doctors' actions in his biography of Justice Emmett Hall, *Aggressive in Pursuit*.

the hospitals, and later in relation to politicians, who were increasingly important for funding the system.

Hughes believed that volunteers were a crucial part of health care, both for their knowledge of local needs and for the opportunity volunteering provided the individuals. "You grow as a person in warmth and understanding, are rewarded with an awareness of belonging and you develop a sense of fulfillment that is indescribable," he said in a 1985 speech to the annual general meeting of the Saskatchewan Health Care Association.

He also became concerned about how the rising cost of health care was eroding the ability of volunteer boards to maintain their influence. In a speech to the Canadian Hospital Association in Vancouver in 1968, at least a decade before politicians were starting to talk about a crisis in health care costs, he said the cost per patient day at a large hospital in Vancouver had risen 50 per cent over the previous five years, 115 per cent over 10 years and 140 per cent over 15 years, and that statistics were similar across the country. He warned the soaring costs were threatening the relationship between trustees and the government; to maintain standards of care, trustees depended on continually increasing levels of government support, which politicians were increasingly loath to provide. He challenged trustees to find ways to slow the cost spiral, lest they be elbowed aside by governments that were responsible to taxpayers for the costs but far less able than trustees to know the needs of patients in local hospitals.

A decade later, when Alberta was considering legislating more political control over the administration of hospitals as a way of reining in costs, Hughes urged trustees to resist the move through a public relations campaign and by directly lobbying individual MLAs. He urged them to understand how the political system worked, and to make it work to their advantage by taking back some of the power that politicians were assuming over the running of their institutions. This is noteworthy as it shows that when Hughes arrived in British

Columbia a few years later, it was not just as a judge schooled in the ways of the law, but as a fully informed student of the political system.

After his move to the coast, he still advocated for trustees to stand up to governments, strong in the knowledge that there is "no real acceptable alternative to the voluntary system of control of the community hospitals of the province. I do not suggest that gives us licence to swing a big stick," he wrote in a 1982 article for *Hospital Trustee*, the magazine for hospital governing boards. "But I do believe that we do not have to be fading violets as we press our case on behalf of the hospital and the community it serves."

In 1979 the Saskatchewan health ministry was facing a crisis in the delivery of cancer treatment because an administrator had been hiring unqualified medical staff. When the government started to sort it out by firing a couple of doctors, patients and their families were outraged and it became a political issue. Rather than try to repair the old cancer agency, the government decided to create a new foundation to oversee cancer treatment and research in the province. Premier Allan Blakeney tapped Hughes to be the first chairman of the Saskatchewan Cancer Foundation and to sort out what had become an administrative and political muddle. He was picked for his experience in health care administration and because the government needed someone with his stature to show it was taking the problems seriously.

This would not be the last time he was brought in to untangle someone else's mess. His reputation would grow to the point that just bringing in Hughes was proof that a government was earnest about tackling a problem. In Hughes, politicians found a happy confluence of someone they could appoint who was good for their image and at the same time enormously able.

Or, as one admirer puts it, "Ted spent a lot of time in the window."

Thatcher v. Thatcher

MURDOCH ALEXANDER "SANDY" MacPherson got out his old shotgun when his brother called with the news that JoAnn Wilson had been bludgeoned, hacked and shot to death. He laid out four shells on the living room floor.

"If he was going to come after me, I would go down fighting. It was the old army training," he told Maggie Siggins, who wrote *A Canadian Tragedy*, a detailed and compelling account of the shocking saga, which appeared a year after Colin Thatcher, a prominent politician and rancher, was convicted of murder in the death of his ex-wife.

MacPherson was the Regina-based Court of Queen's Bench judge who presided over two rancorous custody hearings during the Thatcher divorce. The divorce itself was uncontested, but Thatcher fought virtually every other aspect of the split, inside and outside the courtroom, before finally killing his former wife in the garage of her Regina home in January 1983. Hughes presided over the division of property. Thatcher v. Thatcher was his last case before leaving Saskatchewan and the bench.

Thatcher, son of former premier Ross Thatcher, was a member of the legislature and had until recently been a cabinet minister in the Saskatchewan government. He was also a rancher with a large acreage near Moose Jaw. As Siggins details in her gripping account, he was a philanderer and a bully who was used to getting his own way, whether it was with his wife, the media or the police, who treated him with the respect they felt was due a family that was as close to royalty as was possible in Saskatchewan.

In the months after the divorce was filed in 1980, MacPherson made a number of orders giving JoAnn custody of two of the three Thatcher children—their daughter, Stephanie, and youngest son, Regan. The third child, Greg, at 14, was deemed old enough to decide for himself which parent he wanted to live with. Regan ran away and disappeared. JoAnn naturally suspected, correctly as it turned out, that Colin was hiding him. He had smuggled Regan out of the country. JoAnn's lawyer went to court to try to force Colin to obey the earlier custody order. Colin stalled, ignored the orders or actively interfered with JoAnn's attempt to find and take custody of Regan. Only his status as a sitting MLA saved Thatcher from being jailed for contempt for refusing to obey judicial orders. Instead, as detailed in another book on the case, Heather Bird's *Not Above the Law*, he was fined $6,000. He paid the fine but continued to obstruct JoAnn's attempts to find their son.

"Although we obtained a lot of orders giving to her rights to have custody of the children, the only child she really had custody of was the daughter, Stephanie," says Gerry Gerrand, JoAnn's lawyer during the divorce.

Of the second Thatcher custody hearing, MacPherson told Siggins, "In my 20 years on the bench, this is the worst matrimonial case that has come into the court, the most interminable, the most bitterly fought and the most expensive."

Hughes was assigned the case involving division of property because unlike many of the judges based in Regina, he did not know the Thatchers personally. "They were southern Saskatchewan people, if you like, and I was from the north. There is a bit of a dividing line there as to who you know," Hughes says.

He heard the case over several days in July 1980 and finished writing his judgment in the library of the Victoria courthouse after he left Saskatoon. It was delivered in late October and was the first rendered under the new Matrimonial Property Act, which called for an equal division of assets acquired during a marriage. The act was brought in to protect the spouses of farmers, primarily women, who could be left with nothing after a divorce despite toiling for years on land that was registered solely in their partner's name.

Earlier legislation—the Married Women's Property Act—also allowed judges to divide a family farm evenly between the partners, but it gave judges more discretion. In at least one case under the previous legislation, Hughes divided a family farm evenly between the husband and wife. But in two other cases he found extenuating circumstances that led him to give a larger percentage of the assets to the husband. In one case it was because the husband had acquired assets before the marriage; in the other it was because assets had been acquired after the separation but before the settlement hearing.

As energy minister in the government of Grant Devine, Colin Thatcher had supported the new legislation. But when Hughes awarded JoAnn half the matrimonial assets, about $820,000, and gave Colin just over three months to come up with the money, he was furious.

Decades later, JoAnn's lawyer described Ted's judgment as a "death warrant" for his client.[1]

---

1 Gerrand used this phrase at a tribute luncheon for Hughes at the Union Club in Victoria in November 2014. Although jarring, it was not meant in any way to be a criticism of Ted's judgment.

"Thatcher was infuriated from the beginning of these proceedings about the prospect of his wife getting anything—assets or custody of the children," Gerrand says. "The trial was difficult because we didn't have the procedures we presently have to prove the identity and valuation of properties in a simple way," he adds. "My client and I had to lead evidence to prove essentially the existence, ownership and value of every quarter of land, every piece of machinery and every head of cattle, and Ted sat on the bench patiently listening to all of this evidence. At the end of the trial he reserved judgment, and some weeks later he rendered a judgment awarding to my client one half of the matrimonial property."

The trial was held in a large courtroom on the second floor of the Victoria Avenue courthouse in Regina. Hughes recalls there were entrances on both sides but no aisle in the middle. "Throughout the whole time, she and her friends and lawyers came in one door and sat on one side, and he and his on the other side—a very, very bitter performance."

Adding to the intensity, Gerrand and Tony Merchant, Colin Thatcher's lawyer, had a history outside the court. Merchant was an influential Liberal who later gained national prominence for his aggressive pursuit of class-action cases and numerous brushes with the Law Society of Saskatchewan.[2] Gerrand had also been active as a Liberal. His father was a Liberal MLA, and Gerrand managed Liberal campaigns before deciding that the way the game of party politics was played in Regina was incompatible with being an ethical lawyer. He publicly disapproved of Merchant's dual role as a talk-show host and

2 One run-in related to an abduction charge in 1983 after Merchant helped Colin remove Stephanie, then nine years old, from the home of a family friend after JoAnn was murdered. He pled guilty to a lesser charge of mischief and was granted an absolute discharge. The law society then reprimanded him and fined him $1,000 and $5,000 in costs. He was more recently suspended for three months in 2014 for disobeying a court order.

practising lawyer. In her book, Siggins surmised that Merchant, an influential Liberal and, at the time, the brother-in-law of Otto Lang, political minister for Saskatchewan in the Trudeau government, effectively blocked any chance Gerrand had of becoming a judge.

"I totally alienated myself with Tony Merchant in every imaginable way, and I saw who was being appointed to the bench," Gerrand says. "They were the individuals who played the political game very well."

All of which made for a tense courtroom, but Gerrand says Hughes handled it with his usual aplomb. "He had the skills to see what was coming down in trying the first case under the Matrimonial Property Act, being litigated by parties that were significantly at odds, and with a husband who had by that time demonstrated a preparedness to breach orders of the court.

"It was a difficult trial for him to handle but Ted, Mr. Justice Hughes as he then was, has an aura about him of demanding judicial respect in the courtroom, and I think things went as reasonably well as they could in the circumstances."

It wasn't the first time Tony Merchant had appeared before Hughes in a divorce case. In 1974 he represented a man who was being cited for contempt of court for failing to comply with a maintenance order. He was supposed to have started paying his former wife $150 a month more than a year earlier.

For Hughes, it was a case of "enough is enough." Either the former wife was entitled to the enforcement of the order through a contempt citation "or she is entitled to conclude that the Rule does not mean what it says or if it does mean what it says, then the Court is without the fortitude to invoke it." Not lacking in fortitude, Hughes found the deadbeat husband to be in contempt and ordered him jailed immediately.

It wasn't just the tension in the courtroom that made the Thatcher case difficult. In addition to sorting out what the Thatchers owned and what it was worth, Hughes had to determine the intention behind all the gifts and bequests from Colin's parents, large and small. In every case he found that Colin's father, Ross, had never anticipated that the marriage would end, so even property that was solely in Colin's name was still intended to be for the family. This meant that, under the new legislation, it would be divided evenly between the spouses.

"One of the sad things was Colin's mother, Ross's widow [Peggy Thatcher], had to give evidence about what the intention was when each year a sterling silver service place setting was given to JoAnn and Thatcher. Who was the gift really intended for? They could agree on nothing," Hughes said.

Colin and his mother also asserted that Ross had set up a secret trust that meant the property left in his will would not be part of Colin's assets until after Peggy died. This would have meant a significant portion of the family ranch would be taken out of the property settlement. While refusing to call Ross's widow a liar, Hughes said there was no evidence of such a trust, and what evidence there was on the issue pointed to its being a recently concocted fabrication.

The only significant issue on which he ruled against JoAnn was the question of legal and court costs for the divorce. She wanted Colin to pay them, but Hughes ruled each party should pay their own costs. "While I acknowledge that the costs incurred as detailed to the court by the applicant (JoAnn) are large in amount, the fact is that the division that has been made places a large amount of money in her hands," he wrote.

Or at least it might have done, if she hadn't been killed first.

In the months following Ted's ruling, JoAnn's car was vandalized, her tires were repeatedly slashed and sugar was poured in her gas tank. She got anonymous threatening phone calls. Meanwhile, Colin was continuing to refuse, despite repeated court orders, to divulge where he had hidden their son Regan.[3]

---

3 Regan later became a lawyer, and in 2015 was appointed to the Court of Queen's Bench in Manitoba.

Then on May 17, 1981, JoAnn was in her kitchen, finishing the dinner dishes, when a bullet from a high-powered rifle blew through the window and smashed into her shoulder.

In the aftermath, Tony Merchant threatened to sue the Regina police after an officer suggested, on a police radio call overheard by someone listening on a scanner, that Colin might be a suspect in the shooting, a reasonable supposition under the circumstances.

Now terrified, JoAnn caved in to the pressure, giving Colin permanent custody of their youngest son and agreeing to a lower property settlement that gave her former husband more time to pay.

Even that couldn't keep her safe. When she returned home on the evening of January 21, 1983, JoAnn was attacked in her garage, repeatedly hacked with something akin to a meat cleaver and then shot in the head. After an investigation that went on for a year, Colin was arrested and charged with her murder. A jury found that he had either killed her himself or hired someone else to do it. He was sentenced to life in prison with no eligibility for parole for 25 years. Thatcher appealed all the way to the Supreme Court of Canada, which ruled that it didn't matter which version the jury believed: as long as they thought he was responsible for her death, they could find him guilty of murder.

Thatcher continued to maintain his innocence and was given parole in 2006.[4] He returned to his family ranch near Moose Jaw

4 All of Thatcher's children testified on his behalf at his bid for early release in 2000. He was eventually granted the right to apply for early parole under the Criminal Code's faint-hope clause, which was later eliminated by Stephen Harper's Conservative government. At Thatcher's second hearing in 2003, Gerrand testified that he still considered Thatcher a threat because in a recording between Thatcher and a criminal associate, Thatcher described Gerrand as "a guy I could do, that guy I could do." Thatcher v. Thatcher was the last matrimonial case Gerrand took on.

and released a book about the case in 2009, *Final Appeal: Anatomy of a Frame.*[5]

For his part, Hughes has no doubt that justice was done, in the murder trial and in the hearing on which he sat in judgment. "I never reproached myself for doing what I did, because I think it was what the law called for. But he was a very angry man."

5 When word started circulating that Thatcher was writing a book, the Government of Saskatchewan passed the Profits of Criminal Notoriety Act, making it illegal for criminals to profit from their crimes. Thatcher took the government to court, arguing that the new law didn't apply to his book because it was about his dealings with the justice system. He lost and had to turn over to the government a $5,000 advance from his publisher and any potential profits.

A New Opportunity and a Bitter Crash

"There is not a day goes by but what I wish the whole event had never taken place. Up until the summer of 1977 every day on the Bench had been a happy one for me."

TED HUGHES in a letter to the commissioner for judicial affairs in 1980

LIFE IN SASKATOON was good for Ted and Helen in 1977. Helen was on city council. She had started the work for which she would later be awarded the Order of Canada, building bridges between the growing Indigenous population in Saskatoon and the wider community. Ted was by then an experienced judge, steadily adding to his solid reputation for competence on the bench and his stellar portfolio of community service. He seemed to be firmly on a path that would keep him on the bench in senior positions until he retired, possibly still living in the town where he was born.

In March it looked like the next step up that ladder was imminent. At the close of a conference in Ottawa, Hughes was approached by Edward Ratushny, who was then a special advisor to Ron Basford, the federal minister of justice. Ratushny's job was to screen potential candidates for judicial appointments. He told Hughes in confidence that Alf Bence, the Chief Justice of the Court of Queen's Bench in

Saskatchewan, had submitted his resignation. He wanted to know whether Hughes would be interested in the job should it be offered to him.

In a memo to file that Hughes wrote five years later, he detailed how he had been on his way home and didn't have time for a long conversation with Ratushny. The approach surprised him. He had not expected to be under consideration for the job but would have been honoured to take it on. It was exciting news.

Hughes flew back to Saskatoon and arranged to return to Ottawa, where he met with Ratushny again, over dinner, on April 6. They talked about the conditions under which he would be prepared to serve. He was pleased to hear that he would not have to move to Regina, even though, unlike the situation with Melfort 15 years earlier, it was a move he would have been prepared to make. Ratushny made it clear others were under consideration, and Hughes commented confidentially on potential candidates.

It wasn't the first time the two had met. As a student at the University of Saskatchewan, Ratushny had listened to Hughes lecture, and as a young lawyer in Saskatoon, Ratushny argued a case before Hughes.

Their other connection was Otto Lang, who brought Ratushny to Ottawa as his executive assistant and later appointed him to the role in which he was acting when he approached Hughes. Lang had been dean of the University of Saskatchewan law school when Ratushny was a student there.[1] He had also articled at Ted's firm, Francis, Woods, Gauley and Hughes, while Ted was practising there as a young lawyer, and Ted had taught courses at the School of Law while Lang was dean. Finally, three years earlier, Lang had elevated Hughes to the Court of Queen's Bench.

---

1 Lang, a Rhodes Scholar, was the youngest dean ever appointed at the School of Law when he was named to the position before his 30th birthday.

In 1977, Lang was no longer the justice minister. He had been moved to the transportation portfolio, and Ron Basford was the justice minister, with Ratushny reporting to him. In theory, Basford would make the recommendation to the prime minister for a new Chief Justice of the Saskatchewan Court of Queen's Bench. But Lang remained the political minister for Saskatchewan in the Trudeau cabinet. That meant he effectively controlled the tap at the Ottawa end of the patronage pipeline that still delivered most appointments to the bench.

The bar association screening committees set up a decade earlier created a pool of qualified candidates, but appointments were still made by the politicians in Ottawa, and more often than not they had a connection to the governing party.[2] For most of the 20th century, this meant that federally appointed judges had Liberal connections. By 1977, most of the judges on the Saskatchewan Court of Queen's Bench in Saskatoon and Regina were Liberal appointees, and many of them had solid credentials of service to the party.

Increasingly, however, there were some exceptions, some cross-party appointments, including Hughes when he was elevated to the Court of Queen's Bench by Lang. So when Ratushny suggested that Ted could be given a new appointment by a Liberal government, despite his background as a Progressive Conservative, he believed he had a real chance at the job. Although he was never offered the position, his hopes were raised by the detailed level of negotiations he had with Ratushny, which included where he would be based in the job

---

2 Gerry Gerrand, a Regina lawyer with Liberal connections, sat on a judicial review committee from 1992 to 1996 and was chair for the last three years. In a 2016 interview he said, "You could approve or you could highly approve. The government in power, apparently faithfully, made its appointments from the list of those approved or highly approved. But in every case, with hardly an exception, they were the political supporters of the government in power. So in that respect, the system hasn't changed."

and whether he would be prepared to retire early to make way for new blood in another 10 years.

Three weeks later, while Ted was working in Regina, that hope started to crumble. He discovered that Bence's pending retirement was no longer a secret. Neither was the fact that Hughes was being considered for the job.

While working alone in the judges' library, he was approached by Kenneth MacLeod, a fellow Queen's Bench judge who had previously been a Liberal member of the Saskatchewan Legislature. MacLeod told him that he had been talking with his Liberal connections and that he, Ted, was not going to get the job of Chief Justice. He explained that while he was personally well liked, his previous political affiliation and his lack of service to the Liberal Party took him out of the running for such a plum post.

Hughes was shocked to find himself at the centre of gossip and what he perceived to be scheming against him by his colleagues. The next morning he went to see Bence, who, like Hughes, was a Diefenbaker appointment, and told him that he had no stomach for what now appeared to be a nasty backroom fight over the job. He asked Bence whether he should call Ratushny and withdraw his name from consideration.

While Hughes was still in the room, Bence called Ottawa and discovered that Ratushny had gone back to teaching and was no longer in the job. His replacement told Bence that Basford's recommendation had already gone to the prime minister, and a decision was expected within 48 hours. Under the circumstances, Bence recommended that Hughes hang tight. So he waited.

Months went by.

In the meantime, another colleague on the Court of Queen's Bench, Frederick Johnson, came up to Ted in the hall of the Regina courthouse and asked if he had been approached about replacing Bence. Hughes said he had. Johnson had twice run unsuccessfully as a

Liberal, once for a seat in the provincial legislature and once federally, before being appointed to the bench. He told Hughes that he had not been approached and walked away.

Finally, on August 9, 1977, the announcement was made: Johnson would be the new Chief Justice.[3] Hughes read about it in the *Star-Phoenix*.

After the announcement, Hughes confirmed to his satisfaction what he had suspected: some of his fellow judges with Liberal connections, and other prominent Saskatchewan Liberals, had intervened to scupper the appointment that was on its way to being delivered to him. In his 1982 memo to file, he wrote that later in August he met Lang in his Saskatoon home. Lang told him he had been obliged to intervene with the prime minister's office on behalf of Liberals in Saskatchewan who were outraged that such a plum patronage post was being wasted on a former Progressive Conservative. Lang also confirmed to Hughes that Edward D. Bayda, a Saskatchewan Court of Appeal judge with Liberal connections, was among those who had contacted him. Years later their roles were reversed, albeit somewhat indirectly, when, as BC's deputy attorney general, Hughes lobbied federal bureaucrats in a bid to have a Supreme Court of Canada vacancy filled from British Columbia. At the time it was widely anticipated in Saskatchewan that the job would go to Bayda, who by then was the Chief Justice of the Saskatchewan Court of Appeal.[4]

Lang remembers it differently. He wanted Johnson for the Chief Justice job, not for political considerations, but because he was a better candidate. "I thought that Fred was the better person for the role. He was always a person of about the most mature judgments you could ever expect. In that sense, he was miles ahead of Ted."

---

3 Johnson was appointed lieutenant-governor of Saskatchewan four years later.

4 Details are in the chapter "Making Room at the Top for BC."

Regardless of the motives behind the choice, the effect on Hughes was the same. He was dealing with perceptions, both his own and those of his colleagues. For Hughes, the long weeks waiting for news of the appointment had been dreadful. He hated the sense that he was the object of gossip, a feeling that was confirmed when MacLeod called one day in June to apologize for comments he made about Ted at a cocktail party, which had been overheard by someone outside his circle. For a man who had always earned accolades for his work, the notion that he was being unfairly mocked by his colleagues for what they perceived as his misplaced ambition and his naivety was intolerable.

"I very nearly became paranoid over the thing," he says. "I used to go over to the Bessborough Hotel and stand in the window and watch these guys at the end of a day on a Friday going over to John's Place on the corner, and I just got the idea that they were all conspiring against me. I understand now what they were doing. But I'm just thankful that I got out and started over because I would have broken under it."

In his memo to file, he noted that what transpired was what Ratushny had predicted in "Judicial Appointments: The Lang Legacy," a paper published a year earlier on the risks inherent in the process of gathering information about potential judges prior to appointments: "The inquiries are often of a highly personal nature involving matters of integrity, temperament, personal habits, professional competence, work habits and relations with other people. Obviously, most people would be reluctant to comment about these things in relation to others except on a strictly confidential basis. There is also the danger of rumours being generated about who is and who is not being considered for appointment and speculation as to the related reasons. There is a very real danger not only of embarrassment but also of serious harm to professional and personal reputations. The approach was taken, therefore, of making these inquiries on a discreet and confidential basis."

In one sense it is odd that Hughes would have been so appalled that party politics would come into play in the appointment of a Chief Justice for the Court of Queen's Bench. Even though he was no longer involved with the Progressive Conservative Party, he got his appointment as a judge through his political connections. And most of the appointments that had been made since had a strong political component.

And perhaps he should not have been surprised that others knew he was in contention for the job. He had discussed other potential candidates with Ratushny, and it seems reasonable to conclude that Ratushny had mentioned Hughes in discussions with others.

But as far as Ted was concerned, he had never asked for the job, so it was grossly unfair for others to criticize him for wanting it.

After the appointment was announced, Hughes decided his position in Saskatchewan was no longer tenable. He met with Basford and submitted his resignation, citing the serious damage to his credibility as a judge and his "complete lack of confidence to effectively continue in the office."

"The environment, for me, had become so poisoned, with people not speaking to me and huddling going on, that I lost the appetite for going to work with those people," Hughes says.

While he wanted out, Ted was not willing to leave without a pension for his 15 years of service as a judge. At the time, judges had to reach a minimum age of 65 before receiving any pension, but Ted was only 50.

In December, the justice minister turned down his request for a partial pension and suggested that the problems Hughes was experiencing would ease over time. Sensing he had little choice, he decided to stay for at least another year.

Meanwhile, Hughes had his first meeting with Johnson, in which he pledged his loyalty to the new Chief Justice for as long as he served the court. Hughes recalls that Johnson told him bluntly he had been a fool to think he had any chance at the job, and he had showed poor judgment in talking to Ratushny, no matter how genuine the circumstances seemed to be.

In the months that followed, Hughes found it increasingly difficult to work in what he felt was the poisonous atmosphere of the Saskatoon courthouse. He was also developing stomach problems because of the strain.

Kenneth Halvorson was then a justice of the Court of Queen's Bench in Regina. He was also a Liberal appointee who had worked on Lang's campaigns. He described what it was like for Ted in the Saskatoon courthouse, where the judges' coffee room had become an unhappy place. According to Halvorson, the judges "sit around every morning and B.S., make fun of each other and everybody else. You know, it's pretty cozy, but it can be a malicious place. Ted was the outsider, because the judges there were all Liberal appointees. He was the only leftover Tory.

"Because they were all a bunch of Liberals, of course they were putting down Tories at every opportunity. If it had been me and the shoe had been on the other foot, I would have just said, 'Oh, screw you guys. You don't know what you're talking about. You're just a bunch of asshole Liberals. In our days under Diefenbaker, we did things differently; the court was better, and now it's not so great with you guys.'

"But Ted wasn't like that. Ted was not an aggressive, pushy kind of guy. He was a nice guy. He sort of sat back and took it as best he could. Then he couldn't take it anymore, so he stopped going to the courthouse. But he had to go, because that's where he worked. So he did his work at home, and that's pretty tough, because you need to be at the courthouse to work and that sort of thing. Anyway, he stopped going, because they just abused him. It was really quite bad, to the point where Ted was getting behind in his judgments. He couldn't go to the courthouse. He couldn't work. He was getting behind." Halvorson recalls being assigned to help Ted catch up with his backlog by assisting him with the writing of some judgments.[5]

After a year, Ted started looking for another job. He had one lined up with the federal government, but the election in May 1979 intervened, and the pension remained a sticking point. With Joe Clark's short-lived minority government in power, Ted could not find anyone to negotiate the issue. It wasn't until the second election in a year brought the Trudeau government back that he was finally able to negotiate a pension. With the knowledge that he now had an assured annual income of $28,000—which was 60 per cent of a full pension—he was ready to go looking for a new career.

Helen was not so ready. She had not wanted to come to Saskatoon in 1950, and now she didn't want to leave. She had been re-elected to council in a landslide and was viewed by some as potentially the next mayor. "I had no choice. But I hated to leave Saskatoon. I really did. I enjoyed what I was doing there. But life is sometimes change, and you don't have a chance to change it," she says.

In his memo to file, Hughes described that time as "the most productive years of my life." He would later prove that assertion false, although he could not then have predicted his extraordinary path forward.

---

5 Hughes said Halvorson was the only Saskatchewan judge to call him to commiserate when he left. He has since moved to Victoria, where he is Ted and Helen's next-door neighbour. Halvorson also worked with Ted as an adjudicator in the Alternative Dispute Resolution process set up to compensate victims of abuse in residential schools.

Part II
British Columbia

A New Beginning: From Master of the Court to Civil Servant

"He became the most respected public servant, I guess, we've ever had in the province."

BOB PLECAS

IN MAY 1980, Hughes got his ticket out. He was hired by the BC Government to be a Legal Officer Specialist at a starting salary of $2,582 a month. That was the bottom end of the normal recruiting range according to the confirmation letter. He was to be employed "on the usual probationary basis for six months."

It was a good job for a public-service-minded lawyer, but when Ted's application was received by the ministry of the attorney general, it raised some eyebrows among career civil servants, who weren't sure that a senior judge used to being the master of his own court would be able to adapt to what was ultimately a subservient role.

Frank Rhodes was the assistant deputy minister in charge of personnel for the attorney general's ministry. Richard "Dick" Vogel was the deputy minister. In a 2012 interview for a retrospective on Ted Hughes' career, Rhodes recalled that Vogel came into his office and said, "'I'm excited about hiring a lawyer out of Saskatchewan who is a retiring—or resigning—superior court judge. His name's Ted Hughes, and he is going to come to Victoria and be a legal officer and work in the area of administrative and constitutional law.'" Rhodes remembered, "That was my job in the ministry, and I had these misgivings. I thought, 'This is going to be a very high-maintenance individual. I've got a superior court judge coming to British Columbia to be a legal officer, and that's going to be a unique challenge.'"

But Hughes was ready for the change and quickly proved that he could be a team player, and a valuable one at that.

"I think that probably some of the people that I worked with right off the bat were wondering what to expect, to have someone who had held judicial office now being their new colleague in a little row of offices without windows, where tasks were as they were distributed—how I was going to fit into that kind of different lifestyle," Ted says. "But I didn't find it difficult. I think it was because I'd decided that that's the way I wanted it, what I wanted to do with my life. I really appreciated the chance I got to come to the department of the attorney general."

Hughes came at a good time. Ministers under Premier Bill Bennett were expected and allowed to run their own ministries with little interference, and the politicization of the public service that was to concern Hughes in later years had yet to firmly grab hold. Similarly, the legal services branch of the ministry was run much like a law firm. Lawyers worked relatively independently on the files they were assigned. The attorney general, Allan Williams, was well respected by the staff and maintained a collegial atmosphere.

Ted's job was to advise and represent the government primarily at administrative tribunals. He could also have appeared for the province in court, but that was a duty he told his new employer he did not want to take on, due to his sense of fair play. "The people in the ministry knew that I was not keen on going to court. If I was told it was part of the job and to get there, I would have gone, but I always felt it was difficult for a litigant on the other side to be facing a counsel who had been a judge and who was now appealing to a judge who was presiding to agree with him. My choice was not to go to court and I never did."

Hughes reported for work on November 1, 1980, at the Weiler Building, a historic five-storey Romanesque former department store near the harbour that had been converted to government offices. By then he had bolstered his resume with not only the ground-breaking Thatcher decision but also the addition of the letters QC after his name. On the last day of October, Roy Romanow, then attorney general of Saskatchewan and later premier, put through a special order-in-council in appreciation of Ted's service in the province, granting him the title Queen's Counsel, an honour usually bestowed on lawyers in a list published at the end of the year.[1]

By the end of November his salary was bumped to $3,345 a month, which was still a sharp cut from his pay as a judge in Saskatchewan. However, with the pension he was now getting from the federal government, and Helen's first ever full-time salary from her job with the provincial ombudsman's office, it was enough to support the lifestyle they had been accustomed to in Saskatoon, and to pay for their children's continuing education. Helen went on to work for the Human Rights Council, and she ran for Victoria city council in 1990, where she served for the next 18 years.

Helen and Ted and their youngest son, Brian, lived in a rented house in the Victoria neighbourhood of Gordon Head so Brian could continue high school. After he graduated, they moved to a

---

1 Romanow wasn't the only one to recognize Ted's and Helen's contributions in Saskatchewan. After moving to Victoria, they flew back to Saskatoon for a farewell reception on the evening of Sunday, November 2, 1980, with the more than 300 people who bought tickets to thank them for their service to the community. Among the speakers were the mayor, Cliff Wright, and a Roman Catholic bishop, James Mahoney, a childhood friend of Ted's.

three-bedroom apartment in Camosack Manor, a midrise building a few kilometres from the legislature. Brian worked for a year in a grocery store and saved enough money to buy his dream car, a new Mazda RX7.

Ted spent part of the winter of 1981 in Fort St. John in northern BC, representing the government at the BC utility commission hearings into BC Hydro's proposal to build a dam on the Peace River at a place called Site C.[2]

While he was there he got a call telling him that his son Keith, who was still in Saskatoon, had collapsed in a snowbank after a bad asthma attack at a bus stop, possibly complicated by a medication issue. Keith was in a coma for a couple of weeks, and he moved to join his parents and brother in Victoria when he was well enough to travel.

Ted and Helen's daughter, Sheila, was living with her family in Duncan, an hour north of Victoria, so three of their children had made the move to the West Coast. Their eldest son, David, was living in Ontario.

Ted was 53 and Helen was 48 when they left their extended family and wide circle of friends in Saskatoon and moved to Victoria. It wasn't long, however, before they started to fill the hole that created in their social life. They bought a run-down cottage on Shawnigan Lake, a popular swimming and water-skiing spot near Sheila's home in Duncan. They built a new cottage and dock that became the centre of family gatherings with their children and grandchildren. They also threw parties at the cottage and invited many of their colleagues, as

---

2 Site C was eventually shelved after the BC Utilities Commission found that BC Hydro failed to make a persuasive case for the need to build the multi-billion-dollar project. It was revived 30 years later by Premier Gordon Campbell, with even more controversy and a much bigger price tag than when it was first proposed, but under a government that was determined it would be built. The premier exempted the project from BCUC scrutiny to remove that possible roadblock the second time around.

they had at their home in Saskatoon. Many became friends. Over the years, their new friends became old and loyal friends as they learned that they could always count on Ted and Helen in a crisis.

Bob Edwards was Ted's immediate supervisor in the constitutional and administrative law section of the ministry of the attorney general. He and Ted soon became close, often lunching together at the Union Club. That friendship continued after Ted was appointed deputy minister, and when Ted left seven years later, he recommended Edwards be appointed in his place, which he was.

Edwards subsequently became a BC Supreme Court judge. In 2007 he died suddenly. His colleagues organized a memorial for him at the courthouse in Vancouver and invited his widow, Wendi Mackay.

She didn't want to go.

"I just said, 'I can't do that, there's no family, there's no kids, there's no relatives, it's just too much for me to take on.' And Ted was on the phone. He said, 'I'm coming, we're going to do this together.'

"He said, 'I'm not going to sit in front of the bar where the lawyers sit. I'm going to sit beside you.'

"He said, 'I'm coming the night before. We're going to go for dinner. I'm going to spend the day with you. We're just going to do this together.'

"And I was like, whoa. I needed somebody and just totally out of the blue he did that, and ever since that time he and Helen have just been rocks in my life."

"Loyalty is a huge thing with Ted," says Susan Brice, a Saanich city councillor, former mayor of Oak Bay and former member of the provincial legislature. She got to know Hughes as a member of the justice reform task force he led in the 1980s. "Ted and I have the kind of friendship, and Helen too, obviously, that if at three in the morning I needed them, I would not hesitate to call them, they would not hesitate to come and help me. Ted gave the eulogy at my husband's funeral.

Our family considers him to be our kind of godfather, not to overplay it, but that's the role that Ted plays in our family."

Ted would often appear for the province to represent claimants at boards of inquiry convened by the human rights branch.[3] In one such case in June 1983, he represented a group of Indigenous people who had been refused service at the Lone Star Hotel in Vancouver. Hughes was up against Angelo Branca, a legendary former Court of Appeal judge who had left the bench four years earlier at the mandatory retirement age of 75. Branca was a former amateur boxer who, as a defence lawyer, won acquittals for 59 of 63 clients accused of murder.[4]

"I wasn't afraid to take him on," says Hughes.

Branca was representing the hotel. Ted's clients were Veronica Butler, a 26-year-old child care worker, and several companions. She and a friend had been refused entry to the Lone Star Hotel and had come back a week later with a white friend and with a reporter watching.

They were again told to leave.

A *Province* newspaper reporter covering the hearing wrote that Branca tried to raise doubts about their sobriety and whether they were properly dressed.

But the inquiry chairman ruled they were turned away because they were Indigenous, a violation of the Human Rights Code. He awarded the complainants a symbolic $500 in damages but, more importantly, ordered the hotel to stop discriminating against Indigenous patrons.

In his new career, Hughes was a civil servant, pledged to political neutrality but still subject to buffeting by the winds of political change.

---

3 This case is described in Dominique Clément, *Equality Deferred: Sex Discrimination and British Columbia's Human Rights State, 1953–84*.

4 Vincent Moore, *Gladiator of the Courts: Angelo Branco.*

In the May 1983 provincial election, voters chose to stay with Premier Bill Bennett and his Social Credit government. But Bennett's return to office brought a new era of turbulent change for the province, and fresh challenges and opportunities for Hughes. Bennett defeated the New Democrats, under former premier David Barrett, with a promise to restrain government spending in the face of a deep global recession that was devastating the province's crucial resource industries. Bennett promised voters that the government would share the pain that was being felt in the private sector.

Two months later he followed up on that promise with a sweeping package of reforms that went far beyond simple economic restraint. Along with the budget, the government brought in 26 bills aimed at trimming the size of the civil service by 25 per cent, curbing the power of unions, eliminating the Human Rights Commission and the Rental Review Board, and giving the province direct control over a number of previously independent authorities, including public school boards and colleges.

The incendiary legislation sparked a province-wide revolt, with public- and private-sector unions and widely disparate social and church groups coming together in what was called Operation Solidarity. Strikes and protests sprang up around the province as opponents vainly tried to stop the elimination of rights and privileges won through generations of struggle. Tens of thousands of protesters covered the lawn of the legislature in Victoria, and the civil service went on strike. Managers and excluded personnel like Hughes were thrown in to fill critical gaps. At one point he was working in a hospital laundry. He also found himself back in a courtroom in New Westminster, but this time filling in for striking clerks. Instead of issuing orders, he was swearing in witnesses and processing exhibits. If there had ever been any doubt about Ted being a team player, the last vestiges were erased during the strike.

Meanwhile, Hughes had a new boss.

Attorney General Allan Williams didn't run again in 1983. When Bennett assembled his new slimmed-down cabinet, Brian Smith was given the job. Smith was a former mayor of the affluent Victoria-region municipality of Oak Bay and a lawyer with higher political ambitions. Before the election he had been in cabinet as minister of education (1980–82) and minister of energy, mines and resources (1982–83). In his new job, Smith was at the centre of many of the legal battles sparked by the restraint legislation. In the midst of the fray, he lost one of his top aides. Deputy Attorney General Richard Vogel, who had been in the job for six years, announced he was returning to private practice.

Hughes had by then cemented his reputation as a well-liked and valuable asset in the ministry, but he was not the obvious choice to replace Vogel as deputy minister, at least not to Smith. The incoming attorney general tried to recruit a high-profile lawyer from private practice, but he couldn't find one willing to take the cut in salary.[5] He also offered the job to Frank Rhodes, who was then the highly valued assistant deputy minister in charge of administration within the ministry. But Rhodes turned it down, citing his lack of legal qualifications for the job. "You don't have to be a pilot to run an airline and you don't have to be a doctor to be the deputy minister of health. But all the important tests in that office come in the area of the law," Rhodes said in a 1999 interview with *BC Business* magazine.

Rhodes recommended Hughes for the job instead. They had gotten to know each other in part because Hughes, like Rhodes, had a habit of coming in to the office on Sunday evening to prepare for the

---

5 Writing in the Vancouver *Province*, December 18, 1983, Barbara McLintock said: "And though both lawyers and ministry staff are pleased with the choice of Hughes for the job, it's no secret he was given it only after a government fishing expedition to the private bar drew not so much as a nibble. The salary being offered a deputy minister in the government ($60,000 to $70,000 a year) was not enough to lure any top lawyers away from their $250,000-a-year private practices."

week ahead. Ted had not expected to be tapped for the post, but was delighted to accept what turned out to be a pivotal role in his professional life and the history of the province.

On December 15, after just three years as a civil servant, the former judge became deputy minister in an office that Rhodes would later describe as "ground zero" for an extraordinary era in BC politics, a time that both reinforced British Columbia's reputation in the rest of Canada for wacky politics and set the stage for the starring role Hughes was to play in the ensuing years, when the integrity of politicians and the political process was increasingly on trial.

But most of that would come later. His immediate concern was to oversee the functioning of a ministry that the premier had mandated be cut by 25 per cent. All ministries faced the same orders, reinforced by Bennett's response to one minister who argued that his ministry had to be exempt from the carnage. Instead of sympathizing, the premier raised his target to 30 per cent.[6]

In interviews for this book, Hughes recalls that his ministry was not affected very much by the knife that was being taken to the rest of the government. But Bob Plecas, the deputy minister charged with implementing the cuts across the government, says Hughes was good at the bureaucratic game of eliminating FTES (full-time equivalents—a way of counting the number of jobs when individual employees have varying hours) without losing any valuable staff, usually by hiring people on contract to do work they had previously done as government employees.

The cost-cutters knew what was going on but they looked the other way.

---

6 Bob Plecas recalls that at the cabinet retreat where the new marching orders to ministers were handed out, the message "went through the room like shit through a goose."

"Bennett wanted me to be firm and do it but he also didn't want me to be stupid and so Ted's argument that we had to put people under contract just made sense," Plecas says. "You had to run the joint. You just had to do some of that stuff. You had to find a way to make it work."

And for Hughes, running the joint was only the beginning.

Breaking Down Barriers

EVEN AFTER HE became deputy to the attorney general, Hughes took on additional assignments outside his normal workload of overseeing a government ministry with thousands of employees and a budget of several hundred million dollars.

He continued volunteering on the board of the Juan de Fuca Hospitals, a group of extended-care facilities in the Victoria region, and he continued to speak and write about the role of hospital trustees.

Shortly after he became deputy, he was asked to lead what would be the first of three inquiries over the next decade into the administration of law and justice in British Columbia. In each case, the committees he led found barriers to equal access to justice for British Columbians, based on income, gender, race, sexual orientation and the part of the province in which they lived.

The first inquiry was a provincial review of legal aid services in the province. Funding for legal aid was being reduced as part of the overall cuts to government services. Hughes and his task force held hearings in communities around the province in 1983 and 1984, and their report led to some of that funding being restored. The task force members who toured with Hughes soon learned to appreciate the way he could handle a hearing and listen respectfully to sometimes hostile witnesses. They also discovered his appetite for work and for pork chops, mashed potatoes and gravy at the often less-than-five-star eateries in more remote corners of the province.

The report they issued recognized that legal aid was an essential service, that people who needed help weren't getting it, that lawyers who did legal aid work were not being paid enough and that the funding mechanism for legal aid was inadequate. It also called for a tax on legal services to help pay for legal aid. That recommendation was rejected by the legal profession and the government at the time but was later implemented.[1]

Stephen Owen was a young lawyer at the time, and director of the BC Legal Services Society, the organization that provided legal aid. He was caught in the middle, trying to make the system work when the government cut its funding. He also sat on the committee with Hughes. "It was really the most progressive and expansive legal aid system in the country, but it ran smack into the restraint program," he says. "The bar was mobilizing to try and get it restored, and Ted became deputy just when that was pretty much in full swing.

"I was this young, know-nothing executive director, and he became a great ally when he became deputy AG in really bringing the bar and the law society and the attorney general's ministry and then the public into a full discussion on legal aid. As much as the bar and the law society were trying to support us, it would have gone from the top five in the country to a really impoverished system if it hadn't been for Ted. He used the authority of his office and his own moral authority to save it."

In 1987 and '88, Hughes led a justice reform committee that again held hearings around the province and issued a report that led to

---

1 The province added the provincial sales tax to legal services in 1992, with the promise that the money would be used to support legal aid. However, the proceeds from the tax went into general revenues and were never fully linked to supporting legal aid.

major changes in the organization of courts. While there was general agreement that access to justice in BC was being hampered by delays and high costs, there was less consensus about what should be done.

One of the issues was familiar to Ted from his days as a judge in Saskatchewan. He had left his home province when the district court and Court of Queen's Bench were being amalgamated, a move that Ted had supported but many of his colleagues opposed. Even though it was already happening in other provinces, the idea of merging the courts was still controversial in British Columbia, where the equivalent courts were the Supreme Court and the County Court.

As in Saskatchewan a decade earlier, many Supreme Court judges, including Allan McEachern, Chief Justice of the Supreme Court and, later, the BC Court of Appeal, opposed the idea of a merger. Many County Court judges were also against the idea, even though it would have meant a small bump in pay. Unlike Supreme Court judges, who travelled the province, County Court judges had their own courthouses and chambers and most of the powers and privileges of a Supreme Court judge.

Susan Brice, then the mayor of Oak Bay, was a lay member of the committee. "I never understood the politics of the judicial world; Ted did," she says. "Our commission ultimately made tactical recommendations but nothing earth-shattering. I think Ted was more interested in at least what we accomplished being able to be implemented."

In the end, there was enough concern about the judges' opposition to a merger of the courts that the justice reform committee recommended a go-slow approach. In the report issued in November 1988, the committee called for a number of reforms to make the courts more efficient and accessible, and said the idea of a merger should be revisited in three years.

But while McEachern and other judges continued to oppose a merger, the governing benchers of the Law Society of British Columbia urged the government to get on with it, to merge the courts immediately. And the NDP justice critic, Moe Sihota, introduced a private member's bill calling for a similar approach. So when the attorney general introduced legislation six months later implementing many of the recommendations in the Hughes report and pushing ahead with a merger, the two courts were merged with almost no further controversy.[2]

Hughes was less successful with one of his personal agenda items, which was to persuade the province to change the name of the BC Supreme Court, which was and is neither supreme in BC nor a court of appeal. The highest court in the province is the Court of Appeal. Hughes preferred the name given to similar courts in other provinces, the Court of Queen's Bench, but the committee's recommendation that the province consider a less confusing name was ignored.

The reform committee was successful in persuading the province to require that legal documents and legislation be written in plain language to make them more accessible by eliminating needlessly confusing wording. Although the idea that legal jargon could be a barrier to justice was not on the committee's agenda at the start, when Kathleen Keating, a lawyer and former journalist who was the chief writer and researcher for the committee, brought it to his attention, Ted was soon persuaded of the value of making legal documents more accessible to ordinary people.

"He saw right away that this was a really important issue that we should be tackling, and it very quickly became a priority for him that the report itself would be written for non-lawyers, that it be easily

---

2 In an obituary of David Hector Campbell in the May 2016 edition of *The Advocate*, published by the Vancouver Bar Association, retired BC Supreme Court Justice Mary Ellen Boyd credits Campbell's effective personal management style with the relatively painless merger. He was the Chief Judge of the County Court and came into the Supreme Court in the newly created role of Associate Chief Justice. He looked after much of the administration of the combined court and the assigning of judges.

accessible to interested people, with or without legal training," says Keating, who went on to work on other commissions with Hughes.

Less than two years after he delivered the report on access to justice, the Law Society of British Columbia asked Hughes to take another look at the justice system, this time through the lens of how women were faring.

Even then it was somewhat controversial for a man to chair a committee on gender issues. Hughes certainly had the look of a silver-haired patriarchal establishment figure, and he was of a generation whose men were often more comfortable with women as housewives than workmates.

But women who had worked with Ted knew he was not easily fitted into that mould. Isabel Lloyd (then Isabel Kelly) was appointed to be the first deputy minister for women's programs in British Columbia around the time Ted became a deputy minister. "I was given an office about the size of a walk-in closet and a secretary, no budget and no staff but with a huge mandate," she says. "At the time, as you may be able to imagine, BC wasn't the most gender-equality-friendly part of the country. So it was a bit difficult usually to get any movement with the government. We had some interesting discussions in cabinet. We fortunately had a few cabinet ministers who were okay, but we had some whose attitudes were out of the last century."

Lloyd asked every minister to appoint someone to work with her on gender equity issues that arose in government. While other ministries sent lower-level officials, Hughes was one of the few deputy ministers, along with Bob Plecas, to consistently play a personal role. "I was always able to count on Bob and Ted," she says.

Maureen Maloney, then dean of the law school at the University of Victoria, understood the concern about having a man as the head of the committee looking into gender bias, but she believed Hughes' reputation and stature were more important than his gender. "I think it was a brilliant stroke of genius," she says of his appointment by the law society. "Ted was a very respected figure in the legal profession. He'd been a judge, he'd been a deputy attorney general, he was a person of wisdom and sound advice and had no grist in any mill." She says the decision of the benchers of the law society made the inquiry into gender bias respectable; their choice of Hughes said: "Look, this is a real issue, we're taking it really seriously and this is a really serious person who is taking it seriously as well."

The committee of three women and three men had a wide-ranging mandate "to study the extent to which gender bias, if it exists, may be found within the legal and justice systems, including substantive law."

There had been only one woman in Ted's class of 50 students when he obtained his law degree in 1950. By 1991, when the gender bias committee was struck, the proportion of women graduating from law school had dramatically increased. Close to half the law students at the UBC law school were women, as were about 30 per cent of the lawyers in Canada.[3] Despite that progress, the Hughes committee found serious problems in the legal profession, and in virtually every aspect of the justice system, including family law, workplace issues in law firms, the attitudes of some lawyers and judges in court and the treatment of female offenders.

"Although the laws, for the most part, are gender neutral, the application of many of these laws creates a situation of systemic bias against women, particularly women of low income status, aboriginal women, lesbians, women with disabilities, and women who are members of visible and immigrant minorities," the committee found, concluding: "The gender bias we have identified not only hurts and degrades women, but also undermines the effectiveness of and respect for our justice system. Gender bias means that women are denied

---

3 Joan Brockman, *Gender in the Legal Profession: Fitting or Breaking the Mould.*

equal access to the courts and that the law does not adequately protect them."

By the end, Hughes was comfortable declaring in a presentation of the report, "I am a feminist."

The gender bias committee's 600-page report, with more than 300 recommendations, was one of the first in Canada to extensively study the issues, and it made headlines across the country.

"People took it fairly seriously, I think, because it was Ted Hughes. You know, this guy, who had nothing in the game, who really took it seriously. He wrote a very good report and I think it did make a big difference," says Maloney.

The reputation that made him an effective voice for the disenfranchised was also crucial when he was called on to look into the affairs of the high and mighty.

Rising from Conflict

TED HUGHES BECAME a national figure in 1991 as the man who brought down a premier. William "Bill" Vander Zalm realized he had to resign after Hughes issued his finding that the premier used his public office for personal gain. Vander Zalm's conclusion was based partly on the sometimes bizarre facts of the case brought out in Hughes' report, but it was also based on the reputation of the author. There was no point in attacking Hughes. He was unassailable.

Hughes had been a judge for 18 years when he arrived in Victoria in 1980, but taking down a premier required more than just a comprehensive knowledge of the law and sound judgment. To tackle Vander Zalm, Hughes needed the stature he had earned while putting out political fires in the provincial government. By the 1990s he had emerged in the public eye in British Columbia as the go-to guy for pulling the government out of ethical and legal quagmires.

Crisis management is part of the daily fare of deputy ministers. For Hughes it was no different. Over the previous decade he had navigated an increasingly difficult series of challenges, often exacerbated by the natural state of tension between the government and its opposition in the legislature. Along the way, he slowly added to his own skills and reputation. That reputation gave him more freedom to operate independently, to the point that by the time Vander Zalm asked him to look into the allegations he faced, Hughes had the stature, the judgment and the skills to pull it off.

"I think that's how I got the opportunities," says Hughes. "People would know that I would say it as it was and there'd be no element of bias that would come into it. It would be what should be done in the circumstances. I'd say it with forcefulness and without fear of what the consequences may be—if, in my judgment, it was the right thing."

In one of the many letters of appreciation Ted received when he resigned in 1995 as BC's first conflict-of-interest commissioner for the legislature, a Victoria lawyer, John D. Waddell, QC, wrote: "I have often thought that it must be satisfying to be considered the most credible man in British Columbia. You simply can't gain that reputation without earning it completely."

Hughes' reputation was earned, but not without help. He had Vander Zalm to thank for much of what he had achieved to that point. While the job of deputy attorney general has always been difficult, Vander Zalm's style of governing, the supporting cast of characters he chose to surround him and the string of crises into which they stumbled created the challenges that propelled Hughes into an increasingly public role.

Part of what Hughes brought to the Vander Zalm decision was the work that he and others had done previously on the thorny issue of conflict of interest. For Hughes, that work began under Bill Bennett, and it multiplied in the fertile political environment produced by Vander Zalm's leadership after he took over as premier in 1986.

Conflict of interest was a serious problem for governments in the 1980s. There was no legal definition of a conflict beyond the prohibition in the Constitution Act against ministers of the Crown doing business directly with a government in which they served, and the breach-of-trust provisions in the Criminal Code.

Allegations of conflict of interest were usually made by opposition members who suggested that cabinet ministers were using their powers to feather their own nests rather than strictly looking after the public interest. The opposition politicians would seize on any apparent conflict and demand the resignation of whatever minister was involved. On a couple of occasions, ministers threatened to sue their accusers for libel, although none of those cases went to court. There was no politically neutral way to assess such allegations. The reaction from government was essentially a political assessment; dumping ministers regardless of the merits of the case against them was often easier than dealing with the public fallout of having the allegations linger.

Two ministers resigned over conflict allegations while Hughes was deputy attorney general and Bennett was premier. Forests minister Tom Waterland and health minster Stephen Rogers both stepped aside over shares they owned in a forestry company. Waterland resigned over what was an obvious conflict with his role as forests minister. Bennett said Rogers was not in conflict, but Hughes was asked to look into whether he had done anything illegal by failing to report that he had control over the forestry shares. Rogers subsequently resigned after pleading guilty to a violation of the Financial Disclosure Act. He received an absolute discharge from the judge, who described the act as so complex that most people would find it incomprehensible.[1]

Both men were later brought back into cabinet in different roles. In one of his first conflict inquiries, Hughes was asked to look into an allegation against Waterland that came up after he left government and took a job as president of the Mining Association of British Columbia. Waterland was in discussions with the mining association about the job while he was still in cabinet as minister of agriculture. During that time he attended a cabinet meeting at which a break in electricity rates for a member of the mining association was approved. Waterland had previously been on record as supporting such a benefit

1 The current Financial Disclosure Act was passed in 1996.

but Hughes accepted his assurance that while he was present at the meeting, he had not taken part in the discussion about electricity rates after he was in negotiations with the mining association. That meant he had not been in an actual conflict of interest.

Nonetheless, in a finding that became part of the basis for later legislation, Hughes said there was an appearance of conflict that was problematic. "In future instances the appearance of conflict, as well as conflict in fact, is to be avoided if today's high level of public confidence in the honour and integrity of those who offer themselves for the very high and prestigious position of elected office is to be maintained," he wrote in the opinion he gave to Attorney General Brian Smith in January 1987.

By then, Vander Zalm had taken over as premier.

On the conflict-of-interest front, Vander Zalm started the year by stepping back from a promise made by his predecessor. In his final Throne Speech before resigning in 1986, Bill Bennett had promised to bring in legislation to create rules for defining conflict of interest. In January 1987, Vander Zalm decided to issue guidelines for cabinet ministers rather than legislate how they should behave. This meant there were now written rules at least, but under Vander Zalm's new guidelines the final arbiter of whether a minister was in conflict was still the premier, just as it was under Bennett.

While slammed by critics on the opposition benches and in the media as being weak and unenforceable, the guidelines did contain Ted's recommendation that the appearance of conflict of interest as well as actual conflict of interest must be avoided. For advice on the application of those guidelines when allegations of conflict arose, the attorney general and the premier turned to Hughes, who won the confidence of both government and opposition by applying his judicial experience to interpret the law and by having the self-assurance to step outside those narrow bounds on occasion to allow for fairness and reason.

Hughes never accepted the commonly held view that politicians deserve to be held in contempt. "It is wrong to tar all elected persons with an image created by a few bad apples in the barrel," Hughes said in a 2004 interview with a *Vancouver Sun* reporter. "The fact is that bad apples appear from time to time in every profession—doctors, lawyers, accountants. Yet I would argue that those professions, like publicly elected office, are honourable professions with 99 per cent performance with honour and integrity."

Hughes' strong belief in the fundamental honour of most politicians was matched by his zeal and determination to protect the honour of the profession. Hughes understood that as a public servant he was serving political masters, but from early on he also loyally served an ideal that his masters were also public servants who had to meet high standards to maintain the public trust. If they failed to meet that standard, he was ready to say so.

One of the first to fall below the bar in Vander Zalm's government was forests minister Jack Kempf. The loud, folksy and bombastic MLA from northern BC had used his constituency allowance to pay for a recreational vehicle, among other improprieties. When the allegations surfaced early in 1987, Vander Zalm asked Hughes and Bob Plecas, then deputy minister in charge of personnel, what he should do. They both said the minister had to go.

After Plecas gave his advice, Vander Zalm objected. Kempf would have been the first minister fired, and the premier did not want to create a precedent if he didn't have to. But when Hughes laid out a thoughtful and well-balanced case for why Kempf had to step down, Vander Zalm was persuaded that he had to act.[2]

---

2 Kempf earned a special mention in the lore of the press gallery after telling a mob of reporters, "I am not innocent of anything." In Gary Mason and Keith Baldrey, *Fantasyland: Inside the Reign of Bill Vander Zalm*. Information on this case is drawn primarily from this source.

"If Ted gave you an opinion, that's all you needed to ever have," says Plecas.

Cliff Michael was the fourth member of Vander Zalm's cabinet to step down over a conflict, and the second that Ted was asked to investigate using the premier's guidelines.[3] Hughes was concerned enough by what he found to bring in the police to investigate, and he subsequently sought an outside legal opinion as well.

Michael was a member of the Economic Development Committee of cabinet. In July 1987 the committee received a delegation from Powder Mountain Resorts Ltd. The delegation was seeking development rights for a ski hill, rights over which the cabinet committee had some influence. After the presentation, Michael approached Roger Tadema, a minor shareholder in the venture who had contacts in the investment community, and asked him for his business card. A couple of weeks later, Michael called Tadema to see whether he could connect Michael with anyone interested in buying some recreational property on Shuswap Lake in which he had an interest. Tadema declined but Michael persisted by sending him some brochures.

The cabinet committee eventually recommended another option for Powder Mountain, leaving Tadema wondering whether his application would have received more favourable treatment if he had helped Michael sell some of his lots. Hughes easily identified that as a perception of a conflict of interest.

Michael proffered the same brochures he sent to Tadema to Klaus Linemayr, who visited Michael's constituency office looking for help to revitalize a mill. While Michael made no direct connection to his sales pitch and Linemayr's request, Hughes again found a perceived conflict of interest.

---

3 Ted's investigation of Tom Waterland was prepared before the guidelines were announced on January 15, 1987.

Hughes said Michael was quite forthright in describing how he kept brochures in his desk at the legislature, something he had done as an ordinary MLA before being brought into cabinet. Hughes acknowledged that it was accepted practice for MLAs not in cabinet to follow their private vocations, at least part-time, but he said they crossed a line when they did so in the legislature or their constituency offices. He urged backbench MLAs to live by a standard that embodied Vander Zalm's conflict guidelines, even though only cabinet ministers were required to do so.

The issue of what constituted a conflict was clouded, however, by the premier's blindness to his own conflicts involving his family business and his friends. Even as he was issuing guidelines for his ministers, Vander Zalm saw no conflict with using his office and position to promote Fantasy Gardens, a theme park owned and managed by his wife, Lillian. The premier's example did little to further the message that Hughes was trying to instill.

Neither the police investigation nor the outside legal opinion found grounds for a criminal charge against Michael, but the MLA resigned as minister of transportation and highways on November 12, 1987, a month before Ted submitted his report on the investigation to Brian Smith. In that report, Hughes concluded that Michael's "judgment failed him badly in not signaling at least an appearance of conflict in making his sales pitch on the indicated occasions. It was a dumb thing to have done for which he paid a big price on November 12, 1987."

"A dumb thing to have done" was not a legal judgment, but it was not unusual for Ted, while staying within the dictates of the law, to stray beyond legal language in his advice and reports. And his wider perspective made him all the more valuable to the government.

While his role as a deputy minister was never to give political advice, Plecas says, Hughes had a rare and valuable ability to understand the political implications of policy decisions. "I would expect, and I really would believe this, that sitting in the AG's office, law and politics are as blended together as a milkshake," says Plecas, who served NDP, Social Credit and Liberal governments in BC over five decades.

It was a natural fit for Hughes. While he had left party politics behind 25 years earlier when he became a district court judge, he maintained an active interest as a spectator with an insider's perspective. Long after he left government, he continued to prefer broadcasts of Question Period over any other form of televised entertainment. "When the legislature's sitting in Victoria, at seven o'clock at night they rebroadcast Question Period, and CPAC broadcasts at eight the federal Question Period, and I never miss. I suspect not many people would say that's on their daily television watching but I just enjoy that. I enjoy listening to the question and wondering how on earth they're going to try to get out of that. I guess that's who I am."

At the same time, he worried about losing the idea of a politically neutral public service. In a 1996 speech to the Institute of Public Administration in Canada, Hughes decried the increasing politicization of the civil service. He recognized that courts have ruled that people who work in the civil service have rights, as all Canadians do, to join or support political parties or candidates. But he warned that for those in management, the exercise of those rights risks their prospects for both advancing their careers and surviving a change of government. He argued that the notion that career civil servants need to be purged when a new political party takes control of the government is antithetical to a professional civil service in which veteran public servants must be able to serve governments of any stripe regardless of their personal opinions.

"Some may say this asks too much of the public servant. He or she should not be required to refrain from exercising political rights available to other citizens. My view is that this is not too high a price to pay for a productive and promising career in the public service. If you feel such a practice calls for too high a sacrifice or for too high a standard, then maybe, just maybe, your future would best develop and unfold outside of government where all possible avenues of political participation are open to you."

Hughes needed the shield of neutrality that he urged senior civil servants to embrace when he stepped into the most politically charged assignments of his career—poking through the affairs of the politicians he worked for to assess whether they were using their public position for private gain.

Calling in the Cops: Peter Toigo and the Expo Lands

EXPO '86 WAS a huge success for the province and the Bennett government. Millions of visitors, including Prince Charles and Diana, the Princess of Wales, came to British Columbia to see the world's fair with a transportation theme that was held between May and October on reclaimed industrial land on the north side of Vancouver's False Creek.

When it was over, attention turned to the future of the 173-acre site. The province formed a Crown corporation, the BC Enterprise Corporation (BCEC), to sell the valuable asset. A consortium headed by Chinese billionaire Li Ka-shing eventually bought the land, and it has since become a major urban-redevelopment project. But that was after Vander Zalm's interference in the sale led to a public fight with two of his senior ministers, which put Hughes in the awkward position of having to call in the police.

After the bidding process was well underway, Vander Zalm intervened several times on behalf of his friend Peter Toigo, a Vancouver developer who had supported Vander Zalm's run for the leadership of the Social Credit Party. Toigo wanted to buy the site but had not proffered a bid before the closing date for offers in the fall of 1987.

Vander Zalm's interference and the apprehension that Toigo was getting confidential information about the bidding process alarmed BCEC president Kevin Murphy and economic development minister

Grace McCarthy, whose cabinet responsibilities included BCEC and the sale of the Expo '86 assets.

In December, McCarthy threatened to resign if the meddling didn't stop. This would have been a major blow to Vander Zalm. McCarthy was a giant in Social Credit because of her role in rebuilding the party following its 1972 loss to the New Democrats under Dave Barrett. Vander Zalm persuaded her to stay, and for a while it looked like the Toigo offer was out of the picture.

When it came back in February, again promoted by Vander Zalm, members of the BCEC board were increasingly worried that the sale they were overseeing was becoming hopelessly and possibly illegally compromised. On Friday, March 18, Murphy and board member Keith Mitchell, a Vancouver lawyer, went to see Attorney General Brian Smith.

McCarthy had told Smith of her concerns back in December, but the new allegations seemed to warrant police involvement. At a breakfast meeting in the Oak Bay Beach Hotel on the following Monday, Smith dropped the whole affair in Ted's lap. The deputy AG would have to decide whether to call the police and launch an investigation of not just the premier's friend but the premier himself.

Ted met with Mitchell later that day and spent three and a half hours with Murphy in his office in Vancouver the following afternoon. At that point he decided to call in the RCMP, and he appointed Vancouver lawyer Len Doust to represent the government in any court actions.[1] This would further insulate the government from any allegations of political meddling in the investigation.

Although police began their inquiries quietly, word of the probe eventually leaked out.

---

1 Doust's role was similar to that of special prosecutors, who are used when there is a chance of a conflict of interest involving the government, politicians or justice officials during a police investigation or prosecution.

On Friday, April 8, the Vancouver radio station CKNW reported that Toigo was being investigated in connection with the sale of the Expo lands. At that point the premier's office was aware of the possibility of an investigation because CKNW reporter George Garrett had called a week earlier to try to get confirmation. Vander Zalm had called Smith into his office and asked if there was a police investigation into Toigo. Smith told him that as the attorney general he could neither confirm nor deny that an investigation was underway into anyone, including the premier.

Hughes was in Campbell River on the Friday the story broke. He was called out of a hearing of the justice reform committee he was chairing and summoned back to Victoria for a meeting with David Poole, the premier's chief of staff. He knew what Poole wanted and that the stakes were high.

Poole was a brash, bright, hard-working young man who was given a lot more power in government than others before him in the same position had received. He spoke for the premier internally—and occasionally to the media—and had no patience for the notion that the ministers he was ordering around deserved to be treated with some deference because they had earned their position by being elected while he had only been appointed. Ministers waiting outside Poole's office for a meeting were sometimes summoned with a snap of his fingers.[2]

Hughes was led to understand Poole had only one question, and if he didn't give the right answer, he would be out of a job. The question would be the same one Smith had refused to answer when the premier had asked it.

He chartered a floatplane back to Victoria. It was a clear day, and on the way he asked the pilot to swing over Shawnigan Lake so he could see his cottage from the air.

---

2 Many of the details in this chapter come from Mason and Baldrey's account in *Fantasyland: Inside the Reign of Bill Vander Zalm*.

Smith was waiting for him in Ted's office at 910 Government Street, across the harbour from the legislature, where he was to meet Poole. He didn't tell Ted what to say. He didn't have to.

"I went in there, and he [Poole] asked me point blank whether Toigo and the premier were under police investigation. I told him that those questions aren't answered unless and until charges have been laid, and then full details are disclosed. But it's most unfair for the criminal justice branch to give out that kind of information when charges do not result. That would most improperly malign people, and I wasn't prepared to answer that question.

"So he said: 'All right. Wait here.' He went away, and I assumed he went to the premier's office. I waited over half an hour, and then he came back and he said to me: 'You can go.' There was nothing more than that."

The police eventually concluded that there were no grounds for any charges, but in the meantime, Vander Zalm had come to believe that the investigation was politically motivated and cooked up by Smith and McCarthy to get at him.

In June, with the investigation in its final days, Smith decided to resign his cabinet post amidst rumours that he was going to be fired in an impending cabinet shuffle, and his ministry was going to be split in half.

Around the same time, Ted slipped on a floatplane ramp and badly injured his knee. He was awaiting surgery when Smith arrived at the hospital. They moved into a supply closet, where Smith went over the speech he planned to give in the legislature the next day.

On June 28, Smith stood in the legislature and said: "This is an office of great sensitivity and neutrality in the administration of justice. I now find I can no longer carry out my duties, as I clearly do not have the support of the premier and his office, who do not appreciate the unique independence that is the cornerstone of the Attorney General's responsibilities in a parliamentary democracy."

Later that day, after Ted's operation, the police and Doust gathered at his bedside. They all agreed there was no point in continuing the investigation.

The next morning, Provincial Secretary Elwood Veitch, the cabinet minister designated as a temporary replacement for Smith, came to Ted's hospital room for a briefing.

Two weeks later, McCarthy resigned her cabinet post after telling Vander Zalm she wouldn't accept a role in the new cabinet being announced the next day unless he got rid of Poole. Despite his earlier denials, Vander Zalm had been planning to fire Smith, and he did split the attorney general's ministry, creating a new ministry of the solicitor general.

Bud Smith, a Kamloops lawyer who had served as Bill Bennett's principal secretary and had run in the 1986 Social Credit leadership race, was named as the new attorney general and Ted's new boss.

The cabinet shuffle announced on July 5 coincided with a shuffle of deputy ministers, but Ted wasn't moved. Vander Zalm continued to have great respect for him even after the investigation of Toigo and his refusal to tell Poole what he knew about it. Bud Smith had also asked that Hughes stay on as his deputy. They worked well together and formed a friendship that survived the political storm which overtook them both in 1990.

McCarthy's refusal to stay in Vander Zalm's cabinet opened up the tourism portfolio the premier had been planning to give her. This was filled by Bill Reid, a move that would lead to one of the most bizarre chapters in BC's political history—and Ted's greatest challenge as a civil servant.

Making Room at the Top for BC

WHEN HIS WIFE Mimi got cancer, Supreme Court of Canada judge William McIntyre decided to step down and spend more time with her. McIntyre had grown up in Moose Jaw and earned his law degree at the University of Saskatchewan four years before Hughes graduated from the same school. But he moved to British Columbia to practise law and was a judge on the BC Court of Appeal when he was elevated to the Supreme Court in 1979.

When McIntyre retired in 1989, Attorney General Bud Smith and Ted Hughes saw an opportunity to start a new tradition of having a permanent British Columbia seat on the top court. Legally, three of the nine seats on the court are reserved for Quebec. By convention, three go to Ontario, one goes to Atlantic Canada and two go to Western Canada.

At the time McIntyre was appointed as a judge from BC, the tradition was that the two seats for the west were rotated through British Columbia and the three prairie provinces. In 1989 it would have been Saskatchewan's turn, and Edward Bayda, who was then Chief Judge of the Saskatchewan Court of Appeal, was being touted in some circles as the obvious choice to replace McIntyre.

Hughes says that despite his history with Bayda, there was nothing personal about his lobbying for an appointment from BC. He and Smith were making an argument based on population and geography rather than the merits of any individual. "Bud and I came to the conclusion that British Columbia was not the Prairies, and that a fair distribution of those two seats on the court would be one for British Columbia and one for the Prairies," Hughes says.

Their view fit the notion that there should be five regions in Canada, rather than four, for the purpose of representation on the Supreme Court of Canada, with British Columbia standing as a region on its own, as do Ontario and Quebec.[1]

Hughes and Smith went to Ottawa to make their case. Ted lobbied bureaucrats he had gotten to know in federal-provincial meetings over his years as deputy attorney general. Smith worked his political contacts, including Marjory LeBreton, whom he knew from working on Progressive Conservative leader Robert Stanfield's federal campaigns years earlier. LeBreton arranged a meeting for Smith with Prime Minister Brian Mulroney.

Smith believes his case was helped by the fact that Saskatchewan premier Grant Devine was seeking a $1-billion wheat subsidy in addition to a seat on the Supreme Court for a Saskatchewan judge. "I remember him [Mulroney] making a note, as only he would, that Devine could have the wheat subsidy or the judge, but not both. And I think Devine eventually chose the wheat subsidy. That enabled Mulroney, then, to appoint Beverley McLachlin, whom he liked, and he thought was a good choice," Smith says.

---

1 The same principle was used in the act passed by the federal government in 1995 that recognized Quebec as a distinct society and British Columbia as a separate region for the purpose of creating a regional veto for amendments to the Canadian Constitution (W.H. McConnell, "Constitutional History," in *The Canadian Encyclopedia*, thecanadianencyclopedia.ca/en/article/constitutional-history/).

Ted also met with John Crosbie, the federal justice minister in Mulroney's cabinet. He was ushered into Crosbie's office about 6 PM, after the House had risen for the day.

"He says to me, 'you must be Hughes,'" Ted recounts. "He goes to the cupboard and pulls out a bottle of Scotch and two tumblers. I loathe Scotch. He fills up a good third of each of the tumblers with straight Scotch, no ice, no mix, and puts it in front of me and says, 'there, sit down.' I had a dilemma. Do I drink the damn stuff, which I loathe? I decided I wanted to accomplish my mission and I drank a third of a glass of Scotch. Straight. It was a small price to pay to make my point."

Whether McLachlin's appointment in 1989 turns out to have been the beginning of a new convention or merely politically expedient at the time won't be known until her replacement is announced. Either way, her work as a justice and chief justice of Canada's top court is a valuable legacy in itself. She had already become Canada's longest-serving chief justice when, in June 2017, she announced her plan to retire in December, nine months before reaching the mandatory retirement age of 75.

As part of his discussions with Ottawa, Smith was asked who he would recommend to replace McLachlin as Chief Justice of the Supreme Court of British Columbia. In what might have been another turning point, Smith recommended Hughes. This time, however, his advice was not taken. The prime minister appointed Justice William Esson of the BC Court of Appeal for the job.

Although he was a former judge, Hughes was seen as an outsider by the judges in BC, some of whom, including Chief Justice Allan McEachern, were already not happy with his role in leading the justice reform committee.[2] So, as it had a decade earlier, a prime minister's decision to choose someone else for a senior judicial appointment rather than Hughes turned out to be a blessing for British Columbia.

2 Email from Bud Smith, June 2016.

While there is little doubt he would have been an excellent chief justice, it's much less clear that anyone else had his unique qualifications to rise to the extraordinary challenges he was about to face in his job as deputy attorney general.

TOP Bill Hughes, Ted's father, in 1916, before being wounded.

BOTTOM, LEFT Ted's father, with Ted's brother, Bill, and cousin Betty Hughes in 1928.

BOTTOM, RIGHT Ted on the porch of his family home on 9th Ave in Saskatoon, aged 10 or 11.

MONTGOMERY'S ARMY OCCUPIES SIRTE

OPPOSITE Ted delivering war news in 1942.

TOP The Larmonths in 1942, Helen's sister, Mary, her father and mother, Norman and Muriel, and Helen.

BOTTOM, LEFT Helen graduating from York House in 1950.

BOTTOM, RIGHT Ted at university.

ABOVE Rev. Norman Larmonth with Princess Elizabeth during her visit to Saskatoon in 1952.

OPPOSITE Ted and Helen stepping out in Saskatoon, 1952.

K
NO SMOKING

OPPOSITE, TOP Ted's political connections—on the stage with John Diefenbaker, Alf Bence and Fiorenza Drew, wife of then-Progressive Conservative leader George Drew, 1950s.

OPPOSITE, BOTTOM Diefenbaker appoints Ted to the District Court in 1962.

TOP The new Saskatoon Courthouse in 1958, the year it opened. COURTESY OF SASKATOON PUBLIC LIBRARY—LOCAL

BOTTOM Now a family of six, Christmas 1965.

ABOVE John and Olive Diefenbaker with the Hughes family in their backyard on Kirk Crescent in Saskatoon, about 1969.

OPPOSITE Letter from Diefenbaker congratulating Helen on her election to Saskatoon city council in 1976.

THE RT. HON. JOHN G. DIEFENBAKER, P.C., C.H., Q.C., M.P.

December 7,
1 9 7 6.

My dear Helen:

With Olive in hospital I have fallen behind with my correspondence. I brought her home on Wednesday but she had to return to hospital Sunday evening by ambulance.

She asked yesterday if I had sent a message of congratulations on your spectacular victory in the aldermanic race. I apologize for not having done so; we were delighted to know of your success.

I only wish there were more people like you and Ted, who do so much for others.

With warmest regards to you and him, I am

Yours sincerely,

Alderman (Elect)
Mrs. Edward Hughes,
59 Kirk Crescent,
Saskatoon Sask.

TOP Ted and Helen, on the occasion of Helen's becoming a member of the Order of Canada in 1982, for her thirty years of service to the city of Saskatoon.

BOTTOM Ted, Garde Gardom, a Social Credit cabinet minister and later BC's lieutenant governor, Dick Vogel and Frank Rhodes in the early 1980s.

TOP Lieutenant-Governor David Lam presenting Ted with the Insitute of Public Administration's award for contributing to the excellence of the public service in Canada, 1990.

BOTTOM Ted, BC's deputy attorney general, in his office at 910 Government St. with his staff, Joanne Palmer (L) and Georgina Wong, about 1990.

TOP Ted, as BC's deputy attorney general, announces in July 1990 that he has asked the RCMP to investigate former attorney general Bud Smith for possible obstruction of justice. LOUISE DENIS, *VANCOUVER SUN*

BOTTOM Ted leaves Faye and Dean Leung's home after an hour-long interview in March 1991, during the Vander Zalm investigation. LES BAZSO, *THE PROVINCE*

TOP Irene Fraser, centre, leads a ceremony in Calgary in 2003 at the start of the Alternative Dispute Resolution process for residential school survivors.

BOTTOM Helen began Souper Bowls for Hope, a fundraiser for street youth in Victoria, and ran it for more than a decade.

OPPOSITE, TOP Ted was invested as an officer of the Order of Canada in 2003.

OPPOSITE, BOTTOM Ted in the Hughes' condo on the harbour in Victoria in 2015. CRAIG MCINNES

TOP Ted looking up cases in the courthouse library in Victoria, 2016. CRAIG MCINNES

BOTTOM Memorabilia from a long and varied career, in the Hughes' condo in Victoria. CRAIG MCINNES

TOP Sheila Hetschko, Ted and Helen's daughter, who died in her sleep in 2010.

BOTTOM Ted at the Hughes cottage in Shawnigan Lake, 2016.

CRAIG MCINNES

Blue Boxes, Secret Tapes and the Wild West

SURREY CITY COUNCIL named William "Bill" Reid its Good Citizen of the Year in 2013. The recognition for his decades of service to the community was announced a month before he died in May at the age of 78. A former used-car dealer, city councillor and MLA for the sprawling suburb of Vancouver, Reid was known as "Mr. Surrey" in the region. But on a Wednesday morning in September 1989, in the Victoria offices of Premier Bill Vander Zalm, his name was mud.

The front-page headline for the September 20 edition of the *Vancouver Sun* said "Minister's pals' firm got money: Campaign manager, friend received recycling grant funds."

Reid was then the minister of tourism and the provincial secretary, and the damning *Sun* story was the first page in a chapter that became known as the "blue box scandal." The allegation was that $277,000 in lottery funds that Reid controlled as the tourism minister had been given to a company called Eco-Clean Waste Systems Ltd. Eco-Clean was owned by George Doonan, Reid's campaign manager in the previous provincial election, and Bill Sullivan, a long-time family friend.

It wasn't the first misstep for a government already buffeted by a series of high-profile resignations and ongoing rumours of a caucus revolt against Vander Zalm, but no one could have imagined when the scandal broke how profoundly it would affect the way the game of politics came to be played in British Columbia. Nor could they have foreseen the bizarre episode it would later lead to, an episode that as much as any reinforced BC's reputation for wacky politics.

For Hughes, it was a test of his judgment and resolve in the spotlight of intense public scrutiny on a stage where careers were being made and broken, and where the ultimate risk was that the popular notion that all politicians are crooks would be reinforced.

Vander Zalm announced Reid's resignation the next day in Penticton, where he was attending the annual meeting of the Union of BC Municipalities. Reid's departure from cabinet was a blow to the premier. Reid was a loyal supporter at a time when Vander Zalm had already alienated many members of his Social Credit caucus with his often arbitrary and occasionally startling leadership style.[1]

The premier asked Claude Richmond, the minister of social services, to investigate what he described as serious allegations that warranted immediate action.

Not surprisingly, the leader of the opposition, former Vancouver mayor Mike Harcourt, objected to what he called an in-house investigation designed to make the whole mess go away. He had reason to be suspicious. Although, as noted earlier, Vander Zalm had brought in conflict guidelines for his ministers two years earlier, there was still no prescribed way to handle a conflict-of-interest investigation, and the premier was still the final arbiter of whether there really was a conflict.

Reid's first reaction when contacted by a CBC reporter in April 1989 and asked about his personal relationship with the principals of the firm he was giving money to was "Yeah, and what's the problem with that?"

---

1 Mason and Baldrey, *Fantasyland*.

But others saw that relationship as a big problem. Richmond called in the provincial comptroller general, Brian Marson. In December, Marson reported that the grant approved by Reid was both irregular and improper because of the minster's close relationships with the men getting the money and the way the grant was made.[2] Eco-Clean had not even applied for a grant, and the money was channelled through a third party. It reeked of an abuse of office.

The Marson report wasn't immediately made public. It was held back because of another investigation that was quietly instigated by Hughes, who called in the RCMP three days after Reid resigned in September. The police investigation was well underway by the time Marson delivered his report on December 12. Bill Stewart, assistant deputy attorney general for the criminal justice branch, asked Howard Dirks, the new provincial secretary, to keep the Marson report under wraps so it wouldn't prejudice the RCMP investigation.

That investigation was already underway, and three weeks earlier, Deputy Commissioner Don Wilson, the commanding officer of the RCMP in BC, had written to Hughes to tell him that Reid might have committed a criminal breach of trust.

On December 12, the same day Marson delivered his report, the RCMP sent a brief to Robert Wright, the Vancouver-region Crown counsel, recommending that Reid be charged with breach of trust by a public officer, and that Reid, Doonan and Sullivan be jointly charged with fraud against the City of White Rock.

In BC, police can't lay a charge on their own except in extraordinary circumstances. Charges have to be approved by Crown counsel.

---

2 Many of the details and direct quotes for this chapter come from Stephen Owen's two-volume report, *Discretion to Prosecute Inquiry,* Volume One: *Report and Recommendations* and *Discretion to Prosecute Inquiry, Commissioner's Report,* Volume Two: *Documents,* and from Ted Hughes' memos to file.

So in the political pressure cooker that surrounded the Reid affair, it was up to Wright, an employee of the government that would be embarrassed by any trial, to decide if the three men should be charged.

Today, when police come across a case involving a politician or an employee of the justice system, a special prosecutor from outside government is appointed to oversee the investigation and to decide whether charges are warranted. In making that decision, special prosecutors use two tests: Is there a substantial likelihood of conviction? And would a prosecution be in the public interest? The same criteria were used to make that decision in 1989, but the internal process could not dispel the publicly held suspicion that somehow insiders were getting special treatment, that justice was being denied.

Wright knew what kind of a hot file he had been handed, so he asked a senior Crown counsel from the commercial crime section to prepare a position. Wright also talked to the police, an accountant and A.G. "Ace" Henderson, a Vancouver prosecutor who later became a BC Supreme Court judge.[3] After these discussions, Wright determined that Reid should not be charged.

Before delivering that opinion to the RCMP, however, Wright sought a second opinion from Richard Peck, a top Vancouver lawyer. Peck agreed that there was no basis for a successful fraud prosecution against Doonan or Sullivan, but he concluded that Reid could be convicted under Section 122 of the Criminal Code, which involves

---

3 A year earlier, Wright and Henderson had prosecuted former premier Bill Bennett, his brother Russell, and Herb Doman, the founder of Doman Industries, on charges stemming from the sale of Doman shares moments before a major news announcement that affected the value of those shares. The three men were acquitted, although they were all later found guilty of insider trading at a hearing held by the BC Securities Commission (David Baines, "B.C.'s Biggest Insider-Trading Case Marks 20 Years," *Vancouver Sun*, November 29, 2008).

the abuse of power by a public official.[4] He said it was a difficult decision, however, and recommended that Wright obtain a second outside opinion.

Wright went to John Hall, another top Vancouver lawyer, who agreed with him that no charges ought to be laid against any of the men.

Wright took all the decisions to William Stewart, the assistant deputy attorney general, criminal justice branch. On January 30, Stewart wrote to Deputy Commissioner Wilson of the RCMP that he would not approve the laying of charges against any of the three men because, based on the evidence, there was no substantial likelihood of conviction. The case against them was too weak.

The police were not happy. Wilson appealed to Hughes, who had deliberately avoided being part of the decision about whether to charge Reid and the others on the chance that he would be involved in an appeal. Hughes now found himself in the middle of two disputes, between the police and Crown prosecutors, and between the government and opposition. While his boss, the attorney general, was legally entitled to decide whether a cabinet colleague should be prosecuted, it would have been politically disastrous for him to get involved. That left Ted as the final arbiter.

Hughes reviewed all of the decisions, and on February 13 he brought the ministry staff and the outside lawyers together for a two-and-a-half-hour meeting. At the end he gave no indication of where he was headed.

On February 23 he hand-delivered a letter to Deputy Commissioner Wilson. He later described it as one of the hardest things he ever

---

4 Section 122 of the Criminal Code states: "Every official who, in connection with the duties of his office, commits fraud or a breach of trust is guilty of an indictable offence and liable to imprisonment for a term not exceeding five years, whether or not the fraud or breach of trust would be an offence if it were committed in relation to a private person" (R.S.C., 1985, c. C-46).

had to do. "The easy thing to have done, I suppose, would have been to have prosecuted," says Hughes. "But if you haven't got a reasonable likelihood of conviction, that's not a fair thing to do to anybody. I think that probably was the toughest decision I had. I remember getting the letter done in Vancouver at 777 Hornby, signing it, taking it and getting a cab and going over to Don Wilson's office at 37th and Heather. He was a gentleman, but he was very displeased with me."

Hughes made the decision, but Attorney General Bud Smith made the announcement that no charges would be laid, throwing the issue immediately back into the political realm.

Moe Sihota was the NDP's justice critic. The 35-year-old lawyer from Vancouver Island was quickly making a name for himself with his sharp tongue and his ability to get under the skin of his political opponents. The decision not to charge Reid was like blood in the water, and he attacked. In the first of a series of acts that would draw Hughes deeper into terra incognita, Sihota charged that the appearance of a cover-up tainted the Reid decision.

"Surely the attorney general's department must have known there would be an impression of a cover-up in the public mind, and in the context of this government's reputation for helping its friends and insiders, justice not only had to be done, but it had to be seen to be done," Sihota said.

The allegation stung Hughes. He wrote to the attorney general two days later and recommended that a public judicial inquiry be held into the process leading to the decision not to lay charges against Reid and the others. "That is a serious allegation that undercuts the very foundations of the criminal justice system in the province and, surely, must shake public confidence in that system," he wrote.

In the same letter, Hughes withdrew a request he had submitted several months earlier to step down from his position of deputy attorney general and move into a position with "less onerous responsibilities": "The honourable course is for me to stay at the helm of the ship at least until the propriety and integrity of events and decisions taken over recent weeks have been pronounced upon, one way or another, by such respected jurist that is decided upon."

The attorney general agreed to both requests, but no judge was willing to take the assignment because of their role in the system. The AG turned to Stephen Owen, who was then the province's ombudsman. In April he agreed to step out of that role to conduct an inquiry into how the decision not to prosecute Reid was made, and to make recommendations about how the process could be improved.

The Owen inquiry was ready to start on May 22. But four days earlier, on May 18, Sihota appeared before a Justice of the Peace in Vancouver and started a private prosecution of Reid, alleging a violation of Section 122 of the Criminal Code, the same section that the police believed Reid had violated. The Owen inquiry had to be adjourned indefinitely over concerns that it could be prejudicial to Reid if Sihota's private prosecution went to trial.

The private prosecution presented a serious challenge for Attorney General Bud Smith and for Hughes. On the political side, it was a declaration that Sihota had to step in as a private citizen because the government was ignoring a crime committed by one of its own members. A month earlier, NDP leader Mike Harcourt and Sihota held a press conference at which they said there was sufficient evidence to charge Reid, and if the government didn't do so, they would.

The government had no written policy at the time on private prosecutions. But Hal Yacowar, the director of policy and legal services for the criminal justice branch, advised that the current practice was that private prosecutions for indictable offences were not allowed to proceed. Instead, if a private information were to be laid, an agent of the attorney general would take it over. Then, if it met the usual criteria for proceeding to court—criteria that in this case Hughes had already deemed to be insufficient—the government would prosecute it. If the information fell below the charging standard, as it had in the Reid case, the government agent would enter a stay of proceedings, effectively quashing the private prosecution.

Officials in the ministry urged Smith to follow the current practice and take over the case to protect the integrity of the justice system. But quashing the private prosecution would be politically risky. It could play into the NDP's claims that the government was protecting Reid for political reasons. That option had become more problematic since word had leaked to the NDP that the RCMP had wanted to charge Reid but were turned down by the ministry of the attorney general.

On June 11, Smith announced that he would not intervene in the private prosecution. He told reporters that the circumstances surrounding the case were unusual enough that there was little chance that letting it go forward would set a dangerous precedent.

The same day, Sihota announced that Peter Firestone, a Victoria lawyer he knew from his law-school days, would prosecute the case. Firestone had called Sihota two months earlier and told him that he thought there was a reasonable chance of conviction. He offered to take on the case for little more than his expenses because he believed Reid should be charged.

"It is my view that there is a 'two-tier' system of justice in this province," Firestone had written to Sihota on May 24, 1990. "From my perspective, this prosecution is not politically motivated but is motivated by a profound sense of injustice in that the rich are treated one way and the poor another."

Firestone soon found that the attorney general's announcement that he would not interfere in the private prosecution did not mean that he was willing to cooperate, at least not in the way Firestone expected. Firestone asked for all the relevant documents used in the decision not to prosecute and the results of the police investigation, documents that he believed he, as a prosecutor, should be entitled to have. The attorney general disagreed. Before the prosecution was launched, Sihota had written to Smith as a member of the legislature with a similar request. The attorney general turned him down.

"Fundamental to our liberty is the fact that no citizen should ever have to worry about any attorney general releasing files to anyone not authorized to have them," Smith responded in a letter to Sihota.

Once the prosecution was launched, the ministry took the position that while it was not conducting the prosecution, it still had a responsibility to oversee it to ensure that the interests of the accused were protected. As a result, Hughes responded to Firestone's request for documents by saying the ministry would be only too happy to supply the documents, but it would require a court to issue a subpoena first. "I trust you will see this as a reasonable course to follow," Hughes wrote.

Far from being reasonable, Firestone believed the position taken by the ministry was simply stonewalling. But he also calculated that if that were so, he could not mount a successful prosecution. "Without the cooperation of the attorney general and his ministry, my job as private prosecutor is impossible," Firestone wrote to Sihota later on the day he received the reply from Hughes. He recommended that the charge against Reid be withdrawn, which it was a few days later.

That left Owen free to reopen his inquiry into the circumstances surrounding the decision not to charge Reid, with another layer of conduct by the ministry to sift through. On July 6 he announced that hearings would resume on July 17.

By then the whole affair had taken a strange twist that brought the conduct of the attorney general, the opposition and the media into question in ways that none of them could have imagined, and that pushed Hughes from the background onto centre stage.

On June 27, Sihota announced he was dropping the private prosecution. A day earlier he had received a package of tape recordings that took his attention in an entirely new direction. The tapes were recordings of intercepted radio-telephone communications. Over the next couple of weeks, Sihota consulted lawyers and personally researched the law on all the issues raised by the tapes' contents, how the recordings were obtained and the consequences of making them public.

Brian Graves, a freelance radio reporter, made the tapes with a scanner. He had been picking up calls made from the phone in Smith's car.[5] Graves gave a copy of the tapes to Debi Pelletier, a Canadian Press reporter. She wrote a story on their contents, but on legal advice that the tapes were illegally obtained, it was never published. Pelletier subsequently passed the recordings on to Sihota.

On July 11, an NDP caucus researcher called Hughes early in the afternoon to say that a courier was on the way to his office to hand-deliver a letter from Sihota, who was going to make a statement in the House that afternoon. Sihota wanted Hughes to come to his office afterward.

The letter foreshadowed an extraordinary new role for Hughes, one that would require him to make decisions that would decide the fate of his boss, Attorney General Bud Smith.

"I am writing to you in confidence with the expectation that you will not share the foregoing with the attorney general," Sihota wrote.

The NDP justice critic made the unusual request because he was about to make some explosive allegations in the legislature. Among them, that Smith had been talking to a senior ministry official about ways to embarrass and discredit Firestone, the private prosecutor in the Reid case, and that he also talked to a friendly reporter in the press gallery about ways to get the story out. Sihota charged that Smith's actions violated the independence and impartiality of his office and may have constituted an obstruction of justice.

---

5 The phone is variously described in reports as a radio phone and a cellphone. It likely was a radio phone, although unlike modern digital cellphones, signals from the analog cellphones of the day could be intercepted and monitored by more sophisticated scanners.

The conversations of interest to Sihota were between Smith and William Stewart, the assistant deputy attorney general, criminal justice branch; Smith and Margot Sinclair, a television reporter with CKVU in Vancouver; and Smith and his wife, Daphne Smith, who, like Bud Smith, was a lawyer.

On the day after Smith announced he would not intervene in the private prosecution, the tapes revealed that Stewart gave Smith some information that appeared to contradict Sihota's description of Firestone as a "prominent defence and Crown Counsel" who had reviewed the Reid matter and found that charges should have been laid. Stewart described Firestone as a "dimwit" who had been fired from an earlier murder case because he couldn't handle the pressure.

"How can we get that out?" Smith asked. "We could do anything we want now."

Smith then called Sinclair and tried unsuccessfully to get her to use that information in a story. The tapes also indicated that he had a close personal relationship with the reporter.

In another conversation, Smith told his wife, Daphne, that he did not believe Reid had done anything wrong.

For Sihota, this was evidence of an attempt to obstruct justice. The attorney general was trying to interfere with the private prosecution Sihota had launched. "It is my submission that the totality of the material I have forwarded to you demonstrates on a prima facie basis that the attorney general violated the standard of independence and impartiality expected of him with respect to this prosecution involving a colleague of his. In so doing, the attorney general not only offended the integrity of his office, but also brought the administration of justice into disrepute," Sihota said in the legislature while Hughes listened on a speaker in his office.

That damning accusation added to the cloud that Hughes felt the ministry and the justice system were under following the earlier complaints about the handling of the decision not to charge Reid. It also meant he was in the tricky situation of having to decide what information he could share with his bosses, the attorney general and the premier.

Later that afternoon, Hughes met Sihota in the NDP leader's office in the East Wing of the legislature and took possession of the tapes. Sihota told Hughes he had consulted experts in wiretap law and was satisfied that no law had been broken when the tapes were recorded or distributed. Hughes made no promises other than to tell Sihota he knew what his responsibility was and he would act on it.

After leaving Sihota, Hughes went to see David Emerson, the premier's deputy minister, and Jerry Lampert, who by then had replaced David Poole as Vander Zalm's principal secretary. He briefed them on the events of the afternoon while being careful not to comment on his thoughts regarding the law.

He then answered an urgent call from Smith, who had been away from the legislature that afternoon and now had to meet the press. What had Hughes told them?

Hughes repeated that he had only said he knew what his responsibility was and he would act on that. He denied Sihota's assertion that he had said he would launch an investigation, even though Hughes already knew that had to happen, and it had to be done in a way that would stand up to the intense public scrutiny it would receive.

He then huddled with senior officials from the ministry. The first decision was that Stewart had to step aside.

About 7 PM, Hughes left them discussing the issues among themselves and went to see Smith. In a memo to file, Hughes wrote, "to say he [Smith] was depressed and despondent is almost to understate it." Ted told Smith that, in his view, the attorney general would have to stand down, since regardless of the strength of the case Sihota had made, he would have to turn it over to the police to investigate.

Smith agreed, but in a request that shows he had his own doubts about the impartiality of the justice system, he asked Hughes to turn the tapes over to the RCMP rather than the Victoria city police, who he felt were too close to the New Democrats.[6]

Hughes went back to meet ministry officials again, and they tossed around names of who could be called in from outside to give legal opinions about any possible charges. Hughes left with some ideas about who it should be but had made no final decision.

The next morning, July 12, he decided to call Neil McCrank, the deputy attorney general in Alberta, to see if he would take on the assignment. McCrank agreed.

Hughes then asked the premier's press secretary to tell the press gallery he would be holding a press conference at 11 AM.

Before the press conference, Hughes went to see Vander Zalm and some of his officials. Jerry Lampert, the premier's new principal secretary, asked what he was going to announce. Hughes said he would rather not say, since he wanted to be able to tell reporters that he had not discussed his plan with his political masters.

Hughes was comfortable talking to reporters, but the press conference he held that morning in the press theatre in the basement of the West Annex of the legislature was his first. It was also a first for the reporters, who had never before been summoned to hear a deputy minister tell them what he had done to determine the fate of his boss.

Hughes started by reading the letter he had written to the attorney general four months earlier when he called for the inquiry that Owen had since taken on. The letter detailed his concerns about the threat to public confidence in the justice system. He read it to put what followed in the context of his assurance "to all British Columbians that there are steady hands of honour and integrity at the helm of the justice system of this province."

---

6 Smith said this in a 2016 interview with the author. He also recalled asking Hughes to get a lawyer from outside BC to assess the evidence.

He was not, he said, speaking only of himself, but of the dedicated and loyal staff in the ministry. Hughes saw himself at the centre of a controversy that not only reflected on his own actions earlier in the Reid case but had much wider implications for the province. "Confidence and respect in the system is a cornerstone of our entire society. The system of justice must be fair and impartial and it must deliver as far as it is humanly possible equal justice to all our citizens. That is the history and the tradition of the justice system of this province and I tell you that that is the state of our justice system here today."

Hughes then announced that Stewart would be stepping aside temporarily as the assistant deputy attorney general, criminal justice branch; that the RCMP would investigate Sihota's allegations; and that the report of the police investigation would be going to McCrank.

After the press conference he met with his new boss, Solicitor General Russ Fraser, who had been given responsibility for the ministry of the attorney general when Smith stepped down. Hughes got no indication at the time that his political masters had any objections to what he had done. But 10 days later, when a story appeared in the *Vancouver Sun* that said he had stepped around his political bosses to order the Smith probe, he got the impression that Fraser thought he had overstepped his bounds.

"Maybe he thought I should be making apologies for it but I did what I did on purpose to keep credibility in the system and if I have to go toe to toe to defend it myself, I am quite prepared to do so," Hughes wrote in a memo to file.

Initially, McCrank was asked to investigate whether there were grounds for an obstruction of justice charge against Smith. Subsequently, he was also asked to give his opinion on whether Sihota or any journalists had broken any laws in recording and distributing the tapes and if so, what charges should be considered.

What had started as a scandal for the government was becoming a potential problem for the opposition, as well. From the moment

Sihota started reading off the transcript of the tapes in the legislature, the Socreds tried to paint him as the real villain of the piece for what they characterized as illegally and immorally eavesdropping on private conversations. As one *Vancouver Sun* reporter put it in a story on July 21, "Sihota dropped the Bud Smith tapes into the legislature like a huge rock into a deep mud puddle. It is still not clear who will be covered with the most mud when the affair has run its course."

Hughes considered the allegations against Sihota important but less urgent than the obstruction allegations, since they didn't affect confidence in the justice system, of which he was a part. He believed that confidence could only be restored through the Owen inquiry, which once again had to be put on hold.

McCrank came back during the third week of August with two reports. In the first he said there was no basis for a charge of obstruction of justice against Smith. He said if Smith had wanted to use his office to interfere with the private prosecution of Reid, he could have simply entered a stay of proceedings. McCrank found that what Smith had done in looking for ways to embarrass Firestone and, through him, Sihota, was in the realm of politics rather than the Criminal Code.

The first draft of his second report said Sihota and Brian Graves, the reporter who recorded the conversations, should both be charged with wilfully disclosing a private conversation.

McCrank's recommendation that charges be laid was not what Hughes wanted to hear. Charges against Sihota and Graves would mean that the Owen inquiry would not be able to proceed, and the clouds hanging over the justice system and, by inference, his own conduct could not be cleared away. But he had committed himself to follow McCrank's recommendations.

Hughes met with ministry officials early in the afternoon on Thursday, August 23. They had the final report on the Bud Smith matter but just the draft version of the report recommending charges against Sihota and Graves. The final report was to be delivered late that afternoon. After the meeting, Hughes reluctantly prepared to approve the charges against Sihota and the reporter. He left a message for Sihota and asked the MLA to come and see him, expecting to tell him that he was going to recommend that he be charged.

Meanwhile, Ernie Quantz, director of operations for the criminal justice branch, had been studying the covering letter that arrived with McCrank's final report on charging Sihota and Graves. He thought the letter offered Hughes a way out that would get the Owen inquiry back on track.

Along with the findings of the police investigation, McCrank had been given BC's two-part guidelines for determining whether a charge should be laid. The first part was to determine whether there was a substantial likelihood of obtaining a conviction. McCrank believed there was, based on the available evidence against Sihota and the reporter. The second was whether such a prosecution would be in the public interest. One aspect of that determination was whether the victims suffered harm. McCrank had no difficulty determining that a number of individuals suffered great damage to their reputations as a result of the taping and release of their conversations.

But McCrank said that he could not determine from his vantage point in Alberta two other aspects of the public interest test; he couldn't say whether the desired result could be obtained without a court proceeding, or to what extent the offence represented a community problem that could be better dealt with in another way.

That put the decision back in Ted's hands. Hughes' primary concern was the damage that was being done to the reputation of the justice system by having it dragged into the political arena. After meeting with officials, he decided that he could justify not charging Sihota and Graves. "I made the decision that Sihota would not be charged because I didn't think it was in the public interest to prolong this political catfight, and that's what it was."

When Sihota arrived at his office, Hughes told him it was a false alarm, that the situation had changed since he left a message earlier, and that the MLA would now have to wait until the next day to find out what he was going to do.

Hughes called a press conference for the next morning with the intention of announcing that no charges would be laid as a result of either of the situations McCrank had been asked to look into. However, McCrank had prepared a draft charge against Sihota and Graves and sent it to Chief Superintendent John Sebastian, who had led the RCMP investigation. While it said charges could be justified, the letter made it clear that the decision to proceed with charges was still in Ted's hands.

Robert Wright, the regional Crown counsel for Vancouver, called Sebastian late Thursday night to tell him of Hughes' decision. Wright reported back to Ted that Sebastian had taken the news well.

But at 7:35 the next morning, Hughes got a call from Deputy Commissioner Don Wilson of the RCMP and Inspector Ernie MacAulay of the RCMP Commercial Crime Division. They were deeply offended they had not been consulted on the decision and threatened to lay charges themselves if Hughes proceeded as planned.

Hughes was worried enough about their reaction that he changed course. He decided to go ahead with a press conference on the morning of August 24 but only to announce that no charges would be laid against Smith. He held back on the Sihota/Graves report until he had had a chance to meet with the RCMP officers to calm them down.[7]

---

7 They never were persuaded that Hughes was right. At the Owen inquiry, Inspector MacAulay dismissed the arguments against laying charges against Reid and others as "disappointingly shallow" and argued that the justice system should instead cast a "very wide net" against official corruption (*Vancouver Sun*, September 12, 1990).

Hughes called the attorney general to tell him about the delay, but it was a short conversation. Russ Fraser was on a phone in his car, and everyone now understood that anyone could be listening.

At the press conference, Hughes released a copy of the first report but held back the second. Afterward, he and a few ministry officials met with the RCMP. Hughes then called another press conference late that afternoon and announced that Sihota would not be charged. For reporters covering the story, a big news day had just exploded, and pundits spent the weekend trying to make sense of it all.

On the following Monday, the Owen inquiry resumed with the added task of looking into Hughes' decision to refer the obstruction-of-justice and wiretapping allegations to McCrank. Owen was also asked to comment on Hughes' application of the public interest test in his decision not to prosecute Sihota.

In December Stephen Owen delivered the affirmation Hughes was hoping for. "There is no evidence that any person, including RCMP officers, attorney general Ministry officials and private lawyers in this case acted with anything but integrity, independence and professionalism in performing their respective duties regarding the process leading to the final decision of Mr. Hughes not to prosecute Mr. Reid. In addition, all the evidence supports the conclusion that former attorney general Bud Smith played no part whatsoever in the decision-making process. In short, the system worked fairly, effectively and as intended."[8]

Owen went on, however, to argue that it wasn't enough for the justice system to work fairly and effectively; it had to be seen by the

8 Although he was exonerated by both McCrank and Owen, Smith decided to leave politics. Vander Zalm brought him back into cabinet as the minister of regional economic development, but he did not run in the next election and turned his attention to his private businesses.

public to do so. To that end, he recommended changes that led to the current special prosecutor system, which brings in outside lawyers to make charging decisions about politicians and people who work in the justice system. Though the government made that change, it did not adopt Owen's recommendation to change the charging standard from requiring a "substantial likelihood" of conviction to a "reasonable likelihood," a change that critics argue would restore even more confidence in the system by allowing more cases of high public interest to be tested in court rather than decided in private.

No doubt Hughes' decision to let one of the government's fiercest critics off the hook didn't sit well with all of his political bosses. But while they grumbled to each other, they left Hughes alone.

Owen also affirmed Hughes' decision to refer the charging questions to the Alberta deputy attorney general. "Indeed, Mr. Hughes' prompt and decisive action on July 12 should have given the public confidence that, despite the many unsettling issues surrounding the taped conversations, the administration of justice was secure in his hands, and that any wrongdoing would be impartially uncovered and dealt with."

By the time the final Owen report appeared, Hughes had followed through on his earlier intention to leave his post as deputy attorney general for a less onerous posting. As it turned out, that was a severe misreading of the road ahead.

Fantasy Gardens

STEPHEN OWEN DELIVERED his interim report exonerating Hughes and the other staff in the attorney general's ministry in September 1990. Hughes was then free to step down as deputy AG, having, as he put it in his letter of the previous March, done the honourable thing by staying at the helm until the verdict was in. He resigned as of October 1, 1990, and immediately assumed the post of complaints commissioner for the BC Police Commission. He soon added the responsibility of chairing the Law Society of British Columbia's committee looking into gender equity in the justice and legal system in the province.

Hughes, now 63, considered both of these part-time assignments, but any hope he might have had of a "less onerous posting" was soon to be dashed by a scandal that was moving quietly forward on a parallel track to the Reid/Smith/Sihota affair.

On March 31, 1990, a week after Hughes wrote to Smith asking for an inquiry to blow away the clouds hanging over the ministry of the attorney general, Premier Vander Zalm was approached in his family's Fantasy Gardens theme park by Faye Leung, a Vancouver real estate agent known for her persistence and big floral hats. She said she had a potential buyer for the money-losing theme park in Richmond near the Fraser River.

Fantasy Garden World had been developed and promoted by Bill and Lillian Vander Zalm on the site of a former nursery they purchased in 1984 for $1.7 million. Depending on the eye of the beholder, it was either the height of kitsch or an enchanting retreat, with extensive gardens, a giant windmill, a miniature train, a reproduction of Noah's Ark, statues depicting the life of Jesus, and a Dutch castle with a drawbridge left over from Expo '86. The Vander Zalms lived in a suite on the grounds.

When Vander Zalm became premier, he turned over the operation of the business to Lillian but kept the majority of the shares in his own name. That wasn't enough to ward off complaints about the propriety of using the property for official events, all of which he rejected. As he had demonstrated with his support of his friend Peter Toigo's desire to buy the site of Expo '86, Vander Zalm had no compunction about using his office to promote the business of his friends or his family. He once told reporters, "I am going to take every opportunity to promote Fantasy Garden World."

But as Fantasy Gardens became connected with Vander Zalm's politics, it attracted a stream of protesters who loved to use the windmill as a backdrop for their demonstrations. Attendance plummeted, and many of the businesses that operated on the site moved away. When Leung came along with her proposition, Fantasy Gardens had been losing money for a couple of years.[1] The Vander Zalms' accountants urged them to sell.

A few days after Leung approached the premier, he wrote to Elwood Veitch, the minister for international trade, asking him to meet with Faye and her husband, Dean Leung, to discuss their contacts for joint ventures in business and housing.

---

1 This and many of the other details in this chapter are from E.N. Hughes, *Report of The Honourable E.N. Hughes Q.C. On the Sale of Fantasy Garden World Inc.*

Two months later, Faye Leung presented Vander Zalm with an interim agreement to buy Fantasy Gardens. The potential buyer was later revealed to be Tan Yu, a Taiwanese businessman who wanted to expand his empire into British Columbia. Vander Zalm agreed to the terms, which called for a price of US$14.5 million in an all-cash deal.[2]

Over the next couple of months, Leung made a number of requests for the premier to use his influence to support the deal. She asked him to send a certificate of congratulations that she could present to Yu's son who was getting married in the Philippines, which he did. She also wanted information for Yu about setting up a trust company in British Columbia. Vander Zalm passed that request along to his finance minister, Mel Couvelier.

On July 30, 1990, she faxed Vander Zalm the news that the Tan Yu Group was coming to BC in two days and urged the premier to show him the VIP treatment he was used to getting at home. During that visit in August, Yu and Vander Zalm finalized the sale of Fantasy Gardens. When the deal was done, the premier delivered on the demand for VIP treatment. He arranged a meeting in his office on September 6 with the Tan Yu Group and the finance minister. Lillian attended and poured tea. It was the only time she sat in on what was supposed to be government business. After the meeting, Vander Zalm arranged for the lieutenant-governor to host a luncheon for his guests at Government House. The sale of Fantasy Gardens was announced the next day.

Neither Finance Minister Couvelier nor the lieutenant-governor was told of the private business Vander Zalm was conducting with the Tan Yu Group. Vander Zalm later told Hughes that there was no conflict since the government officials involved did not know about his personal business.

---

2 At the exchange rate of the time, a US dollar was worth about Can$1.17.

All of this came after the extraordinary night of Friday, August 3, which carried on into the morning of August 4, when the deal was concluded hours after midnight with a handshake and the transfer of an envelope stuffed with American hundred-dollar bills.

Tan Yu was staying in a corner suite on the 19th floor of the Westin Bayshore Hotel near the entrance to Stanley Park. Bill and Lillian Vander Zalm arrived in a limousine that Yu had provided to pick them up at a previous engagement. They were then supposed to be joining him and others in his party, including Faye Leung's husband, Dean, where they were waiting at the Imperial Chinese Seafood Restaurant six blocks away for a 12-course banquet.

When the Vander Zalms got to the hotel, they met Leung, who was waiting in another suite on the 19th floor. She said Yu wanted to change the terms of the deal. Instead of all cash, he wanted US$7 million to take the form of a mortgage that the Vander Zalms would hold with no interest for the first five years.

The Vander Zalms were shocked by the new demands. Dinner was forgotten. They called their lawyer and considered their options, starting with walking away and keeping Yu's US$100,000 deposit. Their lawyer said they could pull out, but with no other offers in hand to buy the money-losing property they should at least consider the new demands and try to negotiate a better deal.

Tan Yu arrived back at the hotel about 11 PM. He was miffed that the Vander Zalms had left him waiting at the restaurant. He was a heavy man. It was a warm evening and he settled into a comfortable chair in his suite in his underwear.[3] The Vander Zalms got another

---

3 Many of the details of what happened during negotiations were pulled together by *Vancouver Sun* reporter Gordon Hamilton for a narrative published June 15, 1991, "One Night with Yu." Others are from the Hughes report on the sale of Fantasy Gardens and contemporary news reports.

shock when they tried to talk to Yu, only to be told that he never negotiated face to face. He usually had his subordinates negotiate for him. So Bill wrote counter-offers on hotel stationery; Leung carried them to Yu and brought back his responses.

Over the next couple of hours they arrived at a new deal. It called for a US$3-million payment on closing and US$11.5 million in vendor financing, of which US$7 million would be in the form of an interest-free loan for five years. For the Vander Zalms, that was significantly less than the all-cash deal the premier thought they had (Hughes estimated $2 million to $3 million in lost interest), but the blow had been cushioned by Leung agreeing to cut her commission in half, from US$2 million to US$1 million, to be paid out in proportion to payments received by the Vander Zalms from the purchaser.

Tan Yu came out of his suite wearing a green silk kimono and shook hands with the Vander Zalms, and they posed for a picture together. No one was particularly happy.

Leung collected all the paper from the desk and garbage can where she and the Vander Zalms had been working on the new deal and saved it. She said later she wanted to be able to show her partners why their commission had been cut. She had no idea it would be the paper trail that Hughes would follow six months later.

After pleasantries and small gifts were exchanged, on Tan Yu's instructions, Leung went down to Yu's safety deposit box and brought back a large brown envelope. Dean Leung opened it and counted out 20 piles of 10 US$100 bills. Bill Vander Zalm took the money, and he and Lillian left sometime after 3 AM.

Later, during the 1991 inquiry into the sale of Fantasy Gardens, when Vander Zalm gave Hughes his first account of that evening, he told him about renegotiating the deal with Tan Yu but left out the part about taking home the envelope with the piles of $100 bills in it. The omission would cost him much more than that.

Without providing any details, Vander Zalm announced on September 7, 1990, that Fantasy Gardens had been sold to the Tan Yu Group. Over the next couple of months, details of the deal dribbled out, including the ongoing relationship the premier had with Tan Yu because of the mortgages he held. Vander Zalm's relationship with Faye Leung soured as she became desperate for cash and started pestering him for money she claimed he owed her as part of the deal for Fantasy Gardens and the sale of an adjoining property. Some of the paper she collected from the hotel room the night of August 3 became part of a court action. As the details emerged, complaints mounted that the premier was in a conflict of interest. Comparisons were drawn to Cliff Michael, who resigned after Ted found that he was in an apparent conflict of interest, at least, for trying to sell real estate to people he dealt with as a cabinet minister.

Vander Zalm angrily rejected that analogy and any other suggestions that he was ever in a conflict of interest. But since Cliff Michael's time, the government had put in place a law dealing with MLAs' conflict of interest. On the morning of July 27, a week before Vander Zalm met Tan Yu to shake on the deal for Fantasy Gardens, his government passed BC's first Members' Conflict of Interest Act. It was pushed through in two days, without the support of the New Democrats, who called it a "scandal cover-up bill" rather than a true prohibition against conflicts of interest. The legislation included aspects of the guidelines that Vander Zalm had brought in for members of his cabinet in 1987, but not the then fairly novel idea promoted by Hughes that activities that generated the appearance of a conflict as well as a real conflict were problematic.

The legislation also created the position of a conflict-of-interest commissioner who would report to the legislature. The choice of commissioner would have to be supported by two-thirds of the legislature, which, except at times of a large majority government, meant that the appointee would have to be supported by some members of the opposition as well as the government. In the third week of September, David Emerson, Vander Zalm's deputy minister, asked Ted if he would take on the job.

Hughes was a natural fit to become the first conflict-of-interest commissioner. He had been involved in developing the principles and drafting the guidelines that preceded the legislation, and he was keen to take on the job when he was approached. But there was a problem. The legislature was not sitting at the time, so he would be appointed acting commissioner, since he could not be ratified by the required two-thirds majority of MLAs. In the absence of approval by the legislature, Hughes said he would take on the job only if the leader of the opposition agreed.

Harcourt refused. It wasn't personal. The NDP believed the bill was flawed and they weren't prepared to support anyone for the position.

That put Ted in a quandary. If the rejection had been personal, he would have stuck to his earlier position and turned the job down. But since it wasn't about him, and since Harcourt had served notice that they would not agree to anyone to fill a job that Ted believed was crucial, he felt both free and duty-bound to take on the role on an acting basis. Since he was already being paid a part-time salary as police commissioner, he told Emerson he would take the job but take no pay for it other than expenses.[4]

The new Members' Conflict of Interest Act came into force in December. In February, Hughes was called on to make his first assessment of whether a member of the legislature was in conflict. He was starting at the top. The member was the premier, who decided

---

4 When Hughes finished his term in 1996, the roles were reversed but the dilemma was the same. The NDP was in government, and the Liberals in opposition refused to approve anyone for the position of conflict commissioner until the legislation was amended.

to ask Ted to review the allegations he was facing over the sale of Fantasy Gardens.

Vander Zalm believed he had done no wrong and that a clean bill of health from Hughes would silence his critics. He was in the fifth year of his mandate and had only a narrow window in which to clear his name before he would have to call an election.

"We're prepared to co-operate fully," he said at a press conference when the review was announced. "We have nothing to hide. We did nothing wrong. We have nothing to be ashamed of. I've prayed hard on this and I feel that's the best solution, and I'm convinced and satisfied that he'll find everything was done properly."

Several friends and advisors told him he was making a mistake. Vander Zalm would later agree. In his self-published autobiography he said calling for the investigation was "the biggest mistake of my entire life."

Although he was the acting conflict commissioner, Hughes stepped outside that role to take the assignment. The Members' Conflict of Interest Act was not in effect at the time most of the events he would be looking into occurred, so he had no authority to investigate them as conflict commissioner.

Ted first suggested that a full public inquiry would be the best route. But Vander Zalm wanted Hughes to act on his own as he had done when making assessments earlier of cabinet members accused of having conflicts. Hughes agreed, but he was not willing to go ahead without the support of Harcourt. He also wanted an assurance from Vander Zalm, who was nearing the end of his term, that he would not call an election before Ted was finished.

Harcourt had already called for Hughes to investigate the Fantasy Gardens sale and readily agreed to Ted's terms. Vander Zalm agreed not to call a snap election during the investigation.

Ted hired Joe Arvay and his partner John Finlay to help with the inquiry. Arvay had worked with Ted at the ministry of the attorney general before going into private practice with Finlay. The three men began a short, intensive investigation with the goal of being able to report back within a few weeks. They started by interviewing Bill and Lillian Vander Zalm on successive days. Hughes described the process as more inquisitorial than adversarial. Sometimes Arvay and Finlay took turns asking questions while Hughes took notes. Sometimes Ted interviewed witnesses on his own.

In what was the first of two interviews, neither Bill nor Lillian mentioned the envelope full of cash, which Hughes learned about later from Faye Leung. She gave Ted a copy of a tape recording she made of a phone call to Vander Zalm in which she talked about the cash and described it as an advance on a commission she and Vander Zalm were to share for helping Tan Yu obtain a property, owned by Petro-Canada, that was next door to Fantasy Gardens. Dean Leung, who was ill at the time and was interviewed in his kitchen in his pajamas, described the scene in which his wife brought the cash from Tan Yu's safety deposit box and Dean counted it out before it was handed over to the premier. He said in broken English that Vander Zalm initiated the exchange: "He says, Mr. Tan Yu, 'If you has [sic] some money you don't want to bring back to Orient, can you leave here.'"

Vander Zalm also failed to recall phoning Wilbert "Bill" Hopper, president and CEO of Petro-Canada, two weeks after the late-night negotiations with Tan Yu to inquire about the former service station site adjacent to Fantasy Gardens. Yu was subsequently able to buy that property without going through the bidding process usually used by Petro-Canada.

When Vander Zalm was interviewed the second time, after Hughes and his colleagues had been told about the cash, the premier explained he had been given the money by Yu for safekeeping, an explanation that Hughes said bordered on the incredible: "If it is true then it will be one of those real life examples of the truth being stranger than fiction."

Vander Zalm said he had not mentioned the cash because it was a private matter that had nothing to do with the sale of Fantasy Gardens. In his report, Hughes noted that the premier had sworn to tell the "whole truth," adding that he might have been more inclined to believe Vander Zalm if he had been forthcoming about the cash in the first place.

A week into Ted's inquiry, Vander Zalm's lawyer, John McAlpine, complained that his client was being denied natural justice because of the expeditious way Hughes was conducting his investigation. McAlpine said he had been denied transcripts of witnesses who had appeared before Hughes and wasn't being given the right to cross-examine them.[5]

Hughes was not sympathetic and threatened to resign. "I will not live with the suggestion that I have been party to a denial of anyone's right to fundamental justice," he wrote back in a fax sent on Friday, March 8.

Hughes said he had recommended an investigation under the Inquiry Act similar to the one held by Stephen Owen, in which everyone affected could be represented by counsel who would attend the hearings and cross-examine witnesses. That wasn't what the premier wanted, so he had agreed to conduct the more streamlined review that was then underway. Given McAlpine's objections, Hughes said he would write to Vander Zalm the following Monday to advise him that he was withdrawing from his review, and he would recommend that the premier immediately convene a full public inquiry. He added that if McAlpine thought his client would prefer to continue with the

5 At the same time he was representing Vander Zalm, McAlpine was working with Hughes on a committee sponsored by the Law Society of British Columbia, chaired by Hughes, that was looking into gender equity in the justice system.

current process rather than expose himself to a full public inquiry, he should get back to Hughes before then.

The review continued with no further complaints.

Since the Members' Conflict of Interest Act was not in effect at the time of the sale of Fantasy Gardens, Hughes used the guidelines Vander Zalm had issued for his cabinet to assess whether he believed Vander Zalm had followed the rules. That meant that the appearance of conflict of interest was an issue for the premier, even though it was not part of the legislation passed by his government.

On April 2, nearly seven weeks after accepting the assignment, Hughes issued his report with the headline-grabbing conclusion that the premier was in violation of his own guidelines for avoiding conflicts of interest. "From the very beginning of the negotiations through to the date of the closing, the Premier mixed his public role as chief citizen of this province entrusted with the leadership of the Government of British Columbia with his private business interest," Hughes wrote.

Hughes cited several breaches of the guidelines, including the red carpet treatment given to Tan Yu by the government, the call to the CEO of Petro-Canada, and Vander Zalm's taking the envelope full of cash. Hughes said he was unable to find conclusively what the cash was for, but, nonetheless, he had no doubt that "reasonably well-informed persons could properly conclude that the Premier's ability to exercise his duties and responsibilities objectively in the future might appear to be compromised given the bizarre circumstances in which the money was given to the Premier and the lack of any reasonable explanation."

Hughes found that the fundamental issue wasn't that Vander Zalm did not understand the need to draw a line between his public and private life; it was his "apparently sincere belief that no conflicts existed as long as the public didn't know what was going on."

It wasn't Ted's job to determine what penalty if any Vander Zalm should suffer for his indiscretions. That was a political judgment that would be made by the voters and his colleagues in the government caucus. The consequences unfolded over several days following the release of the report just after the Easter weekend.

For Vander Zalm, the findings should have been no real surprise. The premier's lawyer knew what his client would be asked about in his second interview and the nature of the allegations he would face. Vander Zalm got a clearer picture in that interview on March 24, even though, given his apparent inability to grasp that he had done anything wrong, he may not have understood completely what was coming. He then received a draft copy of the report a week before it was released.

On Friday, March 29, with the report due out in a couple of days, Vander Zalm announced he would stay on as premier until a new leader was chosen, although he didn't actually concede he was ready to resign. That tepid response did not sit well with his caucus, many of whom were already close to being in full revolt. During his term to that point, 11 members of Vander Zalm's cabinet had quit or been fired, the party had lost six straight by-elections and an election had to be called within a few months. *Vancouver Sun* columnist Vaughn Palmer discovered subsequently that the caucus had reached a quiet understanding with Lieutenant-Governor David Lam that if Vander Zalm lost the confidence of his caucus and tried to punish them by calling an election, Lam would turn down his request for an immediate dissolution of the legislature as long as the caucus could quickly pick a replacement.

Hughes' report was released the following Tuesday. Reporters were given copies to read in a lockup before the official release time. Barrie Clark, a former Liberal MLA and radio talk-show host, looked up from his copy and said: "My God, he lied to Ted Hughes. It is over."

And it was. Later that day Vander Zalm bowed to the pressure and resigned.

The Social Credit caucus elected Surrey MLA Rita Johnston to replace him as interim Social Credit leader and premier on April 2, 1991. She was sworn in as the first woman to lead British Columbia, and Ted became known as the man who brought down a premier.

Vander Zalm went away, but not for long.

Vander Zalm: Round Two

WHEN HE STEPPED down, Vander Zalm said contritely that while the findings were not what he expected, "there is no Court of Appeal in these matters. I must live by the guidelines, which I initiated."[1]

That contrition didn't last long. Within days Vander Zalm decided he had been hard done by. His lawyer went to court to try to have the report set aside, arguing many of the procedural points he had made in his letter to Hughes earlier, and also arguing that Hughes had made errors in law in applying the conflict-of-interest guidelines. His petition was rejected by Supreme Court chief justice William Esson on the grounds that Hughes had been retained by Vander Zalm in the role of a respected advisor, with no authority other than the agreement from the premier and the leader of the opposition that he should review the sale of Fantasy Gardens. Since there was no statutory authority for the report, there was no basis on which the court could conduct a review. Justice Esson said that any doubt about the nature of Ted's role was dispelled in the exchange of letters between Hughes and McAlpine,

1 Vander Zalm never really accepted Hughes' verdict. He autographed a copy of the Hughes report for then Vancouver *Province* cartoonist Bob Krieger with the inscription "Remember, this is one man's opinion."

when the premier's lawyer first objected to the procedures he was following.

If Vander Zalm had succeeded in getting Hughes' report set aside in a judicial review, it's not clear what effect that would have had on the political consequences for Vander Zalm, since the impact of the report flowed primarily from Hughes' reputation rather than any statutory authority. And Hughes' reputation was growing while Vander Zalm's was in tatters.

Vander Zalm's next court case provided a victory of sorts for the former premier. In 1992 he was acquitted of breach of trust in connection with the sale of Fantasy Gardens. In what he described as not an easy decision, Judge David Campbell found Vander Zalm not guilty of the criminal charge while agreeing with Hughes' earlier assessment that some of Vander Zalm's activities "might be considered foolish, ill-advised and in apparent or real conflict of interest."

The next time Hughes and Vander Zalm clashed, it was over Vander Zalm's self-published autobiography, *For the People.* Vander Zalm used the 2008 book to settle scores with several people he believed had treated him unjustly through the years, from political opponents to former colleagues, journalists and even the lawyer who represented him during the Hughes inquiry. But in Ted Hughes he ran into a literary subject who had never been willing to have his reputation considered fair game for foul treatment.

Vander Zalm's abuse of Ted's good name started with a parable in the introduction of his book. It was the story of a small-town gossip who seized on appearances to spread tall tales. Naming Hughes, Vander Zalm said one of the messages of the book was that things were not always as they appeared. In other words, he was framed.

In the following 600 pages, the former premier wove together a number of false statements and suppositions to suggest that Hughes was biased against him and that he had an ulterior motive for finding that he had a conflict of interest in the sale of Fantasy Gardens.

He hinted that Hughes picked Arvay and Finlay as lawyers because they were philosophically opposed to him, especially over his attempts to limit access to abortions.[2] He implied that Hughes wanted to impress the New Democrats because he wanted to be appointed conflict commissioner and they had originally opposed his appointment.

Vander Zalm self-published and distributed his book, which got little attention when it came out in 2008. The following year, Hughes saw him being interviewed about it and picked up a copy. As he turned the pages, he was incensed at what he read.

Hughes had never taken lightly anything he perceived to be an assault on his character. At least four times previously he had threatened court action over what he perceived as libellous publications or statements. In Saskatchewan he threatened to sue a newspaper that mischaracterized one of his judgments as a statement that anyone convicted of dangerous driving in his court could expect to be sent to jail. Hughes feared that such a reputation would give others scheduled to appear before him cause to ask for a different judge. The paper refused to retract.

"I was then put in the position where either I took the newspaper to court or took it on the chin," he said five years later in a speech to the Saskatchewan Journalists' Association, in which he used the newspaper's conduct as an example of how not to behave. On the advice of his lawyer, for policy rather than legal reasons, he said, he took it on the chin.

When he was deputy attorney general, he threatened to sue Vaughn Palmer of the *Vancouver Sun* over a comment in one of his columns that Ted's boss, the attorney general, had been given bad advice. For Palmer, a journalist Hughes liked and respected, it was

2 Vander Zalm no longer seemed worried about philosophical differences when he hired Arvay in 2010 to represent him in his successful fight against the Harmonized Sales Tax in BC.

a throwaway line at the end of a column meant as a mild criticism. Hughes took it more seriously. Palmer apologized.

He sued radio host and former Social Credit cabinet minister Rafe Mair over comments he made about Ted and his role in the Bud Smith tapes affair. Mair apologized.

And when Social Credit MLA Jack Weisgerber stood up in the BC legislature in 1992 and suggested that while Hughes was deputy attorney general he had turned down an RCMP request to lay charges linked to the Nanaimo Commonwealth Holding Society bingo scandal, Hughes immediately threatened to sue after Weisgerber repeated the allegation outside the House. Weisgerber apologized for acting on what he said was bad information, and when Hughes said the apology wasn't good enough, he apologized again.

If Hughes had gone to Weisgerber, whom he regarded as a decent man, and told him he had made a mistake, the MLA likely would have apologized without the threat of a lawsuit. But Hughes was annoyed, and his instinct as a lawyer was to use the law to get what he wanted.

"That struck at my integrity," Hughes says. "I was offended that he would suggest that I had played a political role in that decision. I had never had anything to do with it, so I knew that I could be as determined as I wanted to be about knocking it on the head."

Weisgerber also agreed to pay Hughes' $1,500 legal bill, but Hughes returned the cheque after he discovered that it would be covered by Weisgerber's employer.

The government policy to pay legal costs for suits launched in defense of actions taken while in its employ came into play when Hughes decided to sue Vander Zalm over the allegations in his autobiography.

Getting that financial support turned out to be more difficult than it had been when Hughes was still working for the government. Under the rules that applied in 2009, he had to show he had a case and the government had to agree it was in the public interest to pursue it. When he applied for financial backing to sue Vander Zalm, he was turned down. The attorney general's ministry provided a legal opinion that there was a cause for action, but it was not in the public interest to pursue it. A lawyer from outside the ministry was consulted and said there was no case to pursue. Hughes challenged that advice, and the ministry of the attorney general retained former chief justice Donald Brenner to decide. He reviewed all the previous decisions and found that Hughes had a case that was in the public interest to pursue.

Even though the cost was no longer an issue, some of his friends and even Ted's lawyer, Irwin Nathanson, questioned whether suing the former premier was worth the trouble.

"[Nathanson] said to me: 'Ted, do you really want to do this?'

"And I said: 'Irwin, that's why I'm here. Will you take the case?'

"'Sure,' he said, 'I'll take it, but I really wonder if you've thought it through, what it entails and whether it's worth going through all this.'

"I said: 'You're damned right.'"

The suit went to trial in February 2012. Vander Zalm chose to have the case heard before a jury rather than by judge alone, trusting that his populist appeal would win over the five men and two women on the panel as it had charmed British Columbians when he swept to power in 1986. But Hughes' lawyer focused their attention on 1990, when Vander Zalm's already sputtering reign as premier crashed and burned after he used his office to benefit his family business.

Another former premier, Mike Harcourt, testified on Ted's behalf.

In his book, Vander Zalm said that Harcourt's government had appointed Hughes conflict-of-interest commissioner as a reward for his harsh judgment on the Fantasy Gardens sale, a claim that was demonstrably false since Hughes was appointed while the Social Credit Party was still in power.

"I sort of debunked all this stuff and kept looking at the jury and saying Ted Hughes is a man of immense integrity and reputation who

I respect," Harcourt says. "I just said it seven or eight times and looked them in the eyes."

Hughes got a rough ride from Vander Zalm's lawyer over why he launched the suit. "He went at me: 'How sensitive are you? Why would this upset you? You've got a skin that's too thin; do you agree with that?' and all that kind of stuff," says Hughes.

Lillian and Bill came to the trial every day and sat on the front bench at the opposite side of the spectators' gallery from Ted and Helen. After the jury went out, the Vander Zalms left. They did not come back to hear the verdict.

The jury vindicated Hughes. They awarded him $60,000, and Vander Zalm was prohibited from selling or distributing any more copies of the book that contained the offending passages. At that point Vander Zalm's autobiography had sold fewer than 1,200 copies. All of the money, including another $38,000 awarded in costs, went to the province to offset the $200,000 lawyers' bill.[3]

For Ted, it was never about the money. "I just couldn't let that stand."

It might be argued, as Vander Zalm's lawyer did, that Hughes had a thin skin. Going back to his reasons for leaving Saskatchewan, and looking at the number of times he turned to the courts over perceived slights, he certainly spent more time, energy and money worrying about criticism than do most people in high-profile positions. For much of his career, however, he fought for the notion that public servants, elected and appointed, have a duty to act with honour and integrity. Those words had real meaning in his life and work. He also had a much greater reputation to defend. In a sense, he was protecting

3 Twenty years after Hughes' inquiry into access to legal aid, his suit could be viewed as a demonstration that justice in the courts through a civil suit is still only available for those who can afford it. If he had to pay his own legal fees, it would have been an expensive victory.

what had become a valuable trademark. His impeccable personal integrity was a crucial element of his resume, especially later in his career when he was called on to comment on the behaviour of others as the head of public inquiries. So if he was overly sensitive to criticism, it may be because he was like the banks that invest heavily in security—he had valuable assets to protect.

He has also been sensitive about being sensitive. He has said little over the years about his reasons for leaving Saskatchewan, concerned about how that episode would be perceived. So he was enormously gratified when, 20 years after he left the bench in Saskatchewan, the Law Society of British Columbia presented him with the heavy bronze statue of Matthew Begbie that symbolizes the Law Society Award, an honour bestowed every other year for a lifetime contribution of the "truly exceptional in our profession."[4]

Hughes felt validated by the award, which was based on four criteria: integrity, professional achievements, service to the legal profession and efforts to reform the justice system. "It meant more to me to have had my honour and integrity in the profession upheld in, I suppose one might say, a very oblique way, based on what was troubling me in all those years up until that point."

---

4 The statue of Begbie was last awarded in 2016. As with the decision to remove the statue of Begbie from the lobby, mentioned in the Introduction, as of this writing the law society was planning to replace Begbie with a less controversial symbol for the 2018 recipient of the award.

Conflict Commissioner: Some Honourable Members

VANDER ZALM HAD the sequence and the motivation wrong but he was right about one thing. When the legislature returned to the House in May 1991, the New Democrats reversed their earlier position and endorsed Hughes' appointment as British Columbia's first conflict-of-interest commissioner.

Harcourt continued to flay the Members' Conflict of Interest Act as ineffective while endorsing Hughes as an admirable candidate to fill the newly created position of commissioner. The opposition leader promised again that, given the opportunity, an NDP government would bring in the toughest conflict-of-interest legislation in the country.

Hughes stepped down from the police commission and started taking a half-time salary for the now permanent five-year appointment as conflict commissioner.

In October 1991, Harcourt and the New Democrats swept past the battered Social Credit Party under Rita Johnston and soon had the chance to make good on their promise to bring in more comprehensive conflict-of-interest legislation.[1] The amendments they introduced in

1 The NDP won 51 of the 75 seats. The BC Liberals under Gordon Wilson won 17, and the Social Credit Party was reduced to 7 seats. Johnston lost her own seat and retired from politics.

the 1992 spring session put BC on the leading edge of legislating ethical behaviour for politicians and put Hughes in a position to break new ground in its interpretation. The NDP reinstated the principle that was in Vander Zalm's guidelines, which said MLAs must avoid the appearance of being in a conflict of interest as well as actually being in a conflict. British Columbia became the first province in the country to adopt such a provision. The NDP also brought in a clause that would allow members of the public to make a complaint to the commissioner about a potential conflict of interest.

Hughes served his first year as conflict commissioner under the rules of the old act. Harcourt promised that his government would be so compliant that Hughes would be as lonely as the Maytag repairman. Indeed, there were no formal complaints for Hughes to investigate in his first year, but he laid down some important groundwork, including establishing that there are some things elected officials can legitimately do without being considered to be in a conflict, even though their actions have a personal benefit attached. One of those rulings pulled Harcourt's government out of a jam over its promise to get rid of legislation that restricted wage increases for teachers and the public service.

Several members of cabinet, including Harcourt and his finance minister, Glen Clark, had spouses who worked in schools. Many others had spouses who were public servants in other fields. The issue was whether under the new rules they could take part in discussions about a new contract for teachers when that contract would benefit their household finances. Hughes ruled that teachers and other public servants are part of a broad class of electors about whom cabinet ministers could make decisions, even though they might personally benefit because of their individual connections.

Hughes saw his job as being more than just the arbiter of a single piece of legislation. He used his first annual report as conflict commissioner to set out the larger context of what he saw as his underlying challenge. This was the fight to restore the confidence of Canadians in their politicians and to help politicians achieve the preeminent place in society Hughes believed they should have.

In the report he reprinted a speech, titled "A Most Honourable Profession," that he gave in April 1992 to the Certified General Accountants Association of British Columbia. In it he expressed his ambition to turn around the popular view that most politicians are scoundrels. "It doesn't seem to matter that most politicians are honest, hard working and dedicated in their jobs. The fact is that there have been enough allegations of wrong-doing by politicians across this country to cause a 1990 Angus Reid poll to show that 72 per cent of Canadians sampled believe that politicians don't care what ordinary people think and 58 per cent think that politicians are becoming more corrupt and more likely to become involved in situations of conflict of interest."

Hughes saw his role as restoring public faith in politicians by identifying ethical standards of behaviour and encouraging adherence to those standards.

He practised what he preached in terms of respect for the public purse. "This office has not become part of a sprawling bureaucracy in its own right," he wrote in the annual report after spending just a little over half his annual budget of $214,000. His administrative assistant Daphne Thompson, who started working in the office in 1994, later confirmed that when he travelled it was usually economy class, and he was scrupulous about claiming only actual expenses.[2] Hughes and his two part-time assistants handled most of the tasks in the conflict-of-interest office. After he left, more staff were brought in to handle the workload. "I was very different and I think this is all a reflection of being raised on the prairies in the Depression,"

---

2 Daphne Thompson, interview with author, 2016.

Hughes says. "When I was in government here as a deputy and so on, I was really quite surprised at the extent to which consultants were used to do jobs that I felt belonged to the public servants in the office."

With the amended legislation in place, Harcourt's prediction that Hughes would lead a lonely existence was soon proved false. The New Democrats promised the toughest conflict-of-interest legislation in the country and they delivered. But the new law left wide latitude for interpretation, and what was supposed to be a half-time position for Hughes soon took many more hours than that.

Legislators quickly realized they had to question whether many traditional perks of the job were still allowed—including memberships in social and recreational clubs, invitations to lunch and gifts—and what kinds of messages they could write on their official stationery. Often the answers were complicated. Complimentary memberships and passes to sports facilities such as ski hills or golf clubs were, in general, not allowed, but they could be accepted if a club, such as a faculty club or the Union Club in Victoria, where Hughes was a member, was used as a convenient place for an MLA to conduct official business. If such a club had recreational facilities, however, MLAS were advised to either not use them or pay for them separately.

The legislation inserted Hughes into the business of the legislature to the point that *Vancouver Sun* columnist Vaughn Palmer joked in a column on June 2, 1993: "Did you hear about the MLA's prayer? Oh, mighty Hughes, maker of guidelines, giver of rulings, preserver of reputations, we humbly beseech thee to forgive us our sins."

In his second annual report, Hughes was able to say again that he made it through another year without a single complaint of a potential conflict of interest by one MLA against another. But that only told part of the story. The government asked Hughes to rule on whether forestry minister Dan Miller was in a conflict of interest when he awarded timber rights to a mill where he had formerly worked and where he still had seniority rights if he wished to return to work.

That was a clear-cut case for Hughes, and when he reported his findings, Miller became the first minister to be forced out of cabinet under the new rules. Harcourt suspended him for three months for what he called an error in judgment.[3]

Harcourt accepted Hughes' ruling without reservation, but the next decision Ted was called to make on a cabinet minister did not sit so well with the New Democrats. It was the first complaint against an MLA by a private citizen and the first to involve an apparent conflict of interest.[4]

Robin Blencoe, the minister of municipal affairs, represented the riding of Victoria–Hillside. He got into trouble over a massive development planned for a waterfront location north of Victoria. Acting on a complaint from a nearby resident opposed to the plan, Hughes found that Blencoe had an apparent conflict of interest when he intervened in preliminary discussions of the project because of his past associations with the developers, which included relatively small donations one of them had made to his campaign.

Harcourt and the New Democrats were shocked that Hughes considered past donations a trigger for the appearance of a conflict of interest. Blencoe said he thought he was following all the rules. But Hughes found that Blencoe did not seem to appreciate what a difference the addition of a prohibition against an apparent conflict of interest had made in how they had to behave. Neither did Harcourt.

"I don't think any of the members were expecting the expanded

3 Miller came back to cabinet and remained as a senior member of the NDP government through the 1990s. He was selected by the NDP caucus to replace Glen Clark as premier when Clark resigned in 1999.

4 Hughes found that Vander Zalm had an apparent conflict of interest, but that finding was made under the guidelines Vander Zalm had issued for his cabinet, not under the new legislation.

definition that Mr. Hughes has given," Harcourt told reporters after the decision was released in August 1993.

Hughes knew he was breaking new ground. It was the first decision in Canada based on the standard of the appearance of a conflict of interest. It was also the first to find that elected officials might have a personal interest because of benefits they had received in the past rather than any benefits they might receive in the future. But he said that the New Democrats had insisted that they wanted the most rigorous conflict-of-interest rules, so he used that stated intent in interpreting the act. In his third annual report he wrote that, "unlike the position of the member for Victoria–Hillside on this occasion, members henceforth will know the standards resulting from the amendment by which their conduct will be judged."

Despite the howls of the opposition, Harcourt kept Blencoe in cabinet, arguing that the penalty for having the appearance of a conflict of interest should not be the same as having a real conflict.[5]

In 1994, MLAS started filing complaints against each other. Each was essentially a test case launched by members of one party against the other in the hope of enlisting Hughes in their campaign to bring the others down. Most were found after investigation not to be breaches of the act. But that didn't mean they had no impact.

In 1995, Hughes found himself once more with the political future of a premier in his hands. Stories were emerging about contracts for advertising being let by the government to a firm called NOW Communications Group Inc., whose principals had connections with the NDP and the premier before the election.

---

5 Hughes did not say that Blencoe did not have a real conflict of interest. He said that since he had established the appearance of a conflict of interest, there was no need to investigate whether there was a real conflict in order to find that there had been a breach of the Members' Conflict of Interest Act. Two years later Blencoe was fired from cabinet after women who worked for him alleged he had sexually harassed them.

Kim Emerson, a reporter for CKNW radio who worked in the press gallery, went to Hughes to ask him if he thought there was a conflict. Hughes told him that he didn't give opinions off the cuff and that the only way he would do an investigation was if there was an allegation. He said he wouldn't have his office "misused for political or media purposes."[6]

Emerson and his employer, the largest private talk radio/news station in Vancouver, came back with another request that made it clear they were making an allegation. Emerson said NOW had received about $5 million in contracts from the NDP government; that the president of NOW, Ron Johnson, had worked for the party during the 1991 election; and that some of the contracts were being directed through the premier's office. Emerson cited Hughes' decision in the Blencoe investigation to suggest that Harcourt had a similar appearance of a conflict of interest.

Jack Weisgerber, who was now leader of the BC Reform Party, filed a similar request, also citing the Blencoe decision as a precedent.

Harcourt was furious about the allegation, all the more so because it had been levelled by a journalist whom he believed to be politically motivated. "I do not think I have been as angry in my life as I was over the Kim Emerson incident. I seriously considered resigning right then and there. But I decided to stay on because it was the only way I could effectively fight these anti-NDP forces," he later wrote in his autobiography.

Once Hughes was satisfied that the request for an opinion was properly made, he felt he had no choice but to hold a full investigation, even though it was clear that his office was being used for political and journalistic purposes.

Similarly, Harcourt pledged the full cooperation of his office in the investigation, even though he believed the allegations were groundless

6 Details of the investigation are from contemporary media reports.

and Emerson had crossed an ethical line by making allegations rather than just reporting the story. "It affects the trust the people in British Columbia have in the media to offer accurate information and fair comment and fair criticism," Harcourt said at the time. Emerson argued that he was simply seeking information as any journalist would. And Bill Vander Zalm took the opportunity to get a dig in. "If in fact there is a conflict, then he should step down as he suggested I should," he said.

For the next month, Hughes pursued the investigation. This half-time job was taking all his available time. The staff in his office were by then used to seeing him work long hours. "He's definitely not a nine-to-five guy. Especially if there was an investigation going on," says Daphne Thompson.

Harcourt was not overly worried about the outcome of the investigation, although he could not be sure he would be cleared given Hughes' finding on Blencoe. Even so, it was an unwanted distraction. "What pissed me off was it wasted weeks of my time as premier having to prepare and having to testify with Ted, and my staff having to run around and look at 10,000 different advertising and communication contracts. And it was kind of ironic because at the same time they were doing all that to me, [Alberta premier] Ralph Klein was accused of shilling for his wife—her consulting business—when they went on a trade mission to Hong Kong and he was cleared in two days."

Hughes issued his report in April, five weeks after getting the complaint. He found that Harcourt did not have a conflict of interest because, unlike Blencoe, he had no personal interest to serve. While the principals of NOW Communications shared Harcourt's political affiliation, the work they had done for the party in the 1991 campaign had not been for the premier's personal benefit. Hughes also found that Harcourt was not involved in the awarding of the contracts, nor would a reasonably informed person perceive him to have been, which was part of the test for having an apparent conflict of interest.

In addition, while the business given to NOW Communications may well be described as patronage, the Members' Conflict of Interest Act did not prescribe that the commissioner was to act as a "watchdog of patronage," and so, Hughes wrote in his report, "it is generally not my duty to monitor whether government contracts are awarded on the basis of party affiliations." In other words, an action might not pass a political smell test, but that didn't necessarily make it a conflict of interest under the act. The decision made an important addition to MLAS' understanding of what constituted a conflict.

Looking back on his time as BC's first conflict commissioner, Hughes said he might have proceeded differently with the allegations against Harcourt by trying to resolve them without immediately setting up a formal investigation. "As the first conflict commissioner, without precedents to follow, I took a tougher approach in interpreting the new legislation than time and subsequent events have shown to be necessary," he says, somewhat apologetically.

Certainly the conflict commissioner who followed Hughes in the position had a strikingly different approach. H.A.D. "Bert" Oliver was a retired judge who drove a Rolls Royce and served cookies when he met with MLAS. He took the position that his job was to "catch the shit before it hits the fan."

"I've tried to operate in such a way that you don't read my name or the names of MLAS with problems in the media," Oliver said. "If you do read them, I've fouled up somewhere along the line." In his 10 years in the office, Oliver's only major finding that an MLA had a conflict of interest was in the case of Premier Glen Clark and his handling of an application for a casino licence by a friend.

By the time Oliver took the job in 1997, he had the advantage of both the example of the way Hughes ran the office and the precedents he set in interpreting the legislation in the investigations he carried out. He also had the advantage of dealing with legislators who had been persuaded of the need to avoid conflicts by the examples they had been shown of how they could get into trouble.

When Hughes took the position, he was not only the first in BC but a rarity in Canada. Neither he nor the legislators he watched over had a clear idea of what implementing the legislation would mean. Together they ushered in a new era of enforced ethical behaviour in Canada.

"Increasingly the reality is, and Ted told them this 25 years ago, that it's much better to come over and get advice than to create a mess. And if you did create a mess, or it's thought that you created a mess, the best thing is to request an opinion yourself, which is typically what's been happening for the last seven years or so," says Paul Fraser, BC's conflict of interest commissioner in 2016.

Ron Barclay, who was conflict of interest commissioner for the Saskatchewan legislature in 2016, sums up Hughes' impact in the field. "He's really the role model for all of us. He's in a different league."[7]

---

7 Coincidentally, Barclay articled in Ted's firm in Saskatoon while he was still there.

Smackdown

> "Premier Glen Clark got slapped around the ears like a naughty boy last week, and quite a spectacle it was. The lesson Clark learned the hard way was that you don't mess with Ted Hughes. Clark did and paid the price."
>
> HUBERT BEYER'S "CAPITAL BEAT" COLUMN, APRIL 5, 1996

TED HUGHES WAS nearing the end of his five-year term as conflict commissioner for the BC legislature when Glen Clark took over as premier in February 1996. Clark handily won the NDP leadership after Mike Harcourt announced he was leaving. Harcourt decided he had to step aside in October 1995 after reading the Parks report on the Nanaimo Commonwealth Holding Society (NCHS) bingo scandal.[1] The report by forensic accountant Ron Parks detailed how a fundraising arm of the NDP systematically and illegally misused donations to charity. Neither Harcourt nor any members of his caucus were directly linked to the scandal, but the party was badly singed. It was the final blow for Harcourt, a popular mayor of Vancouver who was already

1 "On that October Sunday afternoon," Harcourt wrote in his autobiography, *A Measure of Defiance*, "I decided I would make one last contribution. I took a bullet for the New Democratic Party, and in a sense, for British Columbia."

bitter and disillusioned about the way he was being treated, by both the media and his own party, after his move to provincial politics. In November he called reporters to the press theatre under the premier's office in the West Wing of the legislature. He announced his resignation and left without taking questions.

Clark was a former union organizer who was first elected to the legislature in 1986 and was appointed to the cabinet after Harcourt and the NDP crushed the remnants of the Social Credit Party in 1991. He was among those identified in the media as a "gang of six" who were deemed to be undermining Harcourt's leadership over the previous year and scheming to force him out.[2] Clark was relatively young—he was 38 when he was sworn in as premier—photogenic, brash, articulate and meteorically bright, and he had a reputation for being a class warrior who occasionally was too clever by half.

Three weeks before Harcourt's announcement, Hughes wrote to the Speaker of the legislature, Emery Barnes, announcing that he intended to leave on January 26, 1996. That date was four months before the end of his five-year term, but he would have already served five years by then because of the six months he was acting commissioner before being permanently appointed to the job. Hughes noted that there would be an election in the spring and cited the need for a new conflict commissioner to have time to get up to speed before then.

In the frenzy following Harcourt's announced departure, the need to replace Hughes as conflict commissioner got little attention. Nothing was done. Shortly before he had planned to be out the door,

---

2 Although Harcourt identified Clark in *A Measure of Defiance* as one of the ministers who failed to understand the concept of following their leader, he said that contrary to published reports, Clark was gratifyingly loyal in Harcourt's final months in office. He also said, contrary to the pundits' interpretation, the gang of six was actually an inner cabinet working with him rather than a cabal plotting his demise.

Hughes got a call from Harcourt asking him to stay on until the end of his term in May. Hughes agreed.

In January, Hughes issued his final annual report as conflict commissioner. He used it to comment on the first five years of British Columbia's conflict-of-interest legislation and to call for additional measures to enhance the reputation of politicians with the public they serve. He recognized that in the face of ongoing transgressions by politicians across the country, his optimism that the conflict legislation under his stewardship would alone be enough to turn the tide of public opinion was misplaced. He argued that in addition to the legal sanctions against conflicts of interest, members should have an aspirational code of conduct that would call for office holders to act with "honesty and uphold the highest ethical standards." He also called for the conflict regulations to be broadened to include senior bureaucrats in addition to elected politicians.

In his look back at how the act had been applied under the Harcourt government, Hughes damned members of the legislature with faint praise. It was to their credit, he said, that in his five years as commissioner only one NDP minister—Robin Blencoe—was found after an inquiry to have a real or apparent conflict.[3] But the government had failed to act on recommendations he had made three years earlier that were designed to clean up constituency-allowance spending, despite numerous opportunities to do so. And the legislature management committee tasked with dealing with the issue had not met in more than 10 months.

"It is my opinion that this occurrence is a prime example, right in our back yard, of what causes the cynicism and suspicion on the part of the public with respect to politics and politicians," Hughes wrote.

3 Hughes also found that Dan Miller had a conflict, but that finding was in response to a reference from cabinet rather than the result of a complaint from another MLA or a member of the public.

Earlier in the report he had commented more generally: "The fact is that something must be done because cynicism is an insidious attitude, which, if left to grow and fester, will gnaw away and weaken the very structure of our democratic society and form of government."

Clark, who was still the NDP House leader and not yet premier, responded on January 24, 1996: "I take the criticism of Mr. Hughes seriously and now that he has brought it to our attention we'll probably want to see if we can fix it."

Shortly after he became premier, Clark and his advisors did turn their focus to the conflict commissioner's issues. But the fix they had in mind had very little to do with Ted's recommendations or the next level of ethical behaviour to which he hoped the legislature would be willing to aspire.

Hughes got his first inkling that something was afoot during a visit seven weeks later from Eloise Spitzer, who had just become the secretary to cabinet. In a memo to file, Hughes recorded that Spitzer told him in confidence that David Mitchell was going to be named as the next conflict commissioner, and she wanted to know what Ted's plans were. He told her he intended to stay on for the balance of his term and that he would be looking for work on inquiries and arbitrations. She said there should be some of that work coming up, including a possible inquiry into the NCHS bingo scandal.

David Mitchell was a historian and biographer who had been elected as a Liberal in 1991. He was briefly House leader, then split with the party after about a year and continued to sit as an independent MLA. In February 1996 he announced he would not be running again. When Mitchell's name was first floated by Spitzer, Hughes thought he would be a good choice to replace him as conflict commissioner when he was ready to leave.

Two weeks later, on March 25, Ted was at home when he got a call from the premier. Based on his conversation with Spitzer, Ted thought Clark might be calling to ask if he would preside over an inquiry into the NCHS bingo scandal or to talk about some other work when he was finished as conflict commissioner in May. But Clark was calling to talk about Mitchell. He wanted to announce his appointment as the new conflict commissioner the next day, and he wanted Hughes to step aside almost immediately to allow that to happen. The legislature was being called back for a few days, and Clark wanted to put through a motion confirming Mitchell before it rose again, presumably to make way for an election.

Hughes was taken aback by the request. He was leaving and he had no problem being replaced by Mitchell, but he wasn't ready to leave just yet. And as he started to consider the request, he really did not like the idea that a so-called independent officer of the legislature could be pushed aside as a bit player in a political drama.

The call ended with Hughes saying he would think it over.

At 9:20 the next morning he got a call from Spitzer to confirm that Mitchell could take over his office on April 1, six days later. Hughes denied ever agreeing to that date. He said he was upset by the premier's call and wondered why Mitchell's appointment could not be announced that day with a start date at the end of May when Ted's term was up.

Spitzer told Ted he would continue to be paid until the end of his term and could do some other work for her office, but it was not the kind of work Hughes was hoping to get into. There is no direct indication in Ted's memos to file that he was being offered other work as an inducement to cooperate, but there was certainly a parallel conversation about what the future might bring over the next couple of months if he were no longer the conflict commissioner.

Spitzer called twice again that morning with more explanations, and at about 10:45 AM her boss, Doug McArthur, who was deputy minister to the premier, came to Ted's office. McArthur was also from Saskatchewan. He had been minister of education in Saskatchewan's NDP government when Ted and Helen left Saskatoon, and in that role he had worked with Helen. He knew Ted by reputation but not in person before coming to BC.

McArthur said Mitchell was coming over on the noon Helijet flight from Vancouver. He said the announcement would be made that afternoon at a press conference and that Mitchell would come and talk to Ted about the situation after he arrived. He also explained, but not to Ted's satisfaction, that the timetable for Hughes' departure was rushed because Mitchell wanted to be able to resign his seat before the announcement so that he would not have to answer questions about his plans in the legislature.

When Mitchell arrived in Victoria, he and Hughes talked about the timing without reaching any agreement. Finally Ted gave up. In a memo to file dictated at 1:50 PM he wrote: "I felt I was being put in the position of obstructing an arrangement that had been worked out between him and the Premier's office and while I may live to regret it, I finally, as we sat staring at each other without comment from time to time, I finally said, 'Whatever is decided, I will fall in line.' In this sense, I guess it could be said that I capitulated but you can only take so much and I feel I have really had my head put on the chopping block since seven last night and I, indeed, have succumbed."

McArthur called to confirm that Hughes and Mitchell had worked out an agreement on transition. Hughes repeated his commitment that he would fall in line with whatever was decided. The press conference was held at 3 PM, about an hour later. As an added insult, Mitchell was appointed with a salary of $85,000, which was $21,000 more than Hughes had been making.[4] The media's and opposition's

4 As conflict commissioner, Ted had been paid $64,000 a year—half of what the other independent officers of the legislature, the auditor general and the ombudsman, were paid for what was considered a part-time position, even though it was much more than part-time in terms of the hours Ted put into it.

reaction to the choice of Mitchell as conflict commissioner was incredulous and hostile.

"I keep waiting for someone to tell me this is April Fool's Day," Liberal House leader Gary Farrell-Collins told reporters.[5] Farrell-Collins was one of the Liberals with whom Mitchell had split, and he saw the appointment, as did most pundits, as a ploy by Clark to use what was supposed to be a non-partisan office to attack the Liberals. Farrell-Collins said the Liberals would "un-appoint" Mitchell if, as expected, they won the election that was likely to be called within weeks.

A dejected Hughes cleaned out his office that evening. But he also had a long talk with Helen, who reinforced his view that what Clark was doing was an affront not primarily to him, although he clearly felt the sting of the ejection, but more importantly to the independence of the office. Clark was using what was essentially a technicality to get around the requirement for the conflict-of-interest commissioner to be approved by a two-thirds vote of the legislature, which would have required the support of the Liberals. Mitchell would be appointed in an acting capacity. Ordinarily, he would have to be confirmed by a vote of the legislature within 20 sitting days, but with an election in the offing, that vote would never be held. The legislature was only going to be sitting for six days before the election was called.

Hughes decided that by capitulating he was letting down the office and the very notions of honour and integrity for which it and he stood.

At one the next afternoon, Hughes notified the press gallery that he was holding a press conference of his own at 2 PM in his cleared-out

5 Farrell-Collins later changed his last name to Collins after separating from his wife. He became the minister of finance in the Liberal government that was elected in 2001.

office. For the reporters who attended, it was an event to remember for the rest of their careers.[6]

"I feel like a gun was put to my head," Hughes told them. "It is a sad day for me today and one that I wish did not have to happen. Yesterday I succumbed to an incredible amount of pressure, and in doing so I now believe I failed this office."

Hughes told reporters he had been a pawn in a political game being played by Clark, McArthur and Spitzer. "Clearly I was an immediate dispensable entity in the drama."

Clark's first reaction was to deny Ted's allegations. "I didn't fire Ted Hughes," he said, while accusing the Liberals of playing politics with the situation.

By the next day, however, the undoing began. The media had a field day with the Hughes press conference. The publicity was bad and the timing worse as the election loomed.

"The shabby treatment of this distinguished public servant counts as Premier Clark's most serious mistake to date," columnist Vaughn Palmer wrote in the *Vancouver Sun* the next day.

"Shame, shame," cried the headline on the *Sun*'s editorial.

Ted was in Vancouver for most of the day on Thursday. When he returned to the office, he found a letter from Mitchell. In his "first official duty as acting Conflict Commissioner" he was writing to congratulate Hughes on his valiant effort to maintain the independence of the office. He said he was advising the government to ask Hughes to consider continuing in the office "until the legislature has approved your replacement—whoever that may be."

At 10 that night, McArthur called Ted and apologized for how the transition had been handled. He asked Hughes if he would talk to Clark later that evening.

---

6 This includes the author, who at the time was a reporter for the *Globe and Mail*.

Clark called about 11 PM. He also apologized for the way things were handled and blamed it on poor communications. He asked Hughes to return to his old post the next day. Hughes accepted the apology on the condition that there be nothing said or done in the future to try to shift the blame for the debacle of the past week onto him.[7]

In a short statement the next day, Hughes said: "This is not about Ted Hughes. He doesn't need this job. This is about public trust and confidence in the public life of this province. That trust and confidence have been shaken by the events that are now in the past."

Interestingly, from the government's perspective, it wasn't about Ted Hughes at the start of the week but it was all about Ted Hughes at the end. The government may have thought carefully about who they were bringing in, but they gave no consideration to who they were pushing out and were surprised if not shocked at the resistance he put up, especially since he had already said he was moving on.

Twenty years later, McArthur, now a professor and director of the School of Public Policy at Simon Fraser University in Burnaby, BC, remembers the week as one of the episodes he managed in public life that did not work out as planned. "Mitchell was a good appointment," he says. "My sense was I was probably fairly impatient with what Ted was doing."

While there was an element of politicking by the premier, Mitchell was deemed to be a legitimate choice for the job. His appointment reflected a change of direction the government wanted to see in the office of the commissioner. While Hughes wanted the scope of the office increased, the government wanted the commissioner reined in.

---

7 When Hughes was reappointed, it was at the old salary. He never got the raise offered Mitchell. He stayed on past the normal end of his term, in May, at Clark's request after the election. After July 1, 1996, he did so as a volunteer, since by then he was being paid as a treaty negotiator and was not going to double dip, even though he was actually doing two jobs.

That was a position that Mitchell had also taken the previous year in a private member's statement in the legislature.[8]

"We did want to make a change from the old judge tradition and try to get people who understand something about the experience of legislators and who understood some of the challenges that they faced in trying to deal with some of these very difficult and sometimes obscure conflicts," says McArthur. "Mitchell just seemed to be, he is a very kind of deliberate, serious guy as he has shown the rest of his life."[9]

When the appointment blew up on them, McArthur fell back on a strategy he adopted years before. "When nothing else works, when all

---

8 In Mitchell's statement on April 13, 1995, he said: "There's nothing wrong with having tough conflict-of-interest legislation. When the government brought in changes to the act, however, we had a good, thorough debate in this House. While I supported the bill in principle, I also expressed the fear that the broad definition of conflict of interest, combined with the wide discretion provided to the commissioner, could make political eunuchs out of the members of any government. Today I fear we are dangerously close to this, and unfortunately, many people, including some members of this House, seem to be confused about what in fact constitutes a conflict of interest.

"The current investigation by the commissioner into allegations made against the Premier, related to his government's relationship with NOW Communications, is a good case in point. I believe this is properly a matter of politics—capital-P politics. I believe the government should be criticized severely for this blatant example—one of far too many—of political patronage. The government should be especially condemned for it, because it promised to rid the province of patronage in the last election campaign. That's why I think this is a matter of politics. But is it a matter that should be referred to an independent commissioner? I think the government deserves to be criticized and deserves to be tarred and feathered and hung in the high court of public opinion—but not necessarily referred to a commissioner of conflict of interest. There has to be an appreciation in the public's mind as to what represents politics and what represents a genuine conflict of interest."

9 After losing the conflict-of-interest job and resigning from the legislature, Mitchell moved away from party politics while maintaining an interest in public policy as an academic, author and commentator.

else has failed, grovel. So I called him up and apologized and grovelled a lot," he says. "For me, this was just one of those many things that goes south on you and you just have to manage your way through it. That's Ted, and maybe it's not fair but that's Ted and you are not surprised."

After the attempt to appoint Mitchell failed, Hughes was ready to leave on his own terms. But with no one else in the wings to take his place, Clark asked Hughes to stay on as acting commissioner, which he did until March 1997. By then, at the age of 70, he was ready to concentrate full-time on his next career.

Part III

Canada and First Nations

Payback: Harvey Pollock and Indigenous Justice

"MEET CANADA'S 'MORAL' authority."

That headline on the front page of the *Winnipeg Free Press* on May 16, 1991, welcomed Ted Hughes to Winnipeg, where he had come to announce the terms of another public inquiry. It reflected a quote from Keith Baldrey, the BC legislature bureau chief for the *Vancouver Sun*. Over the previous decade Baldrey had recorded Ted's rapid rise in BC from a government lawyer to deputy attorney general to an independent authority on legal and ethical behaviour for politicians, with a proven ability to topple premiers.

"If Hughes concludes something happens in a certain way, nobody questions it," Baldrey told a reporter for the *Free Press* assigned to introduce Hughes to its readers. "It's accepted as fact, as if he's the ultimate arbitrator."

Hughes had just finished the Vander Zalm conflict decision and was starting his term as BC's first permanent conflict-of-interest commissioner for the legislature. That was a part-time job, however, leaving Ted time to take on other assignments.

The independent commissions marked a transition for Hughes from the somewhat subservient position he had to assume as an employee serving at the whim of the BC government to a role more akin to the one he filled in his days as a judge, when he was the master of his own court, ruled only by his terms of reference, the law and his own sense of natural justice and fair play.

The complicated case that the Manitoba government brought Hughes in to investigate that spring got its start three years earlier with a slow-speed car chase on icy streets a couple of hours after midnight. Constables Robert Cross and Kathryn Hodgins spotted a stolen white Dodge Aries and were gingerly in pursuit when it turned a corner and disappeared.[1] When they caught up to the stolen car it had been ditched in a snowbank and the thieves had run off. The two officers left their own car and went after them. Other patrol cars joined the hunt and it wasn't long before the two thieves were in custody. The incident should have ended there, but before the night was over, what had started as a simple joyride escalated into a deadly police shooting with racial overtones, a wide-ranging inquiry into justice for First Nations people in Manitoba, and a lawyer who had criticized the police during the inquiry being dragged through the mud on a trumped-up charge of sexual assault. That's where Hughes came in.

John Joseph "J.J." Harper was not the car thief Constable Cross was looking for when he hopped out of his patrol car a little after 2 AM on March 9, 1988. Other than being an Indigenous person in a black jacket, Harper didn't even match the physical description of the thief Cross believed was still at large. But moments after they crossed paths, Harper was dying on the sidewalk, fatally wounded by a bullet from Cross's gun.

Harper was a 37-year-old former chief of the Wasagamack Indian Band and a father of three children. He was the executive director of

---

1 The thieves smashed the window of the Aries on a whim and drove around the neighbourhood for a couple of hours, returning once to the parking lot where they stole the car to buy some liquor. Details of the case and the subsequent inquiry are in Murray Sinclair and Alvin Hamilton, *Report of the Aboriginal Justice Inquiry of Manitoba*.

the Island Lake Tribal Council and a leader in Manitoba's Indigenous community.[2] He had been drinking with friends for the previous several hours, and according to Cross, who was the only witness to the shooting, he wasn't inclined to cooperate when the constable asked him for identification. Instead, he kept walking. When Cross grabbed his arm, Harper spun around and despite having what was later found to be a blood alcohol level of .22, almost three times the legal limit for driving, shoved Cross to the ground. Cross grabbed Harper as he fell. Harper fell on top of Cross and reached for the officer's gun. As the two struggled, the gun went off, fatally wounding Harper in the chest.

Hodgins, Cross's partner of three years, showed up a few minutes later along with other officers who had already captured the car thieves. Within hours an internal police investigation cleared Cross of any wrongdoing in Harper's death. A narrowly focused judicial inquest came to the same conclusion a couple of months later. Even before the inquest was launched, Winnipeg police chief Herb Stephen issued a press release announcing that Harper's death was precipitated by the assault on Cross and there was "no negligence" on the part of the officer.

The shooting and allegations of racist comments and jokes made by the officers involved sparked protests by the Indigenous community in Winnipeg, who viewed them as part of an all-too-familiar pattern of mistreatment at the hands of police. They weren't buying Cross's account of the shooting or the internal investigation that found Harper to blame for his own death. The Aboriginal Justice Inquiry of Manitoba that was launched the following year confirmed their suspicions. The inquiry looked at general conditions in the province and closely examined both the Harper shooting and the murder 17 years earlier of Helen Betty Osborne.

---

2 The Island Lake Tribal Council represents several First Nations bands in northeastern Manitoba, including the Wasagamack, and has an office in Winnipeg.

Osborne was a 19-year-old Indigenous woman who was abducted, sexually assaulted, beaten beyond recognition and stabbed more than 50 times with a screwdriver in November 1971 by four white men in the small town of The Pas, Manitoba. Police took 15 years to arrest any suspects. Only two were charged and only one was convicted, a verdict that was finally delivered just three months before J.J. Harper was killed.

"The justice system has failed Manitoba's aboriginal people on a massive scale," the justice inquiry reported after a detailed examination of the Osborne and Harper cases.

Harvey Pollock, QC, was a respected Winnipeg lawyer who had represented Indigenous clients for much of his career. He spoke for the Harper family during the year-long Aboriginal Justice Inquiry and was blistering in his criticism of the police both in examination of witnesses at the inquiry and in media interviews.

From the police perspective, the justice inquiry was brutal. The police investigation into the Harper shooting was shown to be fatally flawed if not a complete cover-up. Cross's gun had never been fingerprinted to verify his claim that Harper had grabbed it. Notes made at the time were lost or doctored. Stories were changed. Careers were ruined and the officer in charge of the investigation committed suicide the day before he was to testify.

Rather than being chastened by the flaws that were revealed, some officers were bitter about the way they believed they were being abused by participants in the inquiry. "They weren't cross-examining police, they were trampling them. They were supposed to be looking for prejudice, but they wound up hounding us, looking for things that don't exist," one officer complained in an interview the day after Inspector Kenneth Dowson shot himself at home while his wife and three children were out.

In a suicide note, Dowson confirmed that the investigation had been flawed, but he also voiced the contempt many police felt for the inquiry. "This investigation was screwed up from the beginning. I've never seen so many things go wrong," he wrote in a note to his friend Staff-Sergeant Rex Keatinge. "The glasses missed at the scene, the gun not [finger]printed, the photos that weren't taken. And then the media took over and it's downhill from there. The effect on all of us has been devastating, especially [Constable Robert] Cross and those young guys at the scene."[3]

As the Harper family's lawyer, Pollock was among those police blamed for the beating their reputation had taken during the inquiry. At one point the husband of Kathryn Hodgins, Cross's partner, complained to the Manitoba Law Society about comments Pollock made about her in a media interview following her testimony. Pollock received a letter of reprimand for the comments.[4]

So when Pollock's name came up a year later during a domestic disturbance, the attending officers took note. Hodgins was one of the officers answering the call. She and her current partner were summoned to a home in north Winnipeg at 4:30 in the morning on Saturday, October 6, 1990, by a woman who was only ever identified as G.H.[5] She phoned the police because she was having problems with her teenage son and she wanted the police to do something.

---

3 The note Dowson wrote shortly before he killed himself on September 20 was published in the *Globe and Mail* on November 2, 1989.

4 Information on this and other details of the Pollock case comes from E. Hughes, *Report of the Honourable E.N. Hughes Q.C. With Respect to the Process and Procedure in the Investigation, Charge, Arrest, Prosecution, Stay and Subsequent Actions of the October 3, 1990 Harvey I. Pollock Q.C. Case,* and contemporary newspaper reports.

5 Her identity was protected because Pollock was charged with sexual assault, even though it later became clear that she was not alleging that a criminal sexual assault occurred. Without questioning the need to protect the victims of sexual assault, it is interesting that the main harm done to Pollock was the way he was so publicly identified by police when he was falsely charged with the offence.

During the investigation, G.H., who had made six previous complaints to police on various matters, said they would never believe what her lawyer had done to her. She told the police she had gone to his office on Wednesday, October 3, to discuss a claim she was making for injuries from a car accident. While she was showing him her injuries, her lawyer touched a spot on her lower back where she said she had been hurt. Two days after the incident, the day before she called the police about her son, she had complained to the law society about the touch and about the fact that her lawyer had criticized her for drinking before the appointment. In her complaint, she said her lawyer had touched her "on my bum where my spine is broken."

She told Hodgins and her partner that her lawyer was Harvey Pollock.

Hodgins told G.H. that she could complain about what happened to the police, and when she did so, she should call what happened to her a sexual assault. G.H. asked Hodgins to write it down for her so she wouldn't forget.

Hodgins did not want to take the complaint. She recognized that because of her earlier encounters with Pollock she would have a conflict of interest, so she told G.H. to take the complaint to the crime section of the Winnipeg Police Department and wrote down the address for her.

Later that day G.H. called the police, and that evening two other officers came to see her to formally take a written statement. In that statement, the officers said G.H. told them Pollock had rubbed her "on the crack of my bum two or three times." At the inquiry that was to follow, Hughes believed her when she denied using those words. Nevertheless, that was the description that Inspector M.R. Bell, the acting director of the crime section, found on his desk when he came in to work on Monday morning, October 8, which was a statutory holiday. The following day two experienced investigators, Sergeants Ronald

Kushneryk and Donald Feener, were dispatched to re-interview G.H. and a companion who had gone with her to Pollock's office.

By Tuesday afternoon, the two officers reported back to Bell that they had probable grounds to arrest Pollock on a charge of sexual assault. Bell concluded that there had been a sexual assault but suggested a meeting the next morning with Crown counsel before proceeding in case the charge should be common assault instead, based on concerns over an earlier case he had read about in which an accused had touched a woman's breast but there was no sexual intent.

In that Wednesday morning meeting, the officers told Crown counsel that Pollock "put his hands up the crack of her ass." Again, words that G.H. had never used. She later told Hughes that she never thought Pollock had any sexual intent; she just didn't like being touched.

The police were not asking Crown counsel whether a charge should be laid. Rather, they were determining what the wording of the charge should be. They agreed on a charge of sexual assault.

Even before the meeting, one of the officers had phoned Bruce Owen, a reporter at the *Winnipeg Free Press*, and told him that Pollock was going to be arrested so he could be there with a photographer when it happened.

Shortly after 9 AM on Wednesday, October 10, Kushneryk and Feener arrived at Pollock's office, placed him under arrest and read him his rights from a card. They had not interviewed Pollock and did not ask him any questions at that point about what had happened in his office a week earlier.

Pollock was dumbfounded. Other than hearing the charge, he had no idea what he was being arrested for. At first he didn't even know who police were alleging he had assaulted. But he was sure of one thing: this was payback.

His law partner asked if he could bring Pollock down to the station rather than having the police take him in, but the officers refused. One of them knew what was waiting on the street below.

The next day, under the headline "Lawyer charged with sexual assault," the *Winnipeg Free Press* carried a front-page picture of Pollock being put in a police car. The accompanying story noted that "a visibly shaken" Pollock was whistling when he came out of the office and said, "It's nonsense, it's absolute nonsense. It's the police at their best."[6]

The damage was done, even though the case against Pollock lasted only until the first day of the preliminary hearing two months later, when the story that G.H. told from the witness stand wandered substantially away from what the police had alleged. Crown counsel entered a stay of proceedings on the charges against the lawyer.

In May the province appointed Hughes to head a commission of inquiry into the bungled affair. At one point in the hearings, reporters described the somewhat bizarre spectacle of red-faced policemen demonstrating on their own behinds how they believed Pollock had fondled G.H., "while a bevy of lawyers craned their necks for a better view." As one reporter wrote, it might have seemed like a Monty Python farce, but the whole potentially career-ending case against Pollock centred on where and how his hand landed on G.H.'s backside.

In his report, Hughes remarked: "I venture to say that never, ever has a three-second touch, occurring under similar circumstances, attracted so much attention, covered so many hours of discussion, and expended so many thousands of dollars."

Hughes eventually determined that the touch, while inappropriate, was far from a sexual assault. And proving criminal intent would have been a "mission impossible" for the Crown.

So what did happen in Pollock's office on October 3, 1990?

After listening to 25 witnesses over 18 days of hearings, Hughes found that G.H. had gone to Pollock's office with a friend in hopes that she would be getting a cheque to settle her injury suit, but Pollock

---

6 Pollock was known as the whistling lawyer, noted for his virtuosity after winning a world whistling championship in 1977.

was just looking for some more information. On the way, she and her friend stopped for a couple of drinks, which Pollock, who lost a son to a drunk driver, took exception to. He suggested she had a drinking problem and ought to consider joining Alcoholics Anonymous. G.H. didn't appreciate the advice, so a visit that started with G.H. being disappointed ended with her being annoyed.

In the course of showing Pollock her injuries, she mentioned that she had a fractured vertebra. Pollock had not seen any reference to that injury and he asked her to show it to him. She took off her coat and pointed to her tailbone at the base of her spine.

"Like a damn fool I stick my thumb out and touch where she was pointing out to see if she's got a fracture," Pollock said in a 2016 interview.

In his report, Hughes said it was wrong for Pollock to have touched his client. He wasn't a doctor and he couldn't have learned anything useful. He found that G.H. had quite reasonably complained to the law society.[7] And he found her to be honest, even if the events she described didn't unfold quite as she had remembered. He says, "G.H. was an honest witness. However, accuracy and honesty are not always synonymous. A good investigator should be aware of this distinction."

He was less generous when he turned his attention to the conduct of the police, who all at first denied that they had tipped off the newspaper. Then Bruce Owen, the reporter, refused to divulge his source. Hughes warned Owen he would be held in contempt if he didn't comply, even though that was a road the commissioner did not want to go down.

"I was faced with what I was going to have to find Owen in contempt of court—God I didn't want to get into that with all the freedom of press stuff that would flow out of that so I said, 'I'm going

---

7 G.H. ended her note to the law society by saying, "I hate him."

to adjourn until 10 o'clock tomorrow morning and I expect whoever that policeman was to come forward and acknowledge that it happened and we'll go from there once that acknowledgment is made,'" Hughes recalls.

With a showdown looming, Hughes spent a tense night.

"Next morning, Sergeant Kushneryk comes forward and says, 'I was the guy.' It got me out of one hell of a pickle."

In the report he issued in October 1991, Hughes concluded that payback for his role in the J.J. Harper inquiry was indeed the primary motive in the charging of Harvey Pollock.[8] He stopped short of calling it a conspiracy, however, concluding instead that it was allowed to happen under the "woefully inadequate" leadership of Herb Stephen, the chief of police.

Chief Stephen had already agreed to retire following the revelations about police actions in the Harper affair that were brought to light in the Aboriginal Justice Inquiry. When the Hughes report came out detailing yet another shoddy investigation, he immediately tendered his resignation.

Harvey Pollock was able to continue to practise law, first with his son and then his grandson. "For me he was great. I was honoured to know him and to have him judge me," says Pollock.

For Hughes, it was not the last time his investigations led him to conclude that police were not serving and protecting everyone equally.

---

8 In addition to the problem of the motivation of the police, the process that led to the charging of Pollock was weakened by earlier cases that had led police to believe that Crown counsel were reluctant to proceed with charges against lawyers. As a result, when police consulted a Crown counsel on the morning before charging Pollock, they didn't share the file they had compiled. Instead they only told him what they thought he needed to hear. In his report, Hughes criticized police for allowing their unfounded suspicions that lawyers were being given special treatment by Crown counsel to get in the way of carrying out their duties.

Hate and Death

> "The fact is, the Canadian Justice system is, in many respects, a foreign system to Aboriginal people and, as such, must be changed."
>
> E. HUGHES, P. MACKINNON AND D. OPEKOKEW, *Report of the Commission of Inquiry into the Shooting Death of Leo LaChance*

A BRONZE SCULPTURE of Leo LaChance was erected in front of the new courthouse in Prince Albert, Saskatchewan, a few months after it opened in 2001. The inscription below the statue reads: "This sculpture serves to remind those who enter here to respect and honour all cultures—to listen, to hear, to treat all people with respect and dignity."

A decade earlier, LaChance was a 48-year-old Indigenous hunter and trapper from the Big River First Nation, which is about 120 kilometres northwest of Prince Albert. He came into town on January 28, 1991, to sell a few furs. When he arrived a little after six in the evening, the trader who usually bought his harvest was already closed for the day, so he went into the Prince Albert Northern Pawn and Gun Shop next door. The co-owner, Carney Nerland, was behind the counter holding an M-56, a Yugoslavian submachine gun that had been converted to fire single rounds. Nerland was a

25-year-old white supremacist, who had been recorded at an event in Alberta the previous summer describing his shotgun as a "native birth control" device.[1]

Two other men were in the store talking to Nerland. After LaChance came in and asked about selling his furs, Nerland fired two shots into the floor. What happened next is still a matter of dispute. The version accepted by the court at Nerland's trial is that LaChance then left and Nerland fired again, through the door, hitting LaChance. The trapper carried on for another 35 metres and collapsed on the road. A man who saw him collapse came into the gun shop and asked to use the phone to call 911. Nerland refused, so the man went to a nearby restaurant and called for an ambulance. LaChance died later in hospital after telling police he had been shot by some white guys.

When police first interviewed Nerland later that evening, he lied. He said someone else had fired a shot while his back was turned. After he was arrested, he told a police officer: "If I'm convicted of killing that Indian, you should pin a medal on me."

Within a few months of the shooting, Nerland pled guilty to a charge of manslaughter and was sentenced to four years in jail. He claimed the shooting was an accident. He thought the gun chamber was empty when he pulled the trigger a third time. His guilty plea cut short any investigation of whether the shooting was racially motivated, a factor that might have led to a longer sentence or potentially supported a charge of murder.

The large Indigenous community in Prince Albert and northern Saskatchewan was outraged by what many believed was a racially motivated murder and a cover-up by sympathizers in the justice

---

1 Details of the Nerland case are from Barb Pacholik and Jana G. Pruden, *Sour Milk and Other Saskatchewan Crime Stories*, from newspaper reports and from the report of the commission led by Hughes.

system. They demanded an inquiry into how the case moved through the notoriously slow courts so quickly and allowed a white man to get off so lightly for killing an Indigenous man.

Gordon Kirkby, the mayor of Prince Albert, wrote to federal justice minister Kim Campbell and called for an inquiry. Campbell replied that it was up to the province.

In February, almost 10 months after Nerland was sentenced, Premier Roy Romanow's NDP government agreed to call an inquiry and asked Hughes to take the lead role. He was joined by Peter MacKinnon, then dean of law at the University of Saskatchewan, and Delia Opekokew, a Cree lawyer from the Canoe Lake First Nation in Saskatchewan, where she attended residential schools before going to York University and practising law in Toronto.

It didn't take long for the inquiry to stall in court. First, Nerland's lawyer challenged it as being a retrial of his client. That argument failed, but another legal challenge dealt a blow that substantially damaged the ability of Hughes and his fellow commissioners to get to the bottom of the events surrounding LaChance's death.

The commission learned that shortly after the shooting a member of the RCMP intelligence division approached the Prince Albert police and told them that someone involved in the investigation was an informant on white supremacist activities in Saskatchewan. Hughes ordered the RCMP to reveal the name of the informant, but the force appealed his order to the Saskatchewan Court of Appeal, which sided with the RCMP. Justice Calvin Tallis ruled the RCMP was not required to reveal the identity of informants except when it was necessary to establish the innocence of someone accused of a crime. The inquiry appealed Tallis's ruling to the Supreme Court of Canada but the high court declined to hear the case.

Commission counsel Morris Bodner commented at the time that the ruling would severely impair the work of the commissioners. It meant that they were unable to follow up on the question of whether the RCMP was trying to subvert the investigation of the local police by declaring their interest. That question seemed to become even more relevant when the Prince Albert Tribal Council subsequently announced that it had learned that Nerland was the RCMP informant, an allegation the RCMP refused to confirm or deny. Yet when Nerland was released on parole in 1993, prison officials said he had been turned over to the RCMP to be hidden away in the witness protection program. Again the RCMP refused to comment, but the fact that Carney Nerland seems never to have resurfaced under that name appears to confirm the allegation.

"It always seemed interesting that you've got a guy in witness protection and then he was not a witness to anything," says Gerald Morin, a Prince Albert lawyer who represented the LaChance family at the inquiry.[2]

When the commission issued its report in October 1993, there was no mention of the informant. The court decision created a hole in the narrative of what really went on that could not be filled.

"Our theory to a certain extent was that they made [LaChance] dance and then [Nerland] shot through that door," says Morin. But all they could determine for certain was that shots were fired, there were two holes through the floor and one through the door, and LaChance was fatally wounded. And when Nerland confessed to firing the fatal shot in what he described as an accident, the police and prosecutors no longer seemed very interested in why it might have been more than that.

The commission criticized the police and the Crown for not actively pursuing the race question, given what they knew about Nerland.

In what appears now to be another step in Ted's growing appreciation of Indigenous issues in Canada, they also issued a general call

---

2 Morin later became a Provincial Court judge in Prince Albert.

to all Canadians to identify and rectify societal barriers to justice. "It became apparent to us during the hearings that we are still a long way from being a tolerant society... In our view, the goal of achieving a society of tolerance, understanding and cross-cultural respect and sensitivity will not be reached until minority cultures are recognized, accepted and appreciated by the majority culture in this country," the commissioners wrote in their report.

That theme would run through much of the work Hughes took on as a commissioner over the next two decades, including when he was called in next to clean up after a prison riot in Manitoba.

Riot

"By its very nature, a jail is not a happy place."

E.N. HUGHES, *Report of the Independent Review of the Circumstances Surrounding the April 25–26, 1996, Riot at the Headingley Correctional Institution*

THE FIRST SPEECH from the Throne of the NDP government under Premier Glen Clark contained a promise to amend the Members' Conflict of Interest Act to make the appointment of future commissioners a less rancorous undertaking. Lieutenant-Governor Garde Gardom read the speech on Thursday afternoon, April 25, 1996.

Later that day, three provinces over, the canteen officer operating the commissary at the Headingley Correctional Institution just west of Winnipeg noticed a strange trend. Inmates from the basement unit were cleaning her out of dollar tokens by making small purchases with five-dollar tokens. She notified the duty officer, who told her to stop making any sales unless inmates had exact change. The duty officer knew from experience that when inmates started collecting tokens, it was usually for one of two purposes—either to buy drugs or to pay to have another inmate assaulted.[1]

Before the night was out, during a routine drug search of the basement unit, guards found a badly beaten inmate. The guards were then attacked and overpowered and forced to flee for their safety. Several were injured. One guard required 150 stiches. Using keys they took from the guards, the inmates raged through the rest of the prison, freeing their friends, setting fires and assaulting their enemies. They dragged prisoners out of protective custody and beat them for hours. They hacked off fingers and tried to castrate one man.

Police took back control of the medium-security prison the following night after persuading all but eight of the 321 inmates to come out. The rest meekly surrendered when police stormed the prison. Forty prisoners and guards were taken to hospital for treatment of their injuries, and the 60-year-old prison was a smouldering, sodden mess. Damage was later estimated at $3.5 million. It would be months before it could again be used to house prisoners.[2]

Even before police regained control, stories were emerging about lax security, rampant drug use and gangs operating inside. After the riot, the prisoners from Headingley had to be transferred to other institutions, creating a new set of problems. Within a week, up to 700 corrections staff, including guards, counsellors and teachers, began walking off the job at eight provincial facilities, claiming their working conditions were no longer safe. They were replaced temporarily by 200 RCMP officers at a cost of $50,000 a day.

---

1 Details of the riot and the aftermath are from contemporary newspaper reports in the *Winnipeg Free Press* and the *Globe and Mail*, and from E. Hughes, *Report of the Independent Review of the Circumstances Surrounding the April 25–26, 1996, Riot at the Headingley Correctional Institution.*

2 The province eventually budgeted $10 million to renovate and update Headingley.

One of the solutions to the overcrowding—granting early release for prisoners deemed less of a risk to reoffend—also created more problems for the government, as some of the inmates given temporary release started getting into trouble.

Back in British Columbia, Hughes was winding down his work as acting conflict commissioner and looking forward to new challenges. He signed on as a chief negotiator for the Federal Treaty Negotiation Office in Victoria. He also took a part-time job as conflict commissioner for Yukon's Legislative Assembly and later took on the same role for the Northwest Territories. When he was reappointed as BC's acting conflict commissioner after David Mitchell's brief tenure (see "Smackdown"), the position was set to end on June 30, 1996, but he agreed to stay on (without pay after July 1) until the end of March 1997.[3] Yet he still found time to say yes when the Manitoba government called in early May 1996 and asked him to conduct an inquiry into the Headingley riot and all the allegations that had been flying since it erupted. A month later he celebrated his 69th birthday.

Hughes' inquiry was part of the deal to get correctional workers back on the job. The Manitoba Government Employees' Union knew his reputation and viewed the inquiry as a chance for corrections officers to air their grievances without fear of intimidation or losing their jobs.

If the union thought the report would fully support the guards, however, it was mistaken. Hughes told reporters at the time of his first tour of the ransacked jail that he would be going wherever he needed to go, from the inmates to the justice minister, to find the answers he needed.

The inquiry took him longer than expected. He was to report by September but the issues were more complicated than he had

---

3 J. Peter Meekison was appointed acting conflict-of-interest commissioner in May 1997. In August, H.A.D. "Bert" Oliver took over as the permanent commissioner. Oliver was succeeded by Paul Fraser in January 2008.

imagined, and he sought and received an extension to December. He ran into some resistance; a diary disappeared, and for some reason the first set of letters he sent to inmates inviting them to talk to him were never delivered. Eventually he interviewed about 150 inmates, corrections officers, administrators and justice officials and received thousands of pages of written submissions.

What he found was an aging institution that was not designed for the role it now played, a place where staff morale was, in the words of one corrections officer, "lower than a snake's belly in a wagon rut." Headingley was a place where corrections officers often hated their jobs, each other and the inmates; it had an incompetent superintendent, porous security that allowed for a free flow of drugs and gangs that terrorized other inmates, and it was ultimately overseen by a justice minister, Rosemary Vodrey, who was surprisingly ignorant of the miserable state of one of the major institutions in her portfolio.

Individual guards made serious and "grossly irresponsible" mistakes the night of the riot, starting with a failure to log the canteen incident, which meant that when the next shift decided to search the basement unit for drugs, they were unaware that they might be facing a heightened risk.

Their individual actions took place in the context of an institution that for almost two decades was known for terrible staff morale. A bad situation had been made worse in recent years by a policy directive that added aspects of social work to the traditional role of corrections officers, who previously had been responsible only for maintaining order and locking doors. Many of the guards were hired at a time when their size was more important than their intelligence, and they had little interest in or capacity to adapt to a new role in which they were required to take more of an interest in the inmates they were overseeing. And it was all exacerbated by a superintendent who had been promoted beyond his competence and who failed to recognize that his approach to running the prison had allowed gangs to thrive and to easily import drugs and violently force other inmates to join or help them.

Finally, while the situation at Headingley was common knowledge throughout the prison system in Manitoba and among some senior administrators in Winnipeg, Hughes was "confounded" by how ignorant senior government officials and the minister were about what was going on in their jurisdiction.

The Headingley assignment brought Hughes new challenges, but he also recognized familiar themes from earlier inquiries he had headed and from his previous work as a judge. He made specific recommendations for changes to procedures in the jail and to the organization of the Manitoba corrections system. He called for a new union–management committee with an outside facilitator to purge the "hatred, negativity, apathy and the couldn't-care-less attitude that I have identified" and replace it with "trust, honour, decency and respect in the workplace."

He also returned to the observation he had been making since urging Helen to run for city council in Saskatoon 22 years earlier. Namely, that much of the criminal activity by Indigenous Canadians was rooted in social inequality. Hughes cited a survey that found that 70 per cent of the inmates at Headingley were Indigenous, as were 75 per cent of gang members in the province.

The only solution to the gang problem, Hughes said, was to put the resources needed into addressing the legacy issues raised by the Aboriginal Justice Inquiry chaired by Murray Sinclair and Alvin Hamilton five years earlier. "Would the pouring of millions of dollars into economic and social programs that would allow poverty-stricken people with no marketable skills, no job, and no job prospects to participate as law-abiding citizens in Canadian life be a justified and worthwhile expenditure of public funds? Someday the Canadian public has to accept that the answer to those questions is, yes," he wrote in his report.

The day the Hughes report was released, the Manitoba government announced it was adopting two of the main recommendations—the workplace committee and a reorganization of the corrections division. It also promised to bring the issue of gangs and the over-representation of Indigenous people in the justice system to a national forum, without promising any specific initiatives.

The issues rooted in Indigenous poverty, colonization and cultural loss would remain a theme in much of Hughes' work for the next 20 years.

APEC and Chretien: The National Arena

"At this point in the tale, the inquiry into last November's APEC summit has descended into chaos."

EDITORIAL IN THE *GLOBE AND MAIL*, DECEMBER 9, 1998

IT'S POSSIBLE THAT even without the Sgt. Pepper video the police handling of protests at the 1997 APEC summit in Vancouver may have led to a full public inquiry. But the images that were shown over and over of a Mountie grimly blasting a CBC television camera with a stream of liquid pepper spray during a hurried attempt to uproot an otherwise peaceful demonstration gave the inquiry a clear focus in the public mind.

Staff Sergeant Hugh Stewart had only a couple of minutes to clear the road leading out of the University of British Columbia campus before a convoy of world leaders was scheduled to pass by. As he later told the RCMP Public Complaints Commission inquiry into police action during the Asia-Pacific Economic Cooperation (APEC) summit in Vancouver,[1] he wasn't aiming deliberately at the cameraman, but

1 The Asia-Pacific Economic Cooperation was initiated by Australia in 1989 to promote trade and growth between and among 18 economies around the Pacific Rim. Leaders meet annually in a different country. The members are called economies because they include some jurisdictions that are not universally recognized as countries, including Taiwan and Hong Kong.

he was going to do whatever was necessary to carry out his orders in the time he had.

Hughes was conducting the APEC inquiry by the time Stewart testified in December 1999, more than two years after the 30-year veteran of the RCMP earned his nickname by discharging a small fire-extinguisher-sized container of oleoresin capsicum (OC), more commonly known as pepper spray after the cayenne pepper plant from which it is obtained. Ted got called in, as he often was, when the first attempt to right a wrong had gone completely off-track, or as the *Globe and Mail*'s editorial board stated, the inquiry had "descended into chaos."

It was an apt description.

For the Liberal government under Prime Minister Jean Chretien, what was to have been a showcase visit of increasingly important trading partners had turned into a political liability that seemed to get worse with each new revelation. When the government finally decided to launch an inquiry into all the allegations of police misconduct, that too soon plunged onto the rocks. And after Hughes took on the task of unravelling the scores of contradictory stories, conflicting values and uncertain law, even some of his most ardent admirers feared that this time the Mighty Hughes had met his match.

"Ted Hughes' reputation is as someone with the wisdom of Solomon," Norman Ruff, an often-quoted political scientist at the University of Victoria, told a Canadian Press reporter on December 31, 1998, adding that in this case that might not be enough.

The week-long APEC meeting had been held at a number of sites in Vancouver in late November 1997. On the last day the leaders and their advisors met at the Museum of Anthropology on the UBC campus, a venue chosen to give the leaders the feeling of being on a retreat away from the city. Parts of the campus were designated as a security zone and declared to be off limits to protestors or anyone else without a security clearance.

The leaders in attendance at the summit were from 18 countries and economic zones, and included Indonesia's President Suharto and heads of other repressive regimes who had been promised they would be protected from being embarrassed by protests during their visit to Vancouver, a promise that fuelled the opposition to their visit. That opposition was neatly captured by *Vancouver Sun* columnist Stephen Hume on August 8, 2001, when he described the APEC summit as the time "when the dictators of blood-stained regimes came calling and our civil liberties were suspended so that they might not feel unwelcome in our democratic midst."

While the Vancouver Police Department (VPD) and the RCMP planned for the largest event they had ever taken on in the city, with more than 2,000 RCMP officers and several hundred members of the VPD, protesters were also making plans to be heard.

In retrospect, the clashes that followed were pretty tame relative to the destructive and occasionally deadly confrontations that subsequently occurred at international gatherings, such as the WTO riots in Seattle two years later. There were no black anarchists smashing windows and burning cars, no nihilist agendas at play, and the attacks of 9/11 that led to steeply ramped-up global security were four years in the future. Still, the allegations of illegal detentions, improper strip searches, indiscriminate use of pepper spray and the suppression of a legitimate right to protest, even on a relatively small scale, led to serious questions about how police handled their assignments and whether there was political interference from the prime minister's office (PMO) or even from the prime minister himself.

Chretien, who a year earlier had grabbed an anti-poverty protester by the throat when the man got too close to him, reacted to his first question about the RCMP's use of pepper spray with a joke. "For me, pepper, I put it on my plate," he said at a press conference wrapping up the summit.

Back in Ottawa a day later, he gave a more serious answer and defended the use of force by police. "Those who did not follow the law, broke the lines and tried to jump over the fence to disturb the conference, had to face the police," he said. "And the police took a means that was apparently very efficient, and there was nobody hurt, and the conference was not disturbed."

The protesters who had felt the sting of pepper spray and the insult of having their signs taken down had a different perspective. There were initially 49 complaints filed with the RCMP Public Complaints Commission, ranging from the excessive use of force to the suppression of the Charter right to freedom of speech.

Documents obtained by the press in the weeks following the meeting showed that Martha Piper, the president of UBC, had concerns about the way the security plans being put in place were intruding on the students' right to free speech and to protest, rights that the university should be supporting, not suppressing. The documents also showed that Jean Carle, a member of the PMO, was involved in the security planning, contrary to earlier assertions by the RCMP and the PMO that that the office was not involved.

In February, three months after the demonstrations, Shirley Heafey, chair of the RCMP Public Complaints Commission, appointed a three-member panel to investigate the complaints that had been filed against members of the RCMP for their actions during the APEC conference. The panel was headed by Gerald Morin, a lawyer from Saskatchewan who had been a member of the commission for about a year. He had also represented the family of Leo LaChance at the inquiry led by Hughes into LaChance's shooting by white supremacist Carney Nerland five years earlier.

The panel was controversial from the outset. Opposition critics had been calling for a wide-ranging judicial public inquiry rather than a narrowly focused investigation by the RCMP Public Complaints

Commission, which would be restricted to looking into the actions of members of the national police force. The behaviour of politicians would be off limits unless individual police officers implicated them through their testimony.

The first issue was funding for lawyers to represent the complainants. Morin and his fellow commissioners wanted Ottawa to pay the cost for complainants to be represented at the hearings, which were expected to go on for months. They made the request in July and heard back from Solicitor General Andy Scott in September. He turned them down, adding to some complainants' suspicions that the hearings would be little more than a whitewash of the police actions.

The panel tried again in October, writing to Scott that "there are important fundamental issues about who we are as Canadians at stake in this hearing."[2]

He again refused.

Hearings had barely gotten started when they were derailed by two other allegations, both based on reports from people who were eavesdropping on private conversations. An NDP MP overheard the Solicitor General tell a Liberal supporter on a flight from Ottawa to Fredericton that a few Mounties would take the fall for anything that went wrong at the APEC conference. After initially denying the remarks, Scott was forced to resign when his seatmate confirmed that he had said things that could be construed as prejudging the outcome of the inquiry.

Meanwhile, lawyers for the federal government alleged that Morin was biased after an off-duty RCMP officer in Morin's hometown of Prince Albert said he overheard the inquiry chair tell a friend in a casino

---

2 Morin wrote about his experiences with the inquiry in Gerald M. Morin, "Personal Reflections on the Ill-Fated First APEC Inquiry," in *Pepper in Our Eyes: The APEC Affair*, edited by W. Wesley Pue, 159–70.

that police used too much pepper spray against the demonstrators. Morin denied making any such statements, as did casino patrons who had talked to him that evening. But the inquiry was again suspended while the courts determined whether Morin could remain on the panel.

Before that was all resolved, however, the dispute over funding for protesters led down a somewhat bizarre and twisted path to what Morin concluded was unwarranted interference in the independence of the panel by Shirley Heafey when she obtained an outside legal opinion on the issue of funding lawyers to represent the complainants. Along the way, Morin hired a private investigator to look into the background of the Mountie who made the allegations against him and into two mysterious break-ins, one in the inquiry office and the other to his car. Nothing of value was taken either time. When he submitted the $8,000 bill to cover the cost of the investigation, Heafey refused to authorize the expense.

On December 4, Morin resigned. Six days later the other two members of the panel also quit.

Despite renewed calls for a judicial inquiry, Heafey insisted the RCMP Public Complaints Commission would continue. Her problem was that she was out of members to appoint to a panel. She went to see Josiah Wood, a former BC Court of Appeal judge who had returned to private practice in Vancouver.[3] While she was in his office, he called Ted to see if he was interested.

He was. Hughes was then still working part-time as a negotiator for the Federal Treaty Negotiation Office in Victoria, but he was happy to take on a bigger job.

---

3 Wood was then at Blake, Cassels and Graydon. He later returned to the bench as a Provincial Court judge in Duncan, BC, the only one at the time who had previously served on a higher court. He died in 2014 at the age of 73, having never retired.

In a 1999 interview for *BC Business* magazine, he said he had a selfish motive for taking on the APEC inquiry at the age of 71: "In retirement, people pursue hobbies. Well, I'm not a man of hobbies; I'm a man of work. I'd much rather be doing this than sailing around the world. I thoroughly enjoy it. I only hope I'll have the good sense to realize when it's time to quit."

Unlike Morin, Hughes would be conducting the inquiry by himself as a lone commissioner. He decided to take it on even after Heafey called him back to say that she could only offer him about $400 a day, not much more than the hourly rate for some of the numerous lawyers who would be appearing before him.[4] Hughes suspects but was never able to confirm that the salary was deliberately set low by someone in Ottawa who wanted him to turn down the job. "I think when they came back and said they were sorry but all they could pay me was $440 a day, I'm quite sure they felt I would say take your job and stick it, but, a), I saw what the play was and that made me stubborn, and b), I wanted to do it anyway.'"

As well as being offered a salary that was an insult to someone of his stature, Hughes knew he was taking on a job that was tainted by the allegations of outside interference made by the previous chair. For Hughes, that wasn't much of a consideration. "I wouldn't have stood for any interference, so I honestly didn't inquire very much about why it had broken down." And his reputation was such that, other than a bit of ongoing grumbling by some of the protesters,

---

4 Legal costs were the most expensive part of the APEC inquiry, which involved a score of lawyers, most of whom were funded by the federal government. Hughes was likely the lowest paid of any who regularly appeared at the hearings (according to an article in the *National Post*, May 25, 2000). The final bill for the entire process was between $5 million and $10 million, depending on what was included. It was the most extensive and expensive inquiry undertaken by the RCMP Public Complaints Commission.

the question of whether the inquiry was biased was never seriously raised again.

Ted's appointment was well received because of who he was, but it wasn't without controversy. While making the announcement, Heafey stressed again that the role of the inquiry was to look into the conduct of RCMP officers. "The prime minister is not my mandate. I am not going to pretend anything else. My mandate is to look at RCMP conduct," Heafey told a news conference.

Opposition politicians continued to press for a full judicial inquiry. "It's unfortunate that Ms. Heafey decided to put a good driver into a bad vehicle," said Jim Abbott, the Reform Party's critic for the Solicitor General.

Others familiar with Hughes' record were confident he would be able to follow the evidence wherever it led. "If you're investigating police misbehaviour, and you find that they acted inappropriately on a direction, you've got to find that the direction was given. So you follow the evidence there," Stephen Owen told a *Vancouver Sun* reporter in December 1998. "So if there is evidence that the PMO was involved inappropriately, that will come out." By then, Owen had been deputy attorney general of BC and had conducted investigations into security-force killings in several conflict zones.

Rather than dwell on the implosion of the previous panel, Hughes started over. He called together the lawyers representing all the parties and told them that any witness who had appeared before on one of the few days that witnesses were actually heard would have to testify again. He also revisited the issue of providing lawyers for the complainants. Hughes wrote to Lawrence MacAulay, who had replaced Scott as Solicitor General, and said it would be unfair for the government to pay for lawyers for the RCMP and other government departments and not for the protesters. "It must be remembered I am under a directive 'to ensure a full and fair hearing in respect of these complainants,'" he wrote.

Ten days later, MacAulay gave in and agreed the government would pay for up to three lawyers for the complainants.

Hughes also asserted that no one was exempt from being a witness at the hearing, including the prime minister, if the evidence led to his door.

By early March the *Toronto Star* proclaimed that Hughes had taken the APEC fiasco and turned it into a credible inquiry. "This is a man who knows what he is doing... It is finally beginning to look as if Canadians might find out what went wrong 27 months ago."

The hearings were able to get underway in March as scheduled, but not without more controversy.

Jaggi Singh was one of the unofficial leaders of APEC Alert, an ad hoc, non-violent group that organized many of the demonstrations. He was targeted for special attention by the local RCMP even though, as Hughes noted in his interim report, the national threat assessment group didn't consider him to be a threat to the APEC delegates. Singh was a former UBC student who considered himself a full-time political activist. On November 24 he was arrested on an assault charge related to an allegation that at a demonstration two weeks earlier he had shouted through a megaphone directly into the ear of a UBC security guard. Singh was released later that day, but only after signing an undertaking that he would stay away from UBC, which would have prevented him from taking part in any further demonstrations. Singh ignored the undertaking and was arrested again the next day. Hughes later found that the RCMP officer who decided to file an assault charge against Singh as a strategy to keep him off the campus was "terribly wrong." The charge was later dropped.

But when it was time for Singh to testify before Hughes in support of his complaints against the RCMP, he at first said he wouldn't appear unless Hughes met several conditions. Singh was to have been the third witness and his stance threatened to hold up the proceedings.

Hughes was having none of it. He said no one's personal agenda was going to get in the way of his task of assessing the actions of the RCMP. "I consider that to be a display of colossal arrogance and of shameful disrespect for this commission," he said.

When Singh did appear, in mid-April, he started reading a speech. Hughes cut him off. Singh told Hughes he wanted to put his evidence in context and show him what was important.

"I know what's important," Hughes said sharply. "We're ready for you as a witness. Now please take the stand."

Singh continued to spar with Hughes. "After that, every time Singh would get up, he would say, 'I've got a colossal application to make this morning.' He tried his best to bait me but I never let him get under my skin," says Hughes.

By early May, Hughes was increasingly frustrated at the pace of the inquiry, which had heard only nine witnesses with another 130 on the schedule. Hughes suggested he might start sitting on Saturdays or continue without breaks. Later that month he announced new rules. He would not allow witnesses to repeat testimony that had already been heard. Questions would be restricted to specific complaints, and he reserved the right to impose time limits on questions. Time mattered to Hughes. He told the *Globe and Mail* on May 26 that the inquiry had to complete its work expeditiously to maintain public confidence in the process.

The hearings did begin to move more quickly, driven in part by Ted's prodigious capacity for work. When he was writing the report, he told a reporter from the *Saskatoon Star-Phoenix* that the APEC inquiry was "the most intricate and complicated fact pattern I've worked with during my legal career. I work approximately 11 hours a day, six days a week as I draft the report."

But more obstacles lay ahead before he got to that stage. In November the Public Complaints Commission counsel, Marvin Storrow, resigned after it was revealed that he had attended a

Liberal fundraising dinner. He was replaced by Barbara Fisher, a colleague of Storrow's at Blake, Cassels and Graydon, and the hearings carried on.[5]

The issue of whether Chretien would be called to testify continued to hang over the inquiry. Critics argued that if it didn't look into the prime minister's role, the inquiry would not be getting the whole picture. Lawyers for the government insisted that the commission did not have the authority to examine the role of anyone outside the RCMP.

Jean Carle, an aide to the prime minister who was considered to be personally very close to Chretien, testified that he had been involved in security planning, but he denied giving any direct orders to police. No one testified that Chretien himself had been directly involved, a point that proved crucial when Hughes finally ruled on whether he could or should try to subpoena a sitting prime minister.

In January 2000, Fisher told Hughes that since the commission did not have a mandate to look into the actions of the PMO and there was no evidence Chretien gave direct orders to the RCMP, he should not be called as a witness. She said that after 130 witnesses, the inquiry had heard enough. Hughes questioned that advice. He noted that Carle had been involved. "If a member of the Prime Minister's staff involved himself in a security issue... then isn't there a reason for me wanting to hear from the Prime Minister?" Fisher replied that this was a question of the credibility of the previous witnesses, which was an issue for Hughes to address.

Hughes released a written ruling at the end of February. He found that he had the right to call Chretien to testify, but only in narrow circumstances. There had to be evidence that his testimony would shed light on the actions of the RCMP. Since there was no such evidence,

---

5 Fisher later became a BC Supreme Court judge. Storrow was given the Law Society of British Columbia Award in 2012, the same award Hughes received in 2000.

he ruled he could not compel Chretien to testify. At the same time, Hughes recognized that the prime minister's testimony was critical to the wider issue of assuring the public that the inquiry had been able to get the full truth about what happened in Vancouver during the APEC summit. "If the Prime Minister does not give evidence at this hearing, there may well be a 'cloud,' albeit unjustified, over my report," Hughes said. So even though he couldn't compel him to do so, Hughes invited Chretien to answer questions at the inquiry, either in person or by video link.

Chretien declined.

His lawyer wrote to Hughes that the prime minister would not testify because of the precedent it would set. If he were to testify, "there would be no limit to the number of inquiries where a prime minister might be asked to appear not because the evidence warranted an appearance but because it would lend credibility to an inquiry," Ivan Whitehall wrote at the end of February.

In the eyes of a couple of complainants, Chretien's refusal to appear before the inquiry was all the proof they needed that it was inadequate and irrelevant and that the truth about what happened would never be known. They dropped their complaints and walked away.

Final arguments were heard in June 2000.

When Hughes took the assignment in December 1998, he told reporters, "I consider it my 1999 work." That turned out to be optimistic. In fact, the APEC inquiry took him through 2000 and half of 2001. When the hearings wrapped up, he had heard from 153 witnesses on more than 160 sitting days. He also had 700 exhibits to sift through when he sat down to consider the evidence. It took him a year to produce his 453-page report, which with its seven indexes landed with a thud at the end of July 2001.

While it was far from a blanket condemnation of the RCMP, Hughes was sharply critical of the planning that went into policing for the APEC summit and the way it was carried out. He found that

Carle had improperly thrown his weight around with the RCMP, and the Mounties often ignored their responsibility to protect the rights of protesters in their zeal to fulfill their responsibility to protect politicians and maintain order.

While many of the complainants welcomed the findings, others were skeptical that they would have much effect. Jaggi Singh, who by then had moved to Montreal and was out on bail pending charges related to protests there, predicted that "the Hughes report will go down in history as one of the most expensive doorstops ever."

Hughes noted in the report that the RCMP had already "learned considerably from the events of Nov. 25, 1997." But 15 years later it's hard to measure whether the report had much impact. A month after it was released, passenger jets were flown into the World Trade Center and the Pentagon. The skirmishes that sparked the APEC inquiry in Canada loomed less large.

"Once 9/11 came along it just didn't seem like a very important matter that police were using pepper spray when we had the Trade Center exploding," says Hughes.

Residential Schools

> "Mr. Justice Hughes retired from the court in 1980. He was appointed to the court in 1962. So, he's certainly senior and elderly, and of the highest repute. But one wonders how active he's likely to be when he began his career 41 years ago."
>
> REGINA LAWYER TONY MERCHANT, commenting to the *Saskatoon Star-Phoenix* on June 30, 2003, on the appointment of Ted Hughes to head the Alternative Dispute Resolution process for residential school survivors

IF HE HAD been referring to a man of more conventional constitution, the controversial class-action lawyer may have had a point. Hughes was 76 in 2003. The job he had agreed to take on was at the centre of arguably the most shameful chapter in Canadian history, although the enormity of the wrong he was being asked to right had yet to be fully understood by most Canadians.

Residential schools were starting to be recognized for the horrific damage they had done to First Nations, to families and to individual children, who for more than a century were taken from their homes and communities and put into boarding schools designed to strip them of their language and culture. The schools were instruments of an official policy of assimilation and cultural eradication that persisted well into the 20th century.

Beyond that, while it was by no means a universal experience, the largely church-run institutions were houses of horror for many students, who were preyed on physically and sexually by the adults who were charged with their well-being, as well as by their classmates.

Hughes was hired to set up and run the federal government's first serious attempt to provide financial compensation for victims of abuse in residential schools through a process that didn't victimize them further in emotionally fraught and expensive courtroom battles. By the time the Alternative Dispute Resolution (ADR) process was started, there was already a backlog of lawsuits filed against the federal government and churches that Ralph Goodale, the federal minister responsible for Indian Residential Schools Resolution Canada, said would take more than 50 years to clear through the courts.

Tony Merchant was one of the lawyers who had been aggressively signing up former residential school students for a class-action suit. His firm represented about half of the 11,500 former students already suing Ottawa when the ADR program was announced. He described it to the *Star-Phoenix* in June 2003 as "yet another disingenuous stall tactic."

If that was the federal government's intent, they picked the wrong man to adjudicate the program. Hughes started commuting from Victoria to Regina, where the head office of the new program was being set up, for three days a week, a regime he was to follow for the next five years. The Hotel Saskatchewan, the historic railway hotel on Victoria Park, was his second home.[1]

His job was as much administrative as judicial from the start. He had a mandate and a budget but no staff, program or facilities. Office

---

1 When he finished in 2008, the hotel staff who had been serving him in the bar and dining room presented him with a plaque that read, "In Appreciation of your Kindness, Warmth and Generosity that you've shown us at the Hotel Saskatchewan. It has been a Great Honour getting to know you. We wish you all the very Best in your Future."

space had to be acquired, adjudicators hired and trained, and protocols set up for the hearings over which they were to preside. By now, having served as a judge and as a deputy minister overseeing hundreds of employees, and having managed complicated tribunals, Hughes had become a strong administrator.

"He really administered by force of his personality," says Rodger Linka, one of the first adjudicators hired. "He commanded such respect and fondness, but it was mostly that people liked him. He was such a decent man that when he ordered that something be done, they jumped to it."

Which was just as well because Hughes expected nothing less.

"Ted is not somebody you want to disappoint," says Melanie Mahlman, who as president and CEO of the Victoria Hospital Foundation worked with Ted on a successful $25-million fundraising campaign that he co-chaired from 2011 to 2014.[2] Mahlman, like so many others who worked with Hughes, was grateful for his experience and for the consideration he showed his colleagues and employees.

Similarly, Wendi Mackay recalls how Ted stood up for her when he was the deputy attorney general and the minister asked her to work overnight rewriting a speech. When Hughes found out, he called her in and told her that while he was expected to work all hours, she wasn't. He told her to go home and not come back in until she had some rest. She subsequently got a formal letter of apology from the ministry's executive committee after he raised the matter with them. "That really explains the kind of guy that Ted is and how he was always very considerate of other people," she says.

The ADR was an initiative of the federal government, but to allow a measure of independence, Hughes answered to a committee called the

---

2 When the campaign took longer than expected, Hughes moved from being a hands-on co-chair to an honorary role because of other commitments.

Chief Adjudicator's Reference Group or CARG, made up of representatives of the federal government, churches, Indigenous organizations and claimants' counsel. CARG also hired the adjudicators and monitored their training. However, the adjudicators were assigned by Hughes and could only be dismissed with his consent.

Merchant and other lawyers who had anticipated making millions by pursuing lawsuits had reason to be skeptical of the ADR process. Other parties had to be persuaded of its legitimacy as well, including the churches and, most importantly, the abuse victims, their families and communities.

To that end, Irene Fraser was a crucial early hire. Unlike the adjudicators, she was not a lawyer. She was a Métis from Alberta who was working on a justice commission for the Government of Saskatchewan while on leave from the Parole Board of Canada, where she had been working to improve the hearing process for Indigenous inmates. She had been asked to perform a pipe ceremony with Hughes. The ceremony, held in Calgary, was to wish him well and commit him to the program, and to commit the Indigenous community to assist him in his work. Fraser, who had been working most of her career in the Indigenous community, was impressed. "He was a man whose heart was open to whatever was put in front of him. I remember thinking I would like to work with this man, that would be sort of a dream."

Hughes brought her on board and they quickly became a cohesive and effective team. Fraser helped Hughes develop the training for adjudicators and used her contacts to bring in residential school survivors to talk to the adjudicators as part of the training. They both did a bit of everything that had to be done, especially in the early days. "We worked at implementing the ideas that had been put together and the structures that had been given. It was a delightful time, an interesting time and Ted was magnificent," Fraser says. "You work just about 24 hours around the clock. We developed policy, we developed practices, we wrote, we met, I put together the training, we put together the process where we put out the call for adjudicators, we trained adjudicators."

The adjudicators were lawyers who were hired on contract. The initial plan called for 32 adjudicators, who would preside over the hearings, and a chief adjudicator (Hughes), who would review all of the adjudicators' rulings and be in a position to handle appeals. Claimants who entered the ADR process also had the option of going back to court if they didn't like the settlement awarded by the adjudicator.

Dan Shapiro, a Saskatoon litigator, was a member of the first group hired. "It was very unusual and fascinating training. We had historians and judges and cultural experts," he says. "We had survivors. There was a certain amount of cultural training that took place, and Irene took care of that. That was the most fascinating eight or nine days that I ever spent in my work life." Shapiro later became the chief adjudicator of the Independent Assessment Program, which took over from the ADR in 2007.

The ADR process was designed from the start to be less confrontational than the adversarial justice system that residential school survivors would otherwise have to navigate if they were to receive any compensation through the courts. The basic model was in place when Hughes was hired. Claimants who chose to use the ADR process would have their claims investigated to see if they had in fact attended a residential school and that they were who they said they were. Then they would get a hearing before an adjudicator, who would use a point system—not unlike those used by life-insurance companies—to make an award based on the nature of their claim as validated by the adjudicator. The chart was a grim detailing of a range of physical and sexual abuse. Points were also awarded for consequential harm, the lasting legacy of childhood abuse that mentally crippled survivors as adults. "Some felt it was a cold, meat chart kind of thing, but as far as I was concerned it worked well," says Hughes. The federal government had set aside $1.7 billion for the process. This included almost $1 billion for compensation, which for individuals was expected to range from $5,000 to $245,000.

Hughes and Fraser set the tone for the hearings. They were completely in tune over how claimants were to be treated and what the hearings were for.

"My father had been a residential school survivor," Fraser says. "One of the things I would say to the adjudicators is that when I'm watching the hearing, I see my father sitting in the chair and I want to know that you have treated my father with the utmost respect."

Lawyers for the claimants, the churches and the government could be at the hearing and were allowed to make statements, but they were not allowed to cross-examine or directly question the claimants. Only the adjudicators could question the claimants. They had to tread a fine line between ensuring the claimants were telling the truth and letting people who had already been victimized know that the hearing was for their benefit and that they could expect to be fully heard and believed.

As much as possible, the hearings were held in the home communities of the claimants and sometimes in their homes. "You would often be able to interview them in the presence of photos of their family members, and that was a really good way to help to establish enough of a bond that people would feel comfortable sharing their experiences," says Shapiro.

For all the good the ADR process did, it wasn't enough to address all the wrongs of more than a century of residential schools in Canada. In 2005, Ottawa appointed former Supreme Court justice Frank Iacobucci to work with Indigenous organizations, former students and their lawyers, the churches and the government to come up with an agreement that would allow for a more encompassing resolution to the sorry legacy of residential schools in Canada. The Indian Residential Schools Settlement Agreement he negotiated included an expanded arbitration program, called the Independent Assessment Program

(IAP), and a Common Experience Payment for all former students of residential schools regardless of whether they had been physically or sexually abused.[3] The Settlement Agreement also established the National Truth and Reconciliation Commission and set up measures to support healing and to commemorate former residential school students and their families and communities.

The IAP incorporated the successful aspects of the ADR and corrected some of its shortcomings. The ADR had different compensation levels for some provinces based on earlier court rulings; as well, claimants could go through the hearing process, and if they weren't happy with the result they could go back to court. The IAP ruling was binding, and new guidelines made it easier for students to be compensated for abuse by fellow students, not just staff at residential schools.

Dan Ish became the first chief adjudicator for the IAP in 2007. Hughes, who had fallen and required surgery again, this time on his right knee, stayed on into early 2008 with the ADR, which was continuing for those claimants who wanted to stay with the old system rather than jump to the new.

Ish says the IAP process was 80 per cent the same as ADR. At the heart of both was the hearing, which gave the process credibility for its ability to ferret out the truth while encouraging survivors to recount events that had in many cases haunted them all their lives.

"And that all started with Ted and Irene just giving us the bare bones of what these hearings might look like, what we could do to try to create a comfortable, safe and supportive atmosphere and above

---

3 The Indian Residential Schools Settlement Agreement was a multi-party agreement dated May 8, 2006, between Canada, represented by Frank Iacobucci; plaintiffs, as represented by the National Consortium and Merchant Law Group; independent counsel; the Assembly of First Nations and Inuit representatives; the General Synod of the Anglican Church of Canada; the United Church of Canada; the Presbyterian Church of Canada; and Roman Catholic entities.

all, whatever the legal outcome, that the people who appeared before us would know that they had been heard and they had been treated respectfully," says Shapiro, who became the chief adjudicator in the IAP when Ish retired in 2013. "That wasn't in the ADR model and yet Ted, with Irene's support, insured that although it was not written, that was going to be an unwritten rule by which we would all be expected to operate."

Hughes didn't attend hearings. His role was to review the decisions to ensure they were in line with the established standards, and he read transcripts of the hearings. Visitors to the Regina office would often find Hughes and Fraser almost hidden behind piles of folders late in the evening. He also kept the bureaucracy at bay, fighting to make sure that the adjudicators could continue to do their jobs without undue interference.

Adjudicators were given contracts with limits on how much they could work that made sense from the point of view of controlling costs but did not always mesh well with the reality of the job that had to be done. Rodger Linka was on the road near Calgary in his early days as an adjudicator when he got an email from Ottawa telling him that he had used up his contract and was to cease and desist all work for the Government of Canada and head back to Regina. He had two more hearings set up, and the claimants and all the other participants were already in place.

"I got hold of Ted immediately," Rodger remembers, "and he started thundering. He said, 'You do those hearings. I'm telling you that you must do those hearings.'

"I said, 'I know.'

"He said, 'You ignore anything that Ottawa tells you and you do those hearings and I'll get to the bottom of this.'

"He worked tirelessly to get that problem solved, even to the point when things were going wrong of saying, 'I'm on the next plane to Ottawa.'

"That's the kind of guy that he was. If you were on the right side of things, if you had done no wrong, he would fight for you and defend you. That's the quality that really shines out about Ted—he's fearless, he's just so fearless when it comes to righting the wrong."

There was a wrong side to be on, however, Linka adds. "Ted absolutely detested meetings. His idea of a good meeting was one that would end in 15 minutes. Government types think that they are working when they go to meetings. He would get into these meetings that would go on, and all of a sudden he would start shifting in his chair and the look on his face would change—you just couldn't miss the annoyance on his face and he couldn't get out of meetings faster."

During the transition to the IAP process, a new employee was dragging out meetings with questions and arguments Ted thought were a waste of time. He put in a quiet word with the new chief adjudicator, and "that person was no longer with us," Linka recalls.

The hearings were difficult for the claimants, many of whom were telling their stories, which they had never shared with families and friends, for the first time. But they were also emotionally draining for the adjudicators, who day after day were hearing how young, vulnerable children were abused and how that abuse affected their whole life.

"It was gut-wrenching. But that's how it was," says Ken Halvorson, Hughes' former colleague from Saskatchewan, who became an adjudicator and wrote a manual for lawyers who appeared at the hearings. "It was bad enough that it would be a priest, but mostly it was older kids at the schools that abused them. They couldn't get away from it, because they'd go to bed at night and it was the other kids there."

At the same time, adjudicators often found the experience to be uplifting, as the survivors told them that the experience of being able to tell their stories and have someone believe them was as important as the money.

Ish, a former dean of the University of Saskatchewan law school, who became an adjudicator at the start of the ADR, tells of flying into a remote village to hold a hearing at the home of an elderly former student. "He was sick in bed and dying of cancer, and we held the hearing and, true to form, like so many, his son was there with him. He was in his 80s. I was asking questions, and I always tell them it's their day. Of course we had to cover certain things, but if they wanted to talk about things that were not technically really relevant, I'd let them go on to feel like they were getting everything out. So I'd say, 'Here's your turn to tell your story,' and I would always ask what was your worst experience and what was your best, and interestingly, the worst was often not what the claim was about. Often it was not being able to see their parents, that kind of thing. And their best often, for boys, was sports.

"This man had funny stories and we were all listening. When we were finished, he looked at us and said, 'I'd like to thank you for coming because I didn't think I was worth it for people to come up and hear my story and I've never told my story fully to anybody else.'

"That just kind of made it. So when I say there were very sad stories but so many ended sort of like that, sort of on a high note. When I started the whole thing I didn't think there would be this kind of restorative, therapeutic value to it. I really changed my mind about that."

Stan Hagen and the Moral Fixer

"SO, WHY DID they hire Hughes in the first place?"

From a political point of view, the headline on Mike Smyth's column in the tabloid Vancouver *Province* on April 9, 2006, posed a good question, a question that the pundit never really went on to address. Hughes had just delivered a scathing report the Government of BC had commissioned him to write. In it he detailed how the Ministry of Children and Family Development was failing to protect vulnerable children and prescribed significant reforms.

At the press conference following the release of the report, a reporter told Hughes that Premier Gordon Campbell maintained the problems he identified had nothing to do with cuts to funding of services.

"He was wrong," Hughes stated flatly, providing front-page fodder for the next day's newspapers and further enhancing his reputation in the Victoria press gallery as the Mighty Hughes.

"Devastating" was Smyth's review of Hughes' response. "Nobody knows how to smack down a government or a premier like Ted Hughes."

So, back to the headline. Why would a politically astute and message-sensitive government hire someone it knew, or should have known, would write a report that would reflect so poorly on its record?

To start, there was a crisis brewing.

Hughes' appointment followed the government's damning admission in the fall that 713 child deaths had never been properly investigated following a reorganization of the child protection system in which the semi-independent Children's Commission was eliminated in 2002, and the responsibility for such investigations was transferred to the Coroners Service.

In response, Judge Thomas Gove was appointed to head a review of child protection services. Ten years earlier, in 1995, Gove had written a report on the torture and murder of five-year-old Matthew Vaudreuil by his mother when both of them were under the watch and care of the provincial child protection system. That report led to the government bringing all the services for children and families into a single ministry. Gove had to withdraw from the 2005 review, however, because he could not get leave from his court duties.

Hughes was persuaded to accept the assignment despite a schedule that took him to Saskatchewan four days a week as the chief adjudicator of the Indian Residential Schools ADR process. The appointment of Hughes as a replacement to head what was originally a five-member panel gave instant credibility to the government's response to the crisis. Once again he was being put in the window.

Even as the original panel was pared from five to one as a result of potential conflicts for the other members who had connections to the system, Hughes' already firmly entrenched reputation was such that no opposition politician dared suggest that anything he produced would be less than thorough or in any way a whitewash. On the contrary, from a strategic point of view the opposition welcomed Hughes' appointment. Despite prominent roles he had filled since then, Hughes was still best known in BC for his report that led to the resignation of Premier Bill Vander Zalm. Few in the legislature's press gallery would have argued with Smyth's assessment that "at 78, he remains our most respected and fearless watchman on politicians."

From a political perspective, it was the government that had good reason to be nervous about what Hughes might produce. "He has always been seen as somebody who had such credibility and judgment and presence, he was revered by the people who worked around him," says David Emerson, who was deputy minister to the premier when Vander Zalm resigned.[1] "I guess, by extension, governments and politicians who sometimes find themselves in a situation where the truth hurts would look at Ted with great trepidation."

But Stan Hagen, the minister of Children and Family Development who persuaded Hughes to take on the review, had a personal connection from an earlier time, when it was his own behaviour that was under scrutiny.

Hagen, a devout Lutheran who was well liked on both sides of the legislature, was more interested in the details of administration than political intrigue. He was the son of a Norwegian immigrant who had started a prominent travel agency in BC, and he was running his own ready-mix concrete business on Vancouver Island when he was first elected to the legislature under the Social Credit banner in the 1986 election that brought Vander Zalm to power. Hagen was soon in cabinet as the minister of a new portfolio that brought together colleges, universities and labour-market training. Unlike many of his predecessors who dealt with higher education and training, he was respected as a politician who listened to and understood the concerns of post-secondary institutions, even if he couldn't always deliver on their wish lists.

---

1 Emerson, who also had an extensive background in the private sector, ran for the federal parliament and was elected as a Liberal in 2004, serving as a minister under Prime Minister Paul Martin. He was re-elected in 2005, when the Liberals lost power, and crossed the floor to serve in the cabinet of Conservative prime minister Stephen Harper, much to the chagrin of many constituents in his Vancouver Kingsway riding.

But in 1987 he was in trouble. The New Democrats discovered that he was still a director of Comox Valley Ready Mix Ltd., the concrete company he had owned and managed before his election. The company sold concrete to a research farm operated by the University of British Columbia, putting Hagen not just in a potential conflict of interest but also potentially in violation of the Constitution Act, which forbids ministers of the Crown from doing business with the government.

When the NDP raised the issue of Hagen's apparent conflict, Vander Zalm's cabinet happened to be on a retreat, along with deputy ministers and the premier's abrasive chief of staff, David Poole. Poole told Hagen he had to resign to make the issue go away for his boss. It was a devastating blow for Hagen, who loved the job and was blindsided by the allegation, which he explained as an oversight by his lawyer, who had not immediately followed his instructions to remove him from the company's management.

Hagen's deputy was Isabel Lloyd (then Isabel Kelly), who had turned to Hughes in the past when she needed help to save some semblance of the Human Rights Commission during the cutbacks in 1983. She called on him again to help Hagen. "He really needed someone who could say, 'Now wait a minute, all is not lost here,'" she says.

Hughes helped Hagen write a temporary resignation letter and undertook an investigation to see if he had been in conflict. In his report to the premier, Ted said that Hagen had made mistakes and that he had been in violation of the guidelines, but there were extenuating circumstances and there had been no violation of the Constitution Act. That allowed Vander Zalm to bring Hagen back into cabinet with some confidence that he wouldn't be crucified by the opposition.

To that end, Hughes went beyond his legal opinion to state in a memo to Vander Zalm: "I draw on 18 years of experience, where day in and day out I made credibility assessments of my fellow citizens, to tell you that in my judgment Stanley Hagen is an honourable man of high integrity."

Nineteen years later, when Hagen needed a credible investigation into his ministry, he turned to Hughes, knowing that while the former judge and conflict commissioner would not pull any punches, he would give the government and the ministry a fair hearing and come back with a report that looked for solutions rather than just laying blame.

The review turned out to be a much larger task than Hughes had been told to expect, taking months rather than weeks. Hughes found "a child welfare system that has been buffeted by an unmanageable degree of change." He found a "revolving door" of ministers and senior managers, and a parade of new programs, all instituted at a time of funding cutbacks, that were putting untenable pressure on front-line workers and the vulnerable people they were supposed to be looking after.

He recommended a new plan for external oversight with the creation of a Representative for Children and Youth, who would be an independent officer reporting directly to the legislature rather than to the minister responsible for child welfare.

Hughes spent four and a half months on the review, all while commuting to Regina for his other job as the head of the ADR process. And once he was done, he continued to press the government to act on his recommendations, most of which were eventually adopted.

Bob Plecas, the veteran BC bureaucrat who reviewed the system 10 years later, called the report the gold standard and "the blueprint for everybody to follow."

"Is it perfect?" he asked rhetorically in an interview. "Of course not. You can't design an administrative system that is going to stop some guy from taking their kid and smashing their brains against the wall because they are filled up with coke and alcohol. But it's a good model."

This was not the last time Hughes would be called on to look at how tough it is for a government to protect vulnerable children. Or how bureaucratic failures can exact a terrible human price.

Loss

ON A GREY March day, high water in Shawnigan Lake covers the shore end of the dock at the Hughes cottage on the West Arm. The maples have yet to leaf and the grounds are littered with the detritus of winter. For Ted, this is a summer place and the traditional opening weekend is still two months away.

The cottage he and Helen built more than 30 years ago is now aging and undergoing some minor renovations. The dock was rebuilt two years ago. A new lower deck was added the year before. The partner of one of their granddaughters is doing the work, and there is a lot of cleanup to finish before the Victoria Day weekend.

The cottage is a gathering place for the Hughes family, a place where memories have been made for generations of kids and grandkids—of warm days swimming off the dock, barbecues and Ted endlessly driving the water-skiing boat in circles around the lake. Helen and Ted have done most of their entertaining here.

Yet even as it is readied for another summer of fun, the lake cottage is tinged with sadness for Ted. So many memories linger of Sheila Hetschko, Helen and Ted's only daughter, who used to walk the grounds with Ted and work the gardens. She would have taken it over. Now it is in the hands of her children, and the rest of the family have visitation rights.

As an RN, Sheila cared for seniors in a nursing home in Shawnigan Lake and lived nearby in Duncan. There she met her second husband, Barry Hetschko. He would come to visit his grandmother. From the nursing home it was a short drive to the Hughes family cottage.

"She used to come here Sundays when she would come off shift at 4 o'clock, and her kids were always here," says Ted. "It was always a happy time to see her coming in her uniform. She loved it here. I miss her so."

In October 2010, Sheila came home from a late shift and went to bed. Her husband got up and went to work in the morning without waking her. When she didn't show up for work later that day, her employer called to find out where she was. She had died in the night. She had not been sick and no cause of death was ever established. She was 51.

Ted was devastated. He and Helen had seen her two days earlier at a birthday party for the fiancé of one of her daughters. Helen misses her too, but says Sheila was Ted's little girl.

"Sheila and I were very, very close. I came from a family of boys; I had no sister. I had David as the first-born son and just never expected to have a daughter, which I wanted very much," Ted says.

He told a friend: "No day will ever be the same."

Despite his grief, he immediately pitched in. Sheila had four children, one of whom was still in school. Barry worked full-time in Duncan. For the next year and a half, at least once a week Ted would go to Chef on the Run in Victoria, buy dinner and drive 45 minutes over the Malahat to Duncan to help out.

Religion had always played a strong role in Ted's life. He went to Sunday School and was confirmed in the Anglican church. He married the minister's daughter. He and Helen raised their own children as Anglicans. In Victoria he regularly attended and supported St. John the Divine Anglican Church.

But Sheila's death shook his faith.

"To have her taken away, on the basis where medical science has got no explanation for her death, really caused me to stand back and take a look at religious life and the belief in God."

Six years later, Ted still goes to church occasionally, but the nature of his faith has changed. He still believes the church is a force for good in the world as an outlet for serving others. He says God is a force that he taps into from time to time for strength and guidance in pursuit of the common good as he "lives out what remains of his earthly life."

But he no longer believes in a "personal and petitionable" god, a god capable of answering individual prayers.[1] A god that could answer his prayers and keep his children safe.

---

1 Hughes got the phrase "personal and petitionable" from an article in the *Anglican Journal* about former CBC news anchor Don Newman, whose faith was similarly shaken by the death of his son and wife.

Lighting a Candle

THE PHOTO OF Phoenix Victoria Hope Sinclair that opens the report of the inquiry into her death shows a small girl in a big hat with a new toy, smiling shyly at the camera. She looks happy. The picture is undated. She was five when she was beaten to death.

The three-volume report is entitled *The Legacy of Phoenix Sinclair: Achieving the Best for All Our Children*. It is the product of the largest and, at a final cost of $14 million, the most expensive public inquiry ever held in Manitoba. Hughes was 83 when he got a call in March 2011 from Manitoba attorney general Andrew Swan asking him to take it on. Hughes was already well known in Manitoba for conducting the inquiries into the arrest of Harvey Pollack and the Headingley jail riot. And five years earlier he had conducted the review of BC's child protection system.

The Phoenix Sinclair inquiry again brought Hughes into a world that was foreign to his own sheltered upbringing in a happy, stable home in Saskatoon. Phoenix lived in the world experienced by too many Indigenous children growing up in Canada.

The population of Manitoba, like that of Saskatchewan, has one of the highest proportions of First Nations and Métis people in the country. As Ted started to appreciate in earlier assignments, they are more likely to experience poverty, substandard living conditions, neglect and abuse than others, are more likely to end up in prison or be taken into care as children. At the time of the inquiry, 16 per cent of Manitobans were Indigenous. Yet more than 80 per cent of the children in care were Indigenous, and they were being taken into care at a rate 12 times higher than non-Indigenous children.

Phoenix Sinclair was born on April 23, 2000, in Winnipeg to Indigenous teenagers who themselves were neglected and abused as children and had grown up in Manitoba's child welfare system. She was immediately taken into care after her parents, 18-year-old Samantha Kematch and 19-year-old Steve Sinclair, were judged by a social worker to have little interest in the child or capacity to raise her. Over the next five years she was cared for by foster parents, friends of the family, her father, and her mother and a stepfather at different times. Through all of that she was reported to be a healthy, happy child until her mother came to take her back around her fourth birthday. They lived with her mother's new partner, Karl Wesley Mackay, who had a history of domestic violence that social workers could have discovered if they had looked for it in their own central database. Phoenix was often locked in her room at their home in Winnipeg's North End. Her final few months were spent on the Fisher River Reserve north of Winnipeg, where Mackay's family was from. Although other children in the home were treated relatively well, she was often kept locked in a cold basement, where she was sadistically beaten with a handle from a refrigerator and an iron rod. When she died, her mother and Mackay wrapped her lifeless body in plastic and buried it in a shallow grave near the town dump. They repainted the basement and moved away.

Phoenix had become invisible to the community and to the welfare system that was supposed to protect her. A few months after she was killed, a welfare worker noted in her mother's file that Phoenix was "A + W"—alive and well—apparently taking the word of her mother, who was pregnant again. Nine months went by before anyone in authority learned of her death, and then it was only after one of the other children living in the home where she died finally told a relative what had happened.

By the time Hughes started the Phoenix Sinclair inquiry, there had already been half a dozen reviews and a trial, at which her mother and her stepfather were convicted of murder and sentenced to life in prison without a chance of parole for 25 years.

The horrific details of the last few months of Phoenix Sinclair's life had a familiar, ghastly ring for British Columbians who remembered Matthew Vaudreuil. Matthew was also only five when he was killed by his mother after enduring ongoing neglect and abuse, despite the fact that both he and his mother had been in the care of the BC welfare system for most of their lives.

The details of Matthew's death in 1992 sparked an inquiry into child protection services in British Columbia led by Judge Thomas Gove, who titled the report he produced in 1995 "Matthew's Story." Gove used the disturbing details of Matthew's life to tell the story of a dysfunctional system that failed again and again in its primary purpose of protecting a vulnerable child.

Hughes followed the same approach in his inquiry into Phoenix's death. He insisted that those involved in the investigation and the writing of the report never lose sight of the tragic life and death of Phoenix Sinclair, the reason they were there. When told by an associate that Manitoba policy would never permit the picture of Phoenix to be used at the front of the report, Hughes said, "Leave it to me," and it was done.

"That's what I really love about Ted; he never forgets what is truly important and he never lets us forget either," says Kathleen Keating, who worked with Hughes on the report as she had done on several of his earlier assignments.

As usual, his first task was to hire staff. All other things being equal, he wanted a woman to serve as commission counsel. "I felt it was time for a woman to lead one of these major inquiries," he says.

After seeking advice and conducting interviews, he picked Sherri Walsh, a partner in a small Winnipeg firm with a background in social justice issues. Walsh was out in the country with her horse when she got a call on her cellphone from Jeffrey Schnoor, Manitoba's deputy minister of justice, who had Ted sitting in his office. He told Walsh that Hughes had just been appointed commissioner of the Phoenix Sinclair inquiry, and he wanted to interview her for the role of commission counsel. Hughes was flying to Victoria that night, so Walsh drove back into town. They met in her office and hit it off. By the time she drove him to the airport, they had settled on a plan that would consume more of their time and energy over the next two and a half years than either of them had imagined.

As he had while he was heading the residential schools ADR program in Regina, Hughes commuted from Victoria to Winnipeg, where he stayed at the Delta Hotel. It was near the offices acquired for the work of the commission and near the convention centre where many of the hearings were held. He kept a gruelling schedule for someone of any age, but even though he was now in his mid-80s, he always showed up for long days of hearings alert and attentive, with a complete grasp of the testimony and the thousands of pages of material that were being submitted to the inquiry.

"He went back to Victoria almost every weekend. We all commented that that was more travel than any of us had the stamina for. He just had tremendous stamina for anyone of any age. His age was never an issue," says Walsh.

Based on his experience dealing with residential school survivors, Hughes was concerned that people involved with Phoenix Sinclair and who had suffered neglect and abuse in their own lives not be further traumatized by the inquiry. In addition to the usual boardroom found in most lawyers' offices, where potential witnesses were interviewed, the commission staff set up a warm room, with ordinary living room furniture, where sensitive witnesses could be interviewed in a less formal setting.

Hughes agreed to report back in a year. But a series of legal and procedural challenges delayed the start of hearings. The Manitoba Government and General Employees' Union, which represents social workers and child welfare agencies, challenged Hughes' authority to hold an inquiry. Their protest failed. Then the union and First Nations child welfare agencies sought to keep private the identities of the 27 individual social workers and supervisors who had been involved with Phoenix and her mother over the years of her life, again without success. Hughes stood by the principle that the point of a public inquiry is to allow the public to view as much as possible of both the proceedings and the results.

The hearings were televised and were in the news for months.

Hughes' original estimate of a few dozen witnesses soon ballooned into more than 150 potential witnesses, of whom 126 appeared at the inquiry. As in earlier assignments as a judge, a civil servant and an independent commissioner, Hughes found that the actions of individuals were often rooted in larger problems that could not be solved by any decree or order he might make. The scope of the inquiry was officially expanded to include an examination of how poverty and other socio-economic conditions factored into Phoenix's death.

"It's been made clear to us through the course of our investigations that in order to make recommendations to better protect Manitoba children, the focus of this inquiry needs to extend beyond the strict parameters of the operations of the child welfare system," Walsh announced in July 2012.

The addition came more than a year after his appointment, but both Hughes and Walsh knew from the beginning that they would be looking at more than just cracks in the government welfare system. "From the very first day he sat in my office, he said he wanted to do something to address the inequities that exist in the Indigenous community," says Walsh.

What became known as Phase Three of the hearings started with the testimony of a panel of grandmother elders, or *kokum* in the Cree language. "Ted was speaking to them elder to elder, grandparent to grandparent, and that was really tremendous, wonderful to watch and important for the evidence that came out," says Walsh.

By the time the hearings wrapped up, the deadline for reporting had been extended twice. The commission lawyers moved back to Walsh's office, where they worked with Hughes on the report. Kathleen Keating was brought in, as she had been for APEC and other assignments with Hughes, as the primary writer and editor. They were behind and the latest deadline was looming. Hughes told them that he thought he could get another extension but he didn't want to. He was concerned that the longer they took to produce the report, the less value it would have.

"This was not bad time management on Ted's part," says Keating. "There had been so many interruptions in the process, with court applications and so on, that he was committed to meeting that deadline, and we did it."

They worked long days and into the evening in a windowless boardroom surrounded by boxes of files. Ted kept a bowl of candy on the table. He had never been much for exercise. Keating recalls they would buy sandwiches in the food court when they left their hotel in the morning. The sandwiches were their lunch. The leftovers were dinner.

"On the last night before the morning deadline," she says, "Ted did excuse himself at 11 o'clock just because he had a meeting with the premier at 9 AM and he needed to get back to his hotel to prepare for that.

"Throughout that process he read every paper and every transcript that was given to him and he always asked the right questions, he listened to the answers and he was always prepared to change his mind so long as the evidence was there and the result would align with his principles.

"But most importantly, he kept that five-year-old girl at the forefront of everyone's minds. He mentioned her often and he measured every potential recommendation for the potential to help children like her."

Hughes found that Phoenix Sinclair died at the hands of adults who should not have been left in a position to do her harm. They were in that position because several individuals who should have been looking after her welfare made decisions that left her at risk and that were often in violation of the rules and procedures they should have followed. But he also found that those individuals were working in a system that was asking too much of them, with unmanageable caseloads and, at times, poor communication among agencies with shared responsibilities.

With the testimony heard in Phase Three, Ted stretched his mandate from the personal tragedy that started with Phoenix's dysfunctional parents back to the way First Nations and Métis have been treated in the land of their ancestors.

"To Canada, a country that purports to be a leader in the advancement of human rights, both at home and abroad, the foregoing facts have to be a significant national embarrassment. The problem cannot be solved by Manitoba acting alone. With these statistics staring me in the face, I am most uncomfortable being confined to the boundaries of a provincial public inquiry. Included in the recommendations at the end of this chapter will be one addressing the inequity of which I speak. I believe that this is as far as I am empowered to go in the search for a solution to this unacceptable state of affairs. That solution will not be simple and will not be quickly accomplished. But for a multitude of reasons, and especially for the sake of the future of generations of Aboriginal children, that solution must be found," he wrote in the final report, which was delivered in December 2013, six months after Ted's 86th birthday.

After completing the report, Hughes continued to work to try to get the over-representation of Indigenous children in government care on the national agenda. He met with BC premier Christy Clark and Manitoba premier Greg Selinger, who agreed to put the issue on the agenda for a meeting of premiers in Charlottetown in August 2014.

In an interview with the *Winnipeg Free Press* at the time, Hughes compared the issue of Indigenous children in care with missing and murdered Indigenous women. "It's traceable to the same underlying features that have caused the overrepresentation of Aboriginal people in our jails, the suicide rate, inadequate housing and substance abuse," he said. "My hope would be that the action plan the premier proposed to the meeting would be widened to look at those underlying problems. I just think it's a real opportunity to take hold of this problem that the Fathers of Confederation didn't get right 150 years ago. A lot of today's problems were introduced at that time."

In the eight decades since Ted was a boy in Saskatoon with little awareness of what was going on with Canada's Indigenous people, he had come to a point where he considered fallout from colonization to be one of the most important issues in the country, and his work on the file the most important of his career. He got there by paying attention to the people who came into his life through his work as a judge, a treaty negotiator and an independent commissioner looking into the failures of the social and legal systems in which Indigenous Canadians were over-represented and under-served. He got there by listening to their stories with full attention and respect, even when he was unable to help them individually or immediately.

In turn, First Nations and Métis grew to respect Hughes.

"You cannot work as a non-Aboriginal person within the Aboriginal community if you are not respected by the people, if they don't think of you as someone who is fair and someone who is going to have them somewhat in their corner," says Irene Fraser, who helped Ted set up the ADR process for former residential school residents. "By 'in their corner' I don't mean that there's a bias such that it moves beyond the point of fairness, but you have to be seen as being fair."

In February 2015, Hughes wrote an opinion piece for the *Globe and Mail*, laying out in another forum what he believed were the historical roots of the violence and poverty experienced by Indigenous Canadians and what was needed now to repair the damage.

"It's time that Canadians, including their political leaders, come to appreciate what those reasons are, what results flow from them and what would realistically help bring the scales into balance, in order to give aboriginal people an equal chance to participate and succeed in mainstream society," he wrote. "The reasons for the conditions above are rooted in the imposition of a foreign way of life on aboriginal people at the time of European occupation, commonly known as colonization. Another component was the residential school program, which brought misery to so many. There was also cultural dislocation and loss of identity, and segregation on what became known as reserves.

"What have been the results? Widespread, large-scale poverty tops the list, associated with poor and inadequate housing conditions. Families struggle because attaining an acceptable standard of living simply isn't economically viable. Educational opportunities are often deficient. Addictions can take hold. Social exclusion and isolation frequently follow.

"What is the solution? There must be a sensible and achievable one, otherwise life will become increasingly uncomfortable for those of us who owe our presence on these lands to our immigrant forebears. The goal that must eventually be met is equality of opportunity for those disadvantaged by colonization and its results."

The op-ed piece for the *Globe* was Hughes' first return to writing for a newspaper since college. But throughout his career he understood the power of the press and how to use it to his advantage.

Positive Press: The Benefits of a Lifelong Affair with Newspapers

YOUNG TED HUGHES didn't get the gold watch that was the customary reward for a paper carrier with a perfect service record. But there was a war on in 1941 and '42, and years later Hughes said he considered the watch he never received for delivering about 100 copies of the *Saskatoon Star-Phoenix* every afternoon without a single complaint to be his contribution to the war effort.

Delivering newspapers was a serious undertaking in 1941. The contract he signed on the day before his 14th birthday required Ted to buy his papers in advance from the *Star-Phoenix* and make collections from his customers. He was also expected to add to the list of customers by canvassing and "to assist the Company in every way possible in extending the number of subscribers."

Ted's early start in the newspaper business didn't lead to a career in the medium, although he did try his hand at writing for the student paper in university. But it blossomed into a lifelong love of reading newspapers and an understanding of the role of the media and reporters that served him well throughout his long and varied career.

Colleagues noted his habit of scooping up any newspaper he would come across in airports or on the ferry and burying his nose in it. He continues to read up to four papers a day in his 80s. "My pleasure is sitting down with my couple of glasses of beer and reading newspapers," he says. "I enjoy reading the stories of criminal cases that seem to have a national component, stories that involve constitutional issues and I read all the columnists in those four papers.

"I'm glad I have that interest and I hope I don't lose it because I don't watch movies. I don't get many books read, but that's my choice. I just love reading newspapers, and I think because of that I became attuned to media issues, what the issues would be in situations where I was involved. I think the background that I developed in understanding media was of assistance to me."

He was never a publicity hound, but he knew the importance of positive press and he knew how to get his side of any story across when he thought it was time to do so. Or at least he did most of the time. And when he was unhappy, he didn't suffer in silence. He was never shy about invoking the authority of the legal system that he knew so well, but he also knew how to complain effectively.

As a judge, in a way that was unusual at the time and unheard of in recent years, Hughes would talk to reporters he trusted about cases he was presiding over to help them get their stories straight.

Marsha Erb was a court reporter for the *Star-Phoenix* in the 1970s and later became a lawyer and a judge in Calgary. "He was really kind and patient and explained things, and he wanted me to get my articles correct as much as I did, of course. There's nothing worse than as a judge seeing things in the press, and I've seen this a number of times in which I thought, 'Was I there? Was that my case?'

"He would never talk about what he was doing with something or what he was leaning toward or what it was looking like. He would just carefully explain what stuff meant."

Bill Peterson, who later became the editor and publisher of the *Star-Phoenix*, appreciated not only that Hughes would explain procedures, but that he ran his courtroom in a way that made trials easier to cover. “He was an active listener. He would interpret things and sort of summarize things, and I don’t know about the other participants in the trial, but as a reporter that was tremendously useful to me.

“You could tell when the end of the day was drawing near because Ted would move into a mode of, OK, this is what we heard today, this is where we are headed tomorrow, everybody [be] ready for that.

“From a reporter’s point of view he was a great guy because he would talk to you. He would encourage you that if you didn’t understand something that was going on in the trial to come and see him, which was more open than most of the other old-fart judges, but also, God help you if you got something wrong,” Peterson says.

When David William Threinen, the child-killer, was sentenced, the *Star-Phoenix* got it very wrong. Erb was covering the trial. After filing her story, she was shocked to see the headline, which said that Hughes had given Threinen parole. Hughes gave Threinen life in prison with the mandatory parole provision in effect at the time. He had no control over whether the child killer would be paroled, a distinction the headline writer failed to understand.

“It looks like he was letting this guy off or giving him a lighter sentence,” says Erb. “I just about had a heart attack.”

She complained to the city desk but the editor in charge couldn’t see the difference. “So I went roaring over to the courthouse and banged on Hughes’ door, and he was sitting in there with some other judge and I said, ‘I didn’t write that headline.’

“He said, ‘I know you didn’t but I’m going to have to talk to Struthers about this.’[1] He was annoyed, obviously.”

“The headline on the story was dead wrong,” says Peterson. “You have no idea the hell that was raised. In my 20-some-odd years at the newspaper it was the only time we recalled the paper from the

---

1 James Struthers, then executive vice-president of the *Star-Phoenix*.

newsstands in the morning, and it was the result of Ted just raising proper hell with the editor."

Hughes socialized with reporters he got to know in Saskatoon, but he also had definite views about their role and responsibilities. In 1975 he laid them out in a speech to the Saskatchewan Journalists' Association in Saskatoon.

"There is no group of people wielding greater power and influence than you do over the minds of the adult segment of our population," he said. "Indeed, I compare your position of influence over the thinking process of the masses with that of the teaching profession over the youngsters in the classroom... So important is the work that you do, in the sense I have just indicated, that there is no place in your field of endeavour for persons not totally committed to following a life of professionalism."

Ted had a lower profile for the first couple of years after he moved to BC. He still read papers but wasn't in them as often. That changed when he became the deputy attorney general and was thrust into the spotlight during the Vander Zalm years. His willingness to talk to reporters, both in a couple of extraordinary press conferences when the fate of politicians was at stake, and behind the scenes, garnered him great respect in the legislature press gallery. By the time he was asked to determine whether Premier Vander Zalm was in a conflict of interest, there was little doubt which of the two men had greater credibility, even before the report was released.

"I got to know people like Vaughn Palmer, Les Leyne and Jim Hume quite well and felt that they were responsible, trustworthy people, and I was always prepared to engage with them up to a point where it was reasonable and fair and in line with my responsibilities," he says. "I never ran from the media."

What he got in return for his openness was press coverage that occasionally verged on the kind of gushing usually reserved for fan magazines. The positive press was not the result of media management; he earned the accolades.

"Is there anyone as unassailable—as unimpeachable—in this province as Ted Hughes?" Keith Baldrey, the chief political reporter for Global TV in Victoria asked in a 2006 column about the Hughes report on the child protection system.

Under the headline "Saint Ted sets the standards," he wrote: "So when the Liberals asked Hughes to take charge of the child protection system, they must have known where this whole thing was headed. They must have known what is now a tried-and-true maxim of BC politics: whatever Ted Hughes said, that's the way things are and the way things are going to be. There is no point in arguing. Saint Ted has spoken. Time to move on and do what he says."

And when Hughes talked, reporters knew it was worthwhile to listen.

In 2006, when he wasn't happy with the response of the BC government to his report on child protection, he spotted a reporter at a conference of social workers where he was the guest of honour.

"Got your notebook?" he asked Les Leyne, the political columnist for the Victoria *Times Colonist*.

"Yes," Leyne affirmed. And a tape recorder.

"Then we might as well make a little headline," Hughes said.

And they did. The headline the next morning on Leyne's column was "Hughes aims rocket at Liberal MLAs."[2]

---

2 Vaughn Palmer related this story in his *Vancouver Sun* column of October 5, 2006.

Never Shy or Retiring

ON A COLD, rainy day in late November the public library in the basement of the Esquimalt municipal hall is a busy place. The spartan fluorescent-lit reading room has none of the architectural flair of the signature reading rooms of the world, but its utilitarian interior functions well for the residents of this slightly faded suburban neighbourhood and the nearby naval base, who come here to browse the books, catch up with newspapers and magazines or use the computers to access the internet.

Ted Hughes is sitting in front of a metal-sided cubicle by a window overlooking the parking lot. He has a small pile of newspapers, a legal notepad and a large coffee from the nearby McDonald's. With his casual pants and red cardigan sweater, he fits right in here as another old man passing the time.

By most standards, at 88, he is old. But on this day, as he does on many days that he comes here, Hughes is working. He is preparing for the launch of a task force on homelessness that the City of Victoria is about to announce. It is one of two projects he has on the go. The other is a mediation of a tricky property dispute on a local First Nations reserve. For Hughes, this is a relatively light workload after a career in which he often worked at what for most people would have been two full-time jobs.

Brenda Eaton had never worked with Ted before the homelessness project, but as a former deputy minister in the BC government, she knew who he was. "He was always, in my day in government, the fellow that you went to if you had a thorny issue that needed somebody with both the smarts and the credibility to be able to tackle complex problems and come up with something that was both sensible and defensible," she says.

Now 23 years past traditional retirement age, Ted still contributes more than just lending his name and reputation.

"I was impressed, although I had heard about his fairly humble style. He has a huge intellect and huge experience and huge credibility and yet he treats everybody with equal respect. That's not just lip service, it's kind of the way he is," says Eaton.

As an office, the small cubicle in a public place seems incongruous for a man of his stature. It is barely large enough to hold all the letters after his name that reflect the honours he has earned over the years: OC for Officer in the Order of Canada, QC for the Queen's Counsel designation he was granted when he left the bench in Saskatchewan, LLD (Honorary) for the honorary doctor of laws bestowed on him by the University of Victoria in 2005 for a lifetime of service.

But after years on the road working out of hotel rooms and temporary offices, Hughes is used to spare and impersonal surroundings, and he finds this place handy. The library is a couple of kilometres from the small condo on Victoria's Inner Harbour where he has lived with Helen for the past 25 years, and it has level, free parking just outside the front door.

While Ted enjoys the recognition he has received and is fiercely proud and protective of his hard-earned reputation, what really matters is the work, not the trappings. It has never been a chore.

"My work was an absolute pleasure throughout my life, and I think I'm very privileged to be able to say that," he states. "I think maybe the reason that I have been somewhat successful in keeping busy on these kinds of things is because I enjoy doing it so much. To me, arriving at the right decision is almost like a puzzle, getting there. Even at my age of today, I'd much rather be applying myself to a problem that required me to think and write than in going to a movie or going to a sports performance."

For many of the puzzles he tackled that others couldn't solve, it turns out that Ted was the missing piece. He had the stature, the reputation, the judgment and the skills to do what others could not.

Looking back, he describes every phase of his life as a happy time—as a child, a student, lawyer, judge, civil servant and commissioner—with the exception of his final three years on the bench and the personal loss he has felt since his daughter died. The pleasure Hughes finds in his assignments is a crucial element of his extraordinary career.

Faith is another. As a lawyer and a judge, he was exposed to the worst of human behaviour while still believing in the value and possibility of the best. Honesty, integrity and truth never became just words. So when it came time for him to assess the behaviour of politicians, he refused to buy into the pervasive cynicism that many Canadians and too many politicians reserve for that profession.

And he likes people. He takes a real interest in what they have to say, and treats everyone with respect, regardless of their station in life or why they are appearing before him or whether he will be able to rule in their favour.

Hughes has been retiring for a long time. But as of this day, is not retired. A year has gone by since his friends and colleagues gathered at the Union Club to celebrate his life's work with the thought that it might be at an end.

Almost a quarter century has passed since Barbara McLintock wrote in the Vancouver *Province* that "Hughes wants to stay on the job until his 65th birthday in five years, then land a part-time job related to the law."

Three years later, the *Vancouver Sun* ran a story under the headline "Workload, age cited as Hughes retires." But duty called, and again he answered: "Citing 65-hour work-weeks and his age, Hughes, 63, gave notice last year he planned to retire, before a public inquiry was called into the Reid affair. His plans were put on hold when the justice system was called into question over the decision not to proceed with criminal charges against Reid over alleged misuse of lottery funds."

Sixteen years later, in 2006, the Victoria *Times Colonist* reported that Hughes expected his current assignment to be his last. "Hughes, 79, is the chief adjudicator on Indian Residential School abuse claims, commuting from Victoria to Saskatchewan each week. He is slated to step down next summer, and says that will likely be the end of a long and illustrious career that included the release of a major report on BC's child welfare system in April.

"'Certainly a year from now my work days I think will be pretty much behind me,' he said at the time."

Ten years later he sits in the Esquimalt Library with newspapers and his legal pad, trying to solve another problem. In a few weeks he will be finished, at least until the phone rings again.

Appendix 1: List of Reports by E.N. "Ted" Hughes

1973

Citizens' School Inquiry, Saskatoon, SK. Chair, Judge E.N. Hughes. Members, Dr. C.J. Kilduff, Max Macdonald, Bishop James P. Mahoney, Mrs. W.G. Salisbury, Gren Smith-Windsor.

1974

Rural Hospital Committee Report, to the Minister of Public Health (Saskatchewan), Walter E. Smishek. Chairman, Mr. Justice E.N. Hughes. Committee members, Mrs. Marian Fowler, Mr. William Haussecker.

1976–77

Province of Saskatchewan, Committee on the Role and Remuneration of Members of the Legislative Assembly of Saskatchewan. Chairman, Mr. Justice Edward N. Hughes. Members, Judge A. Raynell Andreychuk, Mr. Charles S. Mitchell. Interim report, April 14, 1976. Second interim report, August 18, 1976. Final report, November 14, 1977.

1984

Report to the Attorney General of British Columbia from the Task Force on Public Legal Services. Chair, Hon. E.N. Hughes. Members, Robert D. Adamson, Loretta Chaperon, John Hall QC, E.F. (Ted) Horsey, Michael Jacobsen, Frank Maczko, William L. Ostler, Stephen Owen, Dermod Owen-Flood QC, Richard Peck, Daphne M. Smith. Delivered July 31, 1984.

1988

Access to Justice: The Report of the Justice Reform Committee. Presented to the Attorney General of British Columbia. Chair, E.N. (Ted) Hughes QC. Members, William S. Berardino QC, Susan M. Brice, W. Stewart Fleming, Barbara J. Nelson QC, W. Glen Parrett QC, Richard C.C. Peck QC. November 1988.

1991

Report of the Honourable E.N. Hughes, QC, On the Sale of Fantasy Garden World Inc. April 2, 1991.

Report of the Honourable E.N. Hughes, QC, with Respect to the Process and Procedure in the Investigation, Charge, Arrest, Stay and Subsequent Actions of the October 3, 1990, Harvey I. Pollock QC Case. September 1991.

1992

Gender Equality in the Justice System, Volume I and Volume II. *A Report of the Law Society of British Columbia Gender Bias Committee.* Chair, Ted Hughes. Members, Alison MacLennan QC, John McAlpine QC, Stephen F.D. Kelleher, Marguerite Jackson, Wendy Baker QC.

Report to the Victoria Commonwealth Games Society. March 1992.

1991/92–1995/96

Annual reports of the Commissioner of Conflict of Interest. The final report, 95/96, is for Hughes' final seven months in office and contains general recommendations for improvement.

1993

Review and Evaluation of the December 16, 1992, Palmer Report on the 1986–1987 RCMP Investigation into the Death of Marie Rose Desjarlais. Delivered to Commissioner Norman D. Inkster, RCMP, Ottawa, Ontario. July 9, 1993.

Constituency Allowance Review for the B.C. Legislature, by the Hon. E.N. (Ted) Hughes as Conflict of Interest Commissioner. Interim report, January 1993. Second interim report, April 1993. Final report, June 1993.

Report of Commission of Inquiry into the Shooting Death of Leo LaChance: Relating to the January 1991 Shooting Death of Leo LaChance at Prince Albert, Saskatchewan and the Consequent Plea and Sentence of Carney Milton Nerland for the Crime of Manslaughter. Chair, E.N. (Ted) Hughes. Members, Peter MacKinnon and Delia Opekokew.

1996

Report of the Independent Review of the Circumstances Surrounding the April 25–26, 1996, Riot at the Headingley Correctional Institution. Commissioned on May 7, 1996, by the Hon. Rosemary Vodrey, Minister of Justice, Province of Manitoba. November 29, 1996.

1998

Report of the Board of Inquiry Established under Orders-In-Council 1997/181 and 1997/182 Respecting the Administration and Operation of the Territorial Court of the Yukon. August 28, 1998.

1998

Report to the Attorney General of the Judicial Compensation Committee, Province of British Columbia. Chairman, Mr. E.N. (Ted) Hughes QC. Attorney general appointments: Mr. Vince Collins, Ms. Gayle Raphanel. Chief judge appointments: Mr. Leonard T. Doust QC, Mr. Martin Linsley FCA.

2001

Commission Interim Report Following a Public Hearing into the Complaints Regarding the Events that Took Place in Connection with Demonstrations during the Asia Pacific Economic Cooperation Conference in Vancouver, BC, in November 1997 at the UBC Campus and at the UBC and Richmond Detachments of the RCMP. July 31, 2001.

2002

Chair's Final Report Following a Public Hearing into the Complaints Relating to RCMP Conduct at Events That Took Place at the UBC Campus and the Richmond RCMP Detachment during the Asia Pacific Economic Cooperation Conference in Vancouver, BC, in November 1997. March 25, 2002.

2006

BC Children and Youth Review. An Independent Review of BC's Child Protection System. April 7, 2006.

2008

Ethical and Constitutional Values by which members of the Judiciary should be guided when considering or encountering communications to or from members of the Executive and/or Legislative Branches of the Government.

With research assistance by Brenda Edwards, Legal Officer, Provincial Court of British Columbia. Requested by the Judicial Council of British Columbia. June 3, 2008.

2009

Report on Organizational, Cultural and Process Audit of the Esquimalt Fire Rescue Services. Delivered to the Township of Esquimalt on November 30, 2009.

2010

Report by the Hon. Ted Hughes OC, QC, and Mediator John Rooney, Federal Mediation and Conciliation Service, to the Hon. Lisa Raitt PC, MP, Minister of Labour. Prepared pursuant to their appointment on the 5th day of March, 2010, as mediators under Section 105(1) of the Canada Labour Code, in Collective Bargaining Negotiations Between British Columbia Maritime Employers Association (BCMEA) and the International Longshore and Warehouse Union of Canada (Longshoremen).

2013

The Legacy of Phoenix Sinclair: Achieving the Best for All Our Children. A report of the Commission of Inquiry into the Circumstances Surrounding the Death of Phoenix Sinclair. The Hon. Ted Hughes, OC, QC, LLD (Hon), Commissioner. December 15, 2013.

Appendix 2: Awards Presented to E.N. "Ted" Hughes

1973

Smith-Walshaw Award for work in the health care system (Saskatchewan)

1976

"We're Proud of You" Award from the B'Nai B'Rith Lodge No. 739, Saskatoon, SK, awarded annually to someone in the community who has done outstanding work without being properly recognized

1980

Queen's Counsel

Cosmopolitan Club of Saskatoon Distinguished Service Award for Community Service

1990

Lieutenant Governor's Medal from the Victoria Regional Chapter of the Institute of Public Administration of Canada, awarded for contribution to the excellence of the public service of British Columbia

1992

Canadian Bar Association (BC Branch) President's Medal for service to the legal profession of British Columbia

1993

University of Victoria Faculty of Law Alumni Association Begbie Public Service Award for contribution to the public of British Columbia in advancing justice, law reform and standards of the legal profession

2000

Law Society of British Columbia Award (offered every two years)—the highest award conferred by the Law Society based on criteria of integrity, professional achievement, service and reform

2002

Queen's Golden Jubilee Medal

2003

Officer of the Order of Canada, invested by Her Excellency the Right Honourable Adrienne Clarkson, Governor General of Canada

2005

Doctor of Laws (honoris causa) conferred by the University of Victoria

First Call BC Child and Youth Advocacy Coalition Recognition Award

2008

Generosity of Spirit Award on National Philanthropy Day, presented by the Victoria Foundation

Anthony P. Pantages QC Award, presented by the Justice Institute of British Columbia for significant contribution in the field of justice to the benefit of British Columbians

2009

Leadership Victoria Lifetime Achievement Award

One of 100 Alumni of Influence of the College of Arts and Science, University of Saskatchewan, during the college's first century (1909–2009)

CFAX Community Award Recipient as Citizen of the Year

Chancellor's Community Recognition Award, Royal Roads University

2010

Named by *Canadian Lawyer* magazine as one of the twenty-five most influential Canadians in Canada's justice system and legal profession

2011

Named an Honorary Citizen of the City of Victoria

Doctor of Laws (honoris causa) conferred by University of Saskatchewan

2012

Doctor of Laws, Royal Roads University

Selected Bibliography and Sources

Unless otherwise noted, all direct quotes are from interviews the author conducted in 2014, 2015 and 2016.

Anderson, Alan. Urban Aboriginal Population. Retrieved November 12, 2015, from *The Encylopedia of Saskatchewan* (esask.uregina.ca/entry/urban_aboriginal_population.html).

Archer, John H. *Saskatchewan: A History*. Saskatoon: Western Producer Prairie Books, 1980.

Arnason, Barney N. *It Was a Great Privilege: The Co-Operative Memoirs of B.N. Arnason*. Victoria: British Columbia Institute for Co-operative Studies, 2004.

Beaubier, David W. *Prairie Lawyer, Country Judge*. Saskatoon: Law Society of Saskatchewan Libraries, 2005.

Berton, Pierre. *The Great Depression 1929–1939*. Toronto: McClelland and Stewart, 1990.

Bird, Heather. *Not Above the Law: The Tragic Story of JoAnn Wilson and Colin Thatcher*. Toronto: Key Porter Books, 1985.

Blakeney, Allan. *An Honourable Calling: Political Memoirs*. Toronto: University of Toronto Press, 2008.

Borrie, Gordon. "The Judge and the Public: The Law of Contempt." In *The Canadian Judiciary*, ed. Allen M. Linden. Toronto: Osgoode Hall Law School, 1976.

Brockman, Joan. *Gender in the Legal Profession: Fitting or Breaking the Mould*. Vancouver: UBC Press, 2002.

City of Saskatoon. *Municipal Manual 2015*. Saskatoon: City of Saskatoon, 2015. Retrieved November 12, 2015 (saskatoon.ca/sites/default/files/documents/city-clerk/reports-publications/2015MunicipalManual.pdf).

Clément, Dominique. *Equality Deferred: Sex Discrimination and British Columbia's Human Rights State, 1953–84*. Vancouver: UBC Press for The Osgoode Society for Canadian Legal History, 2014.

Gove, T. *Matthew's Story: The Report of the Gove Inquiry into Child Protection in British Columbia*. Victoria: Queen's Printer for British Columbia, 1995.

Harcourt, Mike, and Wayne Skene. *Mike Harcourt: A Measure of Defiance*. Vancouver: Douglas and McIntyre, 1996.

Harvey, R.G. *Head On! Collisions of Ethics and Politics in B.C.'s Transportation History*. Surrey, BC: Heritage House Publishing, 2004.

Hawthorn, Tom. *Deadlines: Obits of Memorable British Columbians*. Madeira Park, BC: Harbour Publishing, 2012.

Johnson, A.W. *Dream No Little Dreams: A Biography of the Douglas Government of Saskatchewan, 1944–1961*. Toronto: University of Toronto Press, 2004.

Kay, Bill. *The Zalm and I: B.C.'s Backroom Politics*. Surrey, BC: Hancock House Publishers, 1993.

Kirbyson, Geoff. "The Big Picture." *Canadian Lawyer*, August 7, 2007.

Littlemore, Richard. "The Perfect Civil Servant." *BC Business*, November 1999.

Mason, Gary, and Keith Baldrey. *Fantasyland: Inside the Reign of Bill Vander Zalm*. Toronto: McGraw-Hill Ryerson, 1989.

McConnell, W.H. "Constitutional History." In *The Canadian Encyclopedia* (thecanadianencyclopedia.ca/en/article/constitutional-history/).

McLintock, Barbara, and Gerry Kristianson. "The Media and British Columbia Politics." In *Politics, Policy, and Government in British Columbia*, ed. R. Kenneth Carty. Vancouver: UBC Press, 1996.

Moore, Vincent. *Gladiator of the Courts: Angelo Branco*. Vancouver: Douglas and McIntyre, 1981.

Morin, Gerald M. "Personal Reflections on the Ill-Fated First APEC Inquiry." In *Pepper in Our Eyes: The APEC Affair*, ed. W. Wesley Pue. Vancouver: UBC Press, 2000.

Newman, Peter C. *Renegade in Power: The Diefenbaker Years*. Toronto: McClelland and Stewart, 1963.

O'Brien, Jeff. *Saskatoon, the Great Depression, and the Civic Relief Board*. Saskatoon: City of Saskatoon Archives, 2006.

Owen, Stephen. *Discretion to Prosecute Inquiry*, Volume One: *Report and Recommendations*. Victoria: Province of British Columbia, 1990.

Owen, Stephen. *Discretion to Prosecute Inquiry, Commissioner's Report*, Volume Two: *Documents*. Victoria: Queen's Printer for British Columbia, 1990.

Pacholik, Barb, and Jana G. Pruden. *Sour Milk and Other Saskatchewan Crime Stories*. Regina: University of Regina, Canadian Plains Research Centre, 2007.

Pedersen, Jen. *A Seat on Council: The Aldermen, Councillors and Mayors of Saskatoon, 1903–2006*. Saskatoon: City of Saskatoon Archives, Office of the City Clerk, 2012.

Persky, Stan. *Fantasy Government: Bill Vander Zalm and the Future of Social Credit*. Vancouver: New Star Books, 1989.

Plecas, Bob. *Bill Bennett: A Mandarin's View*. Vancouver: Douglas and McIntyre, 2006.

Potter, Simon J. *News and the British World: The Emergence of an Imperial Press System, 1876–1922*. Oxford: Clarendon, 2003.

Quiring, Brett. "Lang, Otto Emil (1932–)." Retrieved November 12, 2015, from *The Encylopedia of Saskatchewan* (esask.uregina.ca/entry/lang_otto_emil_1932-.html).

Ratushny, Ed. "Judicial Appointments: The Lang Legacy." In *The Canadian Judiciary*, ed. Allen M. Linden. Toronto: Osgoode Hall Law School, 1976.

Rayner, William. *Scandal! 130 Years of Damnable Deeds in Canada's Lotus Land*. Surrey, BC: Heritage House, 2001.

Siggins, Maggie. *A Canadian Tragedy. Joann and Colin Thatcher: A Story of Love and Hate*. Toronto: Macmillan of Canada, 1985.

Sinclair, Murray, and Alvin Hamilton. *Report of the Aboriginal Justice Inquiry of Manitoba*. Winnipeg: Aboriginal Justice Inquiry of Manitoba, 1991.

Slade, Arthur. *John Diefenbaker: An Appointment with Destiny*. Montreal: XYZ Publishing, 2001.

Spencer, Dick. *Trumpets and Dreams: John Diefenbaker on the Campaign Trail*. Vancouver: Greystone Books, 1994.

Stewart, Walter. *The Life and Political Times of Tommy Douglas*. Toronto: McArthur and Company, 2003.

Strikwerda, Eric. *The Wages of Relief: Cities and the Unemployed in Prairie Canada, 1929–39*. Edmonton: AU Press, 2013.

The Truth and Reconciliation Commission of Canada. *Honouring the Truth, Reconciling for the Future: Summary of the Final Report of the Truth and Reconciliation Commission of Canada*. Truth and Reconciliation Commission of Canada, 2015. Retrieved from trc.ca.

Vander Zalm, Bill. *Bill Vander Zalm "For the People": The Autobiography of British Columbia's 28th Premier*. Vancouver: Bill Vander Zalm, 2008.

Various. *The 1950 Chronicle* (York House School Yearbook). Vancouver: York House School, 1950.

Various. *Memoirs of Hillsburgh, Rural Municipality No. 289*. Hillsburgh, SK: History Committee, 1960.

Various. *Footprints of the Hughes Family*. Unpublished family memoir, 1992.

Vaughn, Frederick. *Aggressive in Pursuit: The Life of Justice Emmett Hall*. Toronto: University of Toronto Press for the Osgoode Society for Canadian Legal History, 2004.

York House. *75 at 75: Her Influence* (York House School 75th Birthday Book). Vancouver: York House School, 2007.

Index

Abbott, Jim, 232
Aboriginal Justice Inquiry of Manitoba, 206–8, 213, 223
abuse of power, definition, 147
Access to Justice (report), 119–21
Albercan Oil Corporation, 35
Alexson, Delbert: murder trial, 55
Alternative Dispute Resolution. *See* residential schools
APEC summit, 9, 225–37
  Jean Chrétien and, 226–27
  legal costs of inquiry, 231, 232–33
  police conduct, 225–26, 227–28, 236–37
  protests against, 227
  Public Complaints Commission on, 225–26, 228–37
  purpose, 225n1
Arvay, Joe, 169–70, 177
Asia Pacific Economic Cooperation summit. *See* APEC summit

Baldrey, Keith, 204
Barclay, Ron, 191
Barrett, Dave, 114, 135
Basford, Ron, 98, 100, 101, 104
Bayda, Edward, 139
BC Children and Youth Review, 248–50, 252–53
BC Enterprise Corporation, 134–35
Beaubier, David, 35n1
Beer, Henry, 26
Begbie, Sir Matthew Baillie, 6, 181
Bence, Alfred "Alf," 46, 50, 98–99, 101
Bennett, Bill, 109, 114, 116, 117, 127, 128, 134, 138, 146n3
Bennett, Russell, 146n3
Bessborough Hotel, 18, 31–32
Beyer, Hubert, 192
bingo scandal, 192–93, 196
Blencoe, Robin, 186–89, 194
"blue box scandal." *See* Reid, William "Bill"
Bodner, Morris, 216
Boyd, Mary Ellen, 121n2
Branca, Angelo, 113
Brenner, Donald, 179
Brice, Susan, 112, 120
Butler, Veronica, 113

Campbell, David Hector, 121n2
Campbell, Gordon, 111n2, 248
Campbell, Kim, 216
capital punishment, 55n1

Carle, Jean, 228, 235
child protection, 248–50, 252–53
Children's Commission, 249
Chrétien, Jean, 9, 226, 227, 233, 235–36
City Park Collegiate Institute, 20
civil service politicization, 132–33
Clark, Barrie, 173
Clark, Glen
  attempts to replace TH, 195–202
  career, 186n3, 192–93
  conflict of interest, 183, 190
  Members' Conflict of Interest Act, amendment of, 219
Clément, Dominique, 113n3
Collins, Gary, 198
Comox Valley Ready Mix, 251
Concentra Financial Services, 39
conflict of interest
  "appearance of conflict," 128, 131, 148, 167, 172, 183, 185–88
  Blencoe, Robin, 186–89, 194
  cabinet resignations, 127–31
  guidelines, 126–27, 128, 130, 167, 172, 175, 182–83
  Members' Conflict of Interest Act, 167–69, 172, 182–83, 185
  Mike Harcourt, 187–90, 201n8
  Reid, William ("Bill"), 143–60
  Stan Hagen, 251–52
  TH becomes first Commissioner, 167–68
  Toigo investigation, 134–38, 163
  Vander Zalm, William ("Bill"), 131, 162–74
Conservative Party, 9, 23–25, 40–41, 45–46
Constitution Act, 126, 251
Co-operative Commonwealth Federation, 41, 45
Co-operative Trust Company, 39
County Courts of BC, 120–21
Court of Appeal, 46, 121, 139, 216
Court of Queen's Bench
  district courts merged with, 43n6, 120
  name change proposed, 121
  patronage in appointments to, 46–47, 100–102, 104, 105
  pitfalls of appointment process, 103
  TH candidacy for Chief Justice, 98–106
  TH resignation from, 104
  travel for, 60
  treatment of lawyers before, 68
Couvelier, Mel, 164
Cranfield, Dahrlyne, 78–83
Cranfield, Daye, 81–83
Crawford, Neil, 16n2
credit unions, 43
Crosbie, John, 140–41
Cross, Constable Robert, 205–6

Daly, Charles Ulick de Burgh, 30
death penalty, 55n1
Dependents' Allowance Board, 20
Depression years, 15, 17, 28, 35n1
Devine, Grant, 140
Diefenbaker, John, 7, 24–25, 45–51, 60
Dirks, Howard, 145
Disbery, Mr. Justice D.C., 43
district courts, 43n6, 46, 69, 120
doctors' strike, 7, 86–87
Doman, Herb, 146n3
Doonan, George, 143, 145
Douglas, Tommy, 7, 24, 41, 45
Doust, Len, 135, 138
Dowson, Kenneth, 207–8

Eamer, Gilbert "Gib," 40
Eco-Clean Waste Systems, 143–44
Edwards, Bob, 112
Emerson, David, 154, 168, 250

Emerson, Kim, 188–89
Erb, Marsha, 67, 268, 269
Esson, William, 141
Estey, James Wilfred, 34
Ewan, John Alexander, 27
Ewan, Mary, 29, 30
Exchequer Court of Canada, 39
Expo '86 lands, 134–38, 163

Fantasy Gardens, 131, 162–76, 179
Farrell-Collins, Gary, 198
Federal Treaty Negotiation office, 221, 230
Federated Co-op, 39, 43, 48
Financial Disclosure Act, 127
Finlay, John, 169–70, 177
Firestone, Peter, 150–51, 152–53, 157
First Nations. *See* Indigenous people
Fisher, Barbara, 235
Fisher, Ron, 57
Fleming, Donald, 50
Francis, W.B., 38, 40
Francis, Woods, Gauley and Hughes, 37–40, 99
Fraser, Irene, 241–42, 243
Fraser, Paul, 221n3
Fraser, Russ, 156, 160
Friesen, Jake, 42

Gardom, Garde, 219
Garrett, George, 136
Gauley, David Eldon "Tom," 38
Gender Equality in the Justice System (report), 122–24, 162
Gerrand, Gerry, 91, 92–94, 96n4
Globe and Mail, 27, 73, 208n3, 225, 234, 265–66
Goodale, Ralph, 239
Gove, Thomas, 249, 259
Graves, Brian, 152, 157, 158
Grubesic, Robert, 78–83

Hagen, Stan, 248–53
  conflict of interest, 251
  integrity affirmed by TH, 251–52
  political career, 250
Hall, Emmett, 46, 87n1
Hall, John, 147
Halvorson, Kenneth, 105–6, 246
Halyk, Silas, 68
Hanbidge, Dinny, 50
Harcourt, Mike, 144, 149, 182–83, 185–90, 192–94, 201n8
Harper, J.J., 205–8, 213
Havergal College, 27
Headingley riot, 219–24
  Indigenous people's inequality, 223–24
  injuries, 220
  prison staff and, 220–21, 222
Heafey, Shirley, 228, 230, 232
Henderson, A.G. "Ace," 146
Hetschko, Barry, 255
Hetschko, Sheila (TH's daughter), 52, 63, 64, 111, 254–56
Hill Cup, 23–24
Hnatyshyn, John
  neighbour to TH, 47, 53
  supports TH's Queen's Bench appointment, 47–49, 50
  TH witness in burglary of, 76–77
Hnatyshyn, Ray, 47n4, 53, 67, 76
Hnatyshyn, Victor, 68
Hodgins, Constable Kathryn, 205–6
Hopper, Wilbert "Bill," 170
Hotel Saskatchewan, 239
Hughes, Brian Edward (son), 53, 58, 63–65, 110
Hughes, Catherine May (cousin), 16, 17, 18
Hughes, David William (son), 47n4, 52, 53, 111
Hughes, Elizabeth (born Underhill, no relation), 59

Hughes, Florence "Florrie" (mother), 16, 18–19, 20, 52
Hughes, Helen (born Larmonth, wife)
childhood, 26, 27–28
councillor in Saskatoon, 54–57, 98
councillor in Victoria, 110
courtship and marriage to TH, 32–33, 84–85
education, 29–31
as friend, 112
home life in Saskatoon, 52–54, 57–64
honoured by City of Saskatoon, 7
musical interests, 31, 65
Order of Canada earned by, 98
voluntary work, 29, 53–55
work with indigenous community, 55–57, 98
Hughes, John (grandfather), 12, 14
Hughes, Keith Douglas (son), 52, 54, 57, 59, 63, 65–66, 111
Hughes, Mary (born King, grandmother), 16, 17
Hughes, Myrtle Estelle (born Thomas, aunt), 15
Hughes, Percy (uncle), 12–14, 15
Hughes, Sheila Elizabeth (daughter), 52, 63, 64, 111, 254–56
Hughes, Ted: career
awards, 181, 273
background, 7–9
BC Police Commission, 162, 168, 182
becomes Queen's Counsel, 110
Chief Justice, Court of Queen's Bench candidacy, 98–106
Conflict of Interest Commissioner, 168–202
cost-cutting under Bill Bennett, 116–17
Deputy Attorney-General, 116–67
pressed to leave and reinstated, 195–202, 221
judge, 45–51, 67–83, 90–97
lawyer, 34–44
Legal Officer Specialist, 108–16
Leo LaChance inquiry, 214–18
Operation Solidarity, duties during, 114
in politics, 9, 23–25, 40–41, 45
relations with reporters, 268–71
resignation from Court of Queen's Bench, 104
retirement, 4–6, 7–8, 106, 275
Supreme Court of BC candidacy, 141–42
Vander Zalm, false statements about TH, 175–81
Hughes, Ted: cases and inquiries
Access to Justice, 119–21
APEC inquiry, 9, 225–37
BC Children and Youth Review, 248–53
Canadian Industrial Gas and Oil v. Saskatchewan, 73
David Threinen murder trial, 78–81
Daye Cranfield criminal contempt trial, 81–83
Delbert Alexson murder trial, 55
Fantasy Gardens report, 125–26, 162–76
Gender Equality in the Justice System, 122–24, 162
Harvey Pollock case, 204–13
legal aid review, 118–19
Mike Harcourt, 187–89
NOW Communications Group, 187–90
Phoenix Sinclair inquiry, 257–66
Reid/Smith/Sihota affair, 143–62
residential schools, 239–47
Robin Blencoe, 186–89
Stewardesses obscenity trial, 74–75
surgeon's sexual assault trial, 69–72

Thatcher v. Thatcher divorce, 91–95, 96, 97
Toigo investigation, 134–38
Windrem v. Hamill, 72–73
Hughes, Ted: character
feelings on sentencing, 75–76
frugality as public servant, 184–85
meetings deplored, 246
openness, 268–69, 270–71
reputation, 5–7, 9, 89, 123, 125–26, 181, 204, 226, 249–50
respected as judge, 67–68, 69
temperament, 105, 109–10, 240, 241, 246
work ethic, 37, 39–40, 61–62, 68, 231, 234, 245, 260
Hughes, Ted: private life
courtship and marriage to Helen, 32–33, 84–85
daughter Sheila's death, 254–56
driving incidents, 61–62
education, 8, 18, 20, 21–24, 34
family origins and childhood, 12–20
friendships, 112–13
newspaper reader, 267–68
political spectator, 132
religion, 17, 19, 23–24, 256
Saskatoon home life, 52–53, 57–64
Shawnigan Lake cottage, 111–12, 254
Victoria home life, 111–12
views on marriage, 85
voluntary work, 86–89, 118, 240
witness to burglary of Hnatyshyns, 76–77
Hughes, William "Bill" (brother), 16, 18–20
Hughes, William "Bill" (father), 12, 13–15, 16, 17, 18–20
Hume, Stephen, 227, 270

Iacobucci, Frank, 243, 244n3
Independent Assessment Program, 243–44, 246
Indian Residential Schools Settlement Agreement, 243–44
Indigenous people
Aboriginal Justice Inquiry of Manitoba, 206–8, 213, 223
Harvey Pollock case, 204–13
Helen Betty Osborne murder, 206–7
Helen Hughes' work for, 55–57, 98
inequality of, 223, 257–58, 264, 265
J.J. Harper shooting, 206, 207–8, 213
Judge Matthew Begbie statue, 6n1
Leo LaChance shooting, 214–18
Lone Star Hotel's discrimination against, 113
Phoenix Sinclair inquiry, 257–66
residential schools compensation, 8, 238–47
Inquiry Act, 171
Ish, Dan, 244–45

Johnson, Frederick, 101–2
Johnson, Ron, 188
Johnston, Rita, 174, 182

Keating, Katherine, 121–22, 262
Kelly, Isabel, 251
Kematch, Samantha, 258, 259
Kempf, Jack, 129
King, William Lyon Mackenzie, 46
Kirkby, Gordon, 216
Klein, Ralph, 189
Kozaruk, Stephen: murder trial, 42–43
Kushneryk, Sergeant, 213

LaChance, Leo, 214–18, 228
inquiry, 216–18
manslaughter of, 214–15
sculpture erected to, 214

Lampert, Jerry, 154, 155
Lang, Otto, 37n2, 99–100
Larmonth, Mary, 27, 28, 29, 30
Larmonth, Muriel Elizabeth, 19, 26, 27
Larmonth, Rev. Norman Douglas, 19, 26–29, 31–32
Law Society of BC, 6n1, 119, 120, 122–23, 162, 171n5, 181, 235n5
Law Society of Manitoba, 208, 209, 212
Law Society of Saskatchewan, 37n2, 93
LeBreton, Marjory, 140
legal aid, 118–19, 171, 180n3
Legal Services Society, 119
Leung, Dean, 163, 165, 170
Leung, Faye, 162–67, 170
Leyne, Les, 270, 271
Liberal party (federal), 46, 226
Liberal party of BC, 182n1
Li Ka-shing, 134
Linemayr, Klaus, 130
Linka, Rodger, 240, 245–46
Lloyd, Isabel, 84, 122, 251
Lone Star Hotel, 113

MacAulay, Ernie, 159
MacAulay, Lawrence, 232–33
Mackay, Karl Wesley, 258, 259
Mackay, Wendi, 112, 240
MacKinnon, Peter, 216
MacPherson, Murdoch Alexander "Sandy," 90, 91
Magistrates Court, 46n1
Mahlman, Melanie, 240
Mair, Rafe, 178
Maloney, Maureen, 122–23, 124
Manitoba Government and General Employees' Union, 261
Married Women's Property Act, 92
Marson, Brian, 145
Matrimonial Property Act, 92, 94
McAlpine, John, 171
McArthur, Doug, 196–97, 199–202
McCarthy, Grace, 134–35, 137, 138
McClelland, Robert Harold, 49
McCrank, Neil, 155, 156–57, 158, 159
McDougall Gauley, 44n7
McEachern, Allan, 120, 141
McIntyre, William, 139
McLachlin, Beverley, 140, 141
McLintock, Barbara, 115n5, 274
Meekison, J. Peter, 221n3
Melfort, SK, 48–49, 50, 60
Members' Conflict of Interest Act, 167–69, 172, 182–83, 194, 201n8, 219
Merchant, Tony, 93–94, 96, 238, 239, 241, 244n3
Michael, Cliff, 130–31, 167
Miller, Dan, 185–86, 194n3
Mining Association of BC, 127–28
Ministry of Children and Family Development, 248–50, 252–53
Mitchell, David, 195–202
Mitchell, Keith, 135
Monnin, Alfred, 48
Morin, Gerald, 228, 229–30
Moxon, Schmitt, Estey and Robertson, 34
Mulroney, Brian, 140
Murphy, Kevin, 134, 135

Nanaimo Commonwealth Holding Soc., 178, 192–93, 195, 196
Nathanson, Irwin, 179
National Truth and Reconciliation Commission, 244
Nerland, Carney, 214–17
New Democratic Party, 167, 182–83, 186n3, 187–88, 192–95
Norman, George Wesley, 16
North Battleford, 8, 35–37
Northwest Territories, 221

NOW Communications Group, 187–90, 201n8

Oliver, H.A.D. "Bert," 190, 221n3
Opekokew, Delia, 216
Operation Solidarity, 114
Osborn, Albert "Al," 37
Osborne, Helen Betty, 206–7
Owen, Bruce, 210–11, 212
Owen, Stephen, 149, 151, 157, 160–62, 232

Palmer, Vaughn, 7, 173, 177–78, 185, 199, 270, 271n2
Parks, Ron, 192
Pasadena Playhouse, 30
patronage, 46–47, 100–2, 104, 105, 187–90, 201n8
Peck, Richard, 146–47
Pederson, Martin, 40–41
Pelletier, Debi, 152
Petro-Canada, 170, 172
Piper, Martha, 228
plain language, 121–22
Plecas, Bob, 108, 116, 122, 129–30, 131–32, 252–53
Pollock, Harvey, 204–13
  and J.J. Harper inquiry, 207–8
  payback motive for charges against, 213
  sexual assault allegations, 208–12
Poole, David, 136, 137, 138, 251
Powder Mountain Resorts, 130
private prosecution, 148, 149–51
Profits of Criminal Notoriety Act, 97n5
Progressive Conservative Party, 9, 23–25, 40–41, 45–46
Province (newspaper), 113, 115n5, 175n1, 248, 274
Provincial Court, 46n1
Public Complaints Commission, 225–26, 228–37
public service politicization, 132–33

Quantz, Ernie, 158
Queen's Bench. *See* Court of Queen's Bench

Ratushny, Edward, 37n2, 68, 98–100, 101, 103, 104
RCMP
  and APEC summit, 225–26, 227–37
  and Leo LaChance case, 216–17
  in Reid/Smith/Sihota affair, 145–48, 150, 155, 156, 159–60
Regina
  centre for commercial law, 49
  Hotel Saskatchewan "second home" to TH, 239
  TH runs law office in, 39–40
  TH seeks judicial appointment in, 48–51
Reid, William "Bill," 143–61
  breach of trust and fraud alleged, 143–45
  investigation, 144–47
  joins Cabinet, 138
  popularity, 143
  private prosecution by Sihota, 148–57
  RCMP investigation, 145–46, 147
  resignation, 144
  Stephen Owen inquiry, 149, 151, 160
  TH declines to prosecute, 147–48
Representative for Children and Youth, 252
residential schools, 8, 238–47
  churches and, 239, 241, 243, 244n3
  Indian Residential Schools Settlement Agreement, 243–44
  inquiry process, 240–43, 244–45, 247

sexual abuse in, 239, 246
value of inquiry into, 247
Rhodes, Frank, 108–9, 115, 116
Richmond, Claude, 144, 145
Rochdale Principles, 43
Rogers, Stephen, 127
Romanow, Roy, 69, 110, 216
Ruff, Norman, 5, 226

Sallows, Ariel, 35–36, 37
Saskatchewan
cancer agency crisis, 89
civil weddings in, 84
Depression years in, 15, 17, 35n1
doctors' strike, 7, 86–87
honours the Hugheses, 110
Saskatchewan Teachers' Federation, 40, 41–42
Saskatoon
honours the Hugheses, 7
city hospital board, 87
Cranfield and Grubesic murders in, 78–79, 81–83
Depression years in, 17, 35n1
Helen Hughes a councillor in, 54–57
Helen Hughes' indigenous community work in, 55–57
Helen Hughes' indigenous community work in, 98
Helen Hughes' voluntary work in, 53–55
Hughes family home in, 12–16, 52–53
indigenous population of, 55–57
Larmonth family home in, 28, 31
municipal election turnout in, 25
social life in, 59–60
surgeon's sexual assault trial in, 69–72
TH a Progressive Conservative candidate in, 40–41
TH articles in, 34–35
TH befriends Diefenbaker in, 45
TH builds home in, 52–53
TH political outsider among judges, 105–6
Saskatoon Hospital Board, 86–89
Saskatoon Star-Phoenix
founder, 16
opinion of TH, 67, 268–70
reporting on TH, 23–24, 34, 234, 238, 239
TH as delivery boy for, 267
TH reading, 17, 102
Saskatoon Telecable, 82–83
Schnoor, Jeffrey, 260
Scott, Andy, 229
Sebastien, John, 159
Shapiro, Dan, 242, 243, 244–45
Shaughnessy, 27, 28, 29
Shawnigan Lake, 111–12, 254
Siggins, Maggie, 90, 91, 94
Sihota, Moe
and Bud Smith tape recordings, 151–54
charges considered against, 156–59
County Courts merger and, 121
exonerated, 158–61
private prosecution of Bill Reid, 148–51
Sinclair, Margot, 153
Sinclair, Phoenix, 257–66
beating death of, 257, 258–59
inquiry approach, 259–62
inquiry findings, 263–64
Sinclair, Steve, 258
Singh, Jaggi, 233–34, 237
Sissons, William "Hal," 23
Site C dam proposal, 111
Smith, Brian, 115, 128, 131, 135, 136, 137
Smith, Bud
charges considered against, 153–58
exonerated, 157, 160

lobbies for BC Supreme Court seat, 139–40
new Attorney-General, 138
news conference by TH, 155–56
obstruction of justice alleged, 153–54
and private prosecution of Reid, 150–51
resignation, 154
tape recordings of, 151–54
Smith, Daphne, 153
Smyth, Mike, 248
Social Credit party
elections, 114, 182, 193
leadership races, 135, 138, 174
rebuilt by Grace McCarthy, 135
Vander Zalm alienates caucus, 143, 144, 173
special prosecutors, 146
Spitzer, Eloise, 195, 196, 199
Stanfield, Robert, 140
Stephen, Herb, 206, 213
Stephen Owen, 119
Stewardesses obscenity trial, 74–75
Stewart, Staff Sergeant Hugh, 225–26
Stewart, William, 145, 147, 153, 156
St. John's Shaughnessy, 27, 28, 29
St. Laurent, Louis, 46
St. Mark's Hall, 26–27
Storrow, Marvin, 234–35
Struthers, James, 269n1
Sullivan, Bill, 143, 145
Supreme Court of BC, 120–21, 141–42
Supreme Court of Canada, 73, 139–41, 216
Swan, Andrew, 257

Tadema, Roger, 130
Tallis, Calvin, 69, 216
Tan Yu, 164–67, 170, 172
Thatcher, Colin, 90–97
custody battle, 91
divorce from JoAnn Wilson, 90–93
murders JoAnn Wilson, 90, 96
paroled, 96
Thatcher, Peggy, 95
Thompson, Daphne, 184, 189
Thomson, Harold F., 42
Thorson, Joe, 39
Threinen, David: murder trial, 78–81
Times Colonist, 271, 275
Toigo, Peter, 134–38, 163
Trail, BC, 27
Trone, J.L., 26
Trudeau, Pierre, 47n1
Truth and Reconciliation Commission, 244

Union Club of BC, 4, 6, 112
University of Saskatchewan
alumni, 22, 32, 56, 99, 139
chair in Human Rights, 37n2
faculty, 34, 57, 99, 216, 247

Vancouver *Province*, 113, 115n5, 175, 248, 274
Vancouver Sun
opinion on TH, 7
reporting on APEC summit, 227, 232
reporting on TH, 185, 199, 204, 232, 271n2, 275
on Sihota/Smith/Reid affair, 157
TH quoted in, 129
TH threatens lawsuit, 177–78
Vander Zalm, Lillian, 131, 163, 164, 165, 166, 170, 180
Vander Zalm, William "Bill," 125–38, 162–81
cabinet scandals, 126–31
caucus dissatisfaction with, 143, 144
conflict of interest guidelines of, 128, 183

false statements about TH, 175–76, 179–80
Fantasy Gardens affair, 131, 162–74, 176
Peter Toigo scandal and, 134–35
resignation, 125, 173
Vaudreuil, Matthew, 249, 259
Veitch, Elwood, 138, 163
Victoria Hospital Foundation, 240
Victoria *Times Colonist*, 271, 275
Vodrey, Rosemary, 222, 223
Vogel, Richard "Dick," 108–9, 115

Walsh, Sherri, 260, 261–62
Waterland, Tom, 127–28, 130n3
Waygood, Kathryn "Kate," 54
Weisgerber, Jack, 178, 188
Whitehead, Rose, 42–43
white supremacists, 214–17
Williams, Allan, 109
Wilson, Don, 145, 148, 159
Wilson, Gordon, 182n1
Wilson, JoAnn
divorces Colin Thatcher, 90–93
murdered by Colin Thatcher, 90, 96
threats and vandalism against, 95
Winnipeg Free Press, 204, 210, 211, 220n1, 264
women's equity, 122–24, 162, 171n5
Wood, Josiah, 230
Woods, Mervyn J., 38
Wright, Robert, 145–46, 159

Yacowar, Hal, 149
York House, 28, 29–31
Yukon Legislative Assembly, 221
Yund, Robert: murder trial, 42

CRAIG MCINNES is a veteran reporter, editor, and writer. His long newspaper career includes eighteen years with the *Globe and Mail* and fourteen years with the *Vancouver Sun*, where he wrote extensively about public policy issues, science, medicine and social trends. Since leaving daily journalism in 2013, he has continued to work as a writer and editorial consultant for a number of organizations and clients.